C-2867 CAREER EXAMINATION SERIES

This is your PASSBOOK for...

Senior Personnel Clerk

Test Preparation Study Guide
Questions & Answers

NLC®
NATIONAL LEARNING CORPORATION®

National Learning Corporation

212 Michael Drive, Syosset, NY 11791
(516) 921-8888 • www.passbooks.com
E-mail: info@passbooks.com

PASSBOOK® SERIES

THE *PASSBOOK® SERIES* has been created to prepare applicants and candidates for the ultimate academic battlefield – the examination room.

At some time in our lives, each and every one of us may be required to take an examination – for validation, matriculation, admission, qualification, registration, certification, or licensure.

Based on the assumption that every applicant or candidate has met the basic formal educational standards, has taken the required number of courses, and read the necessary texts, the *PASSBOOK® SERIES* furnishes the one special preparation which may assure passing with confidence, instead of failing with insecurity. Examination questions – together with answers – are furnished as the basic vehicle for study so that the mysteries of the examination and its compounding difficulties may be eliminated or diminished by a sure method.

This book is meant to help you pass your examination provided that you qualify and are serious in your objective.

The entire field is reviewed through the huge store of content information which is succinctly presented through a provocative and challenging approach – the question-and-answer method.

A climate of success is established by furnishing the correct answers at the end of each test.

You soon learn to recognize types of questions, forms of questions, and patterns of questioning. You may even begin to anticipate expected outcomes.

You perceive that many questions are repeated or adapted so that you can gain acute insights, which may enable you to score many sure points.

You learn how to confront new questions, or types of questions, and to attack them confidently and work out the correct answers.

You note objectives and emphases, and recognize pitfalls and dangers, so that you may make positive educational adjustments.

Moreover, you are kept fully informed in relation to new concepts, methods, practices, and directions in the field.

You discover that you are actually taking the examination all the time: you are preparing for the examination by "taking" an examination, not by reading extraneous and/or supererogatory textbooks.

In short, this PASSBOOK®, used directedly, should be an important factor in helping you to pass your test.

SENIOR PERSONNEL CLERK

DUTIES:

Performs difficult and varied clerical tasks in the processing and maintenance of personnel forms and records; supervises subordinate clerks; and performs related duties. Under general supervision, an incumbent of this position coordinates and performs various specialized administrative support and clerical functions in the Personnel division of a large department. This is the highest level of this series and requires the incumbent to exercise independent judgment in the performance civil service and reporting procedures within an automated personnel/payroll systems environment. Incumbents may act in a lead capacity or may supervise lower level clerical staff. Does related work as required.

SUBJECT OF EXAMINATION:

The written test is designed to test for knowledge, skills, and/or abilities in such areas as:

1. **Office record keeping** - These questions test your ability to perform common office record keeping tasks. The test consists of two or more "sets" of questions, each set concerning a different problem. Typical record keeping problems might involve the organization or collation of data from several sources; scheduling; maintaining a record system using running balances; or completion of a table summarizing data using totals, subtotals, averages and percent. You should bring with you a hand-held battery- or solar-powered calculator for use on this test. You will not be permitted to use the calculator function of your cell phone.
2. **Preparing written material** - These questions test for the ability to present information clearly and accurately, and to organize paragraphs logically and comprehensibly. For some questions, you will be given information in two or three sentences followed by four restatements of the information. You must then choose the best version. For other questions, you will be given paragraphs with their sentences out of order. You must then choose, from four suggestions, the best order for the sentences.
3. **Public contact principles and practices** - These questions test for knowledge of techniques used to interact with other people, to gather and present information, and to provide assistance, advice, and effective customer service in a courteous and professional manner. Questions will cover such topics as understanding and responding to people with diverse needs, perspectives, personalities, and levels of familiarity with agency operations, as well as acting in a way that both serves the public and reflects well on your agency.
4. **Supervision** - These questions test for knowledge of the principles and practices employed in planning, organizing, and controlling the activities of a work unit toward predetermined objectives. The concepts covered, usually in a situational question format, include such topics as assigning and reviewing work; evaluating performance; maintaining work standards; motivating and developing subordinates; implementing procedural change; increasing efficiency; and dealing with problems of absenteeism, morale, and discipline.
5. **Understanding and interpreting written material** - These questions test for the ability to understand and interpret written material. You will be presented with brief reading passages and will be asked questions about the passages. You should base your answers to the questions only on what is presented in the passages and not on what you may happen to know about the topic.

HOW TO TAKE A TEST

I. YOU MUST PASS AN EXAMINATION

A. WHAT EVERY CANDIDATE SHOULD KNOW

Examination applicants often ask us for help in preparing for the written test. What can I study in advance? What kinds of questions will be asked? How will the test be given? How will the papers be graded?

As an applicant for a civil service examination, you may be wondering about some of these things. Our purpose here is to suggest effective methods of advance study and to describe civil service examinations.

Your chances for success on this examination can be increased if you know how to prepare. Those "pre-examination jitters" can be reduced if you know what to expect. You can even experience an adventure in good citizenship if you know why civil service exams are given.

B. WHY ARE CIVIL SERVICE EXAMINATIONS GIVEN?

Civil service examinations are important to you in two ways. As a citizen, you want public jobs filled by employees who know how to do their work. As a job seeker, you want a fair chance to compete for that job on an equal footing with other candidates. The best-known means of accomplishing this two-fold goal is the competitive examination.

Exams are widely publicized throughout the nation. They may be administered for jobs in federal, state, city, municipal, town or village governments or agencies.

Any citizen may apply, with some limitations, such as the age or residence of applicants. Your experience and education may be reviewed to see whether you meet the requirements for the particular examination. When these requirements exist, they are reasonable and applied consistently to all applicants. Thus, a competitive examination may cause you some uneasiness now, but it is your privilege and safeguard.

C. HOW ARE CIVIL SERVICE EXAMS DEVELOPED?

Examinations are carefully written by trained technicians who are specialists in the field known as "psychological measurement," in consultation with recognized authorities in the field of work that the test will cover. These experts recommend the subject matter areas or skills to be tested; only those knowledges or skills important to your success on the job are included. The most reliable books and source materials available are used as references. Together, the experts and technicians judge the difficulty level of the questions.

Test technicians know how to phrase questions so that the problem is clearly stated. Their ethics do not permit "trick" or "catch" questions. Questions may have been tried out on sample groups, or subjected to statistical analysis, to determine their usefulness.

Written tests are often used in combination with performance tests, ratings of training and experience, and oral interviews. All of these measures combine to form the best-known means of finding the right person for the right job.

II. HOW TO PASS THE WRITTEN TEST

A. NATURE OF THE EXAMINATION

To prepare intelligently for civil service examinations, you should know how they differ from school examinations you have taken. In school you were assigned certain definite pages to read or subjects to cover. The examination questions were quite detailed and usually emphasized memory. Civil service exams, on the other hand, try to discover your present ability to perform the duties of a position, plus your potentiality to learn these duties. In other words, a civil service exam attempts to predict how successful you will be. Questions cover such a broad area that they cannot be as minute and detailed as school exam questions.

In the public service similar kinds of work, or positions, are grouped together in one "class." This process is known as *position-classification.* All the positions in a class are paid according to the salary range for that class. One class title covers all of these positions, and they are all tested by the same examination.

B. FOUR BASIC STEPS

1) Study the announcement

How, then, can you know what subjects to study? Our best answer is: "Learn as much as possible about the class of positions for which you've applied." The exam will test the knowledge, skills and abilities needed to do the work.

Your most valuable source of information about the position you want is the official exam announcement. This announcement lists the training and experience qualifications. Check these standards and apply only if you come reasonably close to meeting them.

The brief description of the position in the examination announcement offers some clues to the subjects which will be tested. Think about the job itself. Review the duties in your mind. Can you perform them, or are there some in which you are rusty? Fill in the blank spots in your preparation.

Many jurisdictions preview the written test in the exam announcement by including a section called "Knowledge and Abilities Required," "Scope of the Examination," or some similar heading. Here you will find out specifically what fields will be tested.

2) Review your own background

Once you learn in general what the position is all about, and what you need to know to do the work, ask yourself which subjects you already know fairly well and which need improvement. You may wonder whether to concentrate on improving your strong areas or on building some background in your fields of weakness. When the announcement has specified "some knowledge" or "considerable knowledge," or has used adjectives like "beginning principles of..." or "advanced ... methods," you can get a clue as to the number and difficulty of questions to be asked in any given field. More questions, and hence broader coverage, would be included for those subjects which are more important in the work. Now weigh your strengths and weaknesses against the job requirements and prepare accordingly.

3) Determine the level of the position

Another way to tell how intensively you should prepare is to understand the level of the job for which you are applying. Is it the entering level? In other words, is this the position in which beginners in a field of work are hired? Or is it an intermediate or advanced level? Sometimes this is indicated by such words as "Junior" or "Senior" in the class title. Other jurisdictions use Roman numerals to designate the level – Clerk I, Clerk II, for example. The word "Supervisor" sometimes appears in the title. If the level is not indicated by the title, check the description of duties. Will you be working under very close supervision, or will you have responsibility for independent decisions in this work?

4) Choose appropriate study materials

Now that you know the subjects to be examined and the relative amount of each subject to be covered, you can choose suitable study materials. For beginning level jobs, or even advanced ones, if you have a pronounced weakness in some aspect of your training, read a modern, standard textbook in that field. Be sure it is up to date and has general coverage. Such books are normally available at your library, and the librarian will be glad to help you locate one. For entry-level positions, questions of appropriate difficulty are chosen – neither highly advanced questions, nor those too simple. Such questions require careful thought but not advanced training.

If the position for which you are applying is technical or advanced, you will read more advanced, specialized material. If you are already familiar with the basic principles of your field, elementary textbooks would waste your time. Concentrate on advanced textbooks and technical periodicals. Think through the concepts and review difficult problems in your field.

These are all general sources. You can get more ideas on your own initiative, following these leads. For example, training manuals and publications of the government agency which employs workers in your field can be useful, particularly for technical and professional positions. A letter or visit to the government department involved may result in more specific study suggestions, and certainly will provide you with a more definite idea of the exact nature of the position you are seeking.

III. KINDS OF TESTS

Tests are used for purposes other than measuring knowledge and ability to perform specified duties. For some positions, it is equally important to test ability to make adjustments to new situations or to profit from training. In others, basic mental abilities not dependent on information are essential. Questions which test these things may not appear as pertinent to the duties of the position as those which test for knowledge and information. Yet they are often highly important parts of a fair examination. For very general questions, it is almost impossible to help you direct your study efforts. What we can do is to point out some of the more common of these general abilities needed in public service positions and describe some typical questions.

1) General information

Broad, general information has been found useful for predicting job success in some kinds of work. This is tested in a variety of ways, from vocabulary lists to questions about current events. Basic background in some field of work, such as sociology or economics, may be sampled in a group of questions. Often these are principles which have become familiar to most persons through exposure rather than through formal training. It is difficult to advise you how to study for these questions; being alert to the world around you is our best suggestion.

2) Verbal ability

An example of an ability needed in many positions is verbal or language ability. Verbal ability is, in brief, the ability to use and understand words. Vocabulary and grammar tests are typical measures of this ability. Reading comprehension or paragraph interpretation questions are common in many kinds of civil service tests. You are given a paragraph of written material and asked to find its central meaning.

3) Numerical ability

Number skills can be tested by the familiar arithmetic problem, by checking paired lists of numbers to see which are alike and which are different, or by interpreting charts and graphs. In the latter test, a graph may be printed in the test booklet which you are asked to use as the basis for answering questions.

4) Observation

A popular test for law-enforcement positions is the observation test. A picture is shown to you for several minutes, then taken away. Questions about the picture test your ability to observe both details and larger elements.

5) Following directions

In many positions in the public service, the employee must be able to carry out written instructions dependably and accurately. You may be given a chart with several columns, each column listing a variety of information. The questions require you to carry out directions involving the information given in the chart.

6) Skills and aptitudes

Performance tests effectively measure some manual skills and aptitudes. When the skill is one in which you are trained, such as typing or shorthand, you can practice. These tests are often very much like those given in business school or high school courses. For many of the other skills and aptitudes, however, no short-time preparation can be made. Skills and abilities natural to you or that you have developed throughout your lifetime are being tested.

Many of the general questions just described provide all the data needed to answer the questions and ask you to use your reasoning ability to find the answers. Your best preparation for these tests, as well as for tests of facts and ideas, is to be at your physical and mental best. You, no doubt, have your own methods of getting into an exam-taking mood and keeping "in shape." The next section lists some ideas on this subject.

IV. KINDS OF QUESTIONS

Only rarely is the "essay" question, which you answer in narrative form, used in civil service tests. Civil service tests are usually of the short-answer type. Full instructions for answering these questions will be given to you at the examination. But in case this is your first experience with short-answer questions and separate answer sheets, here is what you need to know:

1) Multiple-choice Questions

Most popular of the short-answer questions is the "multiple choice" or "best answer" question. It can be used, for example, to test for factual knowledge, ability to solve problems or judgment in meeting situations found at work.

A multiple-choice question is normally one of three types—

- It can begin with an incomplete statement followed by several possible endings. You are to find the one ending which *best* completes the statement, although some of the others may not be entirely wrong.
- It can also be a complete statement in the form of a question which is answered by choosing one of the statements listed.

- It can be in the form of a problem – again you select the best answer.

Here is an example of a multiple-choice question with a discussion which should give you some clues as to the method for choosing the right answer:

When an employee has a complaint about his assignment, the action which will *best* help him overcome his difficulty is to

A. discuss his difficulty with his coworkers
B. take the problem to the head of the organization
C. take the problem to the person who gave him the assignment
D. say nothing to anyone about his complaint

In answering this question, you should study each of the choices to find which is best. Consider choice "A" – Certainly an employee may discuss his complaint with fellow employees, but no change or improvement can result, and the complaint remains unresolved. Choice "B" is a poor choice since the head of the organization probably does not know what assignment you have been given, and taking your problem to him is known as "going over the head" of the supervisor. The supervisor, or person who made the assignment, is the person who can clarify it or correct any injustice. Choice "C" is, therefore, correct. To say nothing, as in choice "D," is unwise. Supervisors have and interest in knowing the problems employees are facing, and the employee is seeking a solution to his problem.

2) True/False Questions

The "true/false" or "right/wrong" form of question is sometimes used. Here a complete statement is given. Your job is to decide whether the statement is right or wrong.

SAMPLE: A roaming cell-phone call to a nearby city costs less than a non-roaming call to a distant city.

This statement is wrong, or false, since roaming calls are more expensive.

This is not a complete list of all possible question forms, although most of the others are variations of these common types. You will always get complete directions for answering questions. Be sure you understand *how* to mark your answers – ask questions until you do.

V. RECORDING YOUR ANSWERS

Computer terminals are used more and more today for many different kinds of exams.

For an examination with very few applicants, you may be told to record your answers in the test booklet itself. Separate answer sheets are much more common. If this separate answer sheet is to be scored by machine – and this is often the case – it is highly important that you mark your answers correctly in order to get credit.

An electronic scoring machine is often used in civil service offices because of the speed with which papers can be scored. Machine-scored answer sheets must be marked with a pencil, which will be given to you. This pencil has a high graphite content which responds to the electronic scoring machine. As a matter of fact, stray dots may register as answers, so do not let your pencil rest on the answer sheet while you are pondering the correct answer. Also, if your pencil lead breaks or is otherwise defective, ask for another.

Since the answer sheet will be dropped in a slot in the scoring machine, be careful not to bend the corners or get the paper crumpled.

The answer sheet normally has five vertical columns of numbers, with 30 numbers to a column. These numbers correspond to the question numbers in your test booklet. After each number, going across the page are four or five pairs of dotted lines. These short dotted lines have small letters or numbers above them. The first two pairs may also have a "T" or "F" above the letters. This indicates that the first two pairs only are to be used if the questions are of the true-false type. If the questions are multiple choice, disregard the "T" and "F" and pay attention only to the small letters or numbers.

Answer your questions in the manner of the sample that follows:

32. The largest city in the United States is
    - A. Washington, D.C.
    - B. New York City
    - C. Chicago
    - D. Detroit
    - E. San Francisco

1) Choose the answer you think is best. (New York City is the largest, so "B" is correct.)
2) Find the row of dotted lines numbered the same as the question you are answering. (Find row number 32)
3) Find the pair of dotted lines corresponding to the answer. (Find the pair of lines under the mark "B.")
4) Make a solid black mark between the dotted lines.

VI. BEFORE THE TEST

Common sense will help you find procedures to follow to get ready for an examination. Too many of us, however, overlook these sensible measures. Indeed, nervousness and fatigue have been found to be the most serious reasons why applicants fail to do their best on civil service tests. Here is a list of reminders:

- Begin your preparation early – Don't wait until the last minute to go scurrying around for books and materials or to find out what the position is all about.
- Prepare continuously – An hour a night for a week is better than an all-night cram session. This has been definitely established. What is more, a night a week for a month will return better dividends than crowding your study into a shorter period of time.
- Locate the place of the exam – You have been sent a notice telling you when and where to report for the examination. If the location is in a different town or otherwise unfamiliar to you, it would be well to inquire the best route and learn something about the building.
- Relax the night before the test – Allow your mind to rest. Do not study at all that night. Plan some mild recreation or diversion; then go to bed early and get a good night's sleep.
- Get up early enough to make a leisurely trip to the place for the test – This way unforeseen events, traffic snarls, unfamiliar buildings, etc. will not upset you.
- Dress comfortably – A written test is not a fashion show. You will be known by number and not by name, so wear something comfortable.

- Leave excess paraphernalia at home – Shopping bags and odd bundles will get in your way. You need bring only the items mentioned in the official notice you received; usually everything you need is provided. Do not bring reference books to the exam. They will only confuse those last minutes and be taken away from you when in the test room.
- Arrive somewhat ahead of time – If because of transportation schedules you must get there very early, bring a newspaper or magazine to take your mind off yourself while waiting.
- Locate the examination room – When you have found the proper room, you will be directed to the seat or part of the room where you will sit. Sometimes you are given a sheet of instructions to read while you are waiting. Do not fill out any forms until you are told to do so; just read them and be prepared.
- Relax and prepare to listen to the instructions
- If you have any physical problem that may keep you from doing your best, be sure to tell the test administrator. If you are sick or in poor health, you really cannot do your best on the exam. You can come back and take the test some other time.

VII. AT THE TEST

The day of the test is here and you have the test booklet in your hand. The temptation to get going is very strong. Caution! There is more to success than knowing the right answers. You must know how to identify your papers and understand variations in the type of short-answer question used in this particular examination. Follow these suggestions for maximum results from your efforts:

1) Cooperate with the monitor

The test administrator has a duty to create a situation in which you can be as much at ease as possible. He will give instructions, tell you when to begin, check to see that you are marking your answer sheet correctly, and so on. He is not there to guard you, although he will see that your competitors do not take unfair advantage. He wants to help you do your best.

2) Listen to all instructions

Don't jump the gun! Wait until you understand all directions. In most civil service tests you get more time than you need to answer the questions. So don't be in a hurry. Read each word of instructions until you clearly understand the meaning. Study the examples, listen to all announcements and follow directions. Ask questions if you do not understand what to do.

3) Identify your papers

Civil service exams are usually identified by number only. You will be assigned a number; you must not put your name on your test papers. Be sure to copy your number correctly. Since more than one exam may be given, copy your exact examination title.

4) Plan your time

Unless you are told that a test is a "speed" or "rate of work" test, speed itself is usually not important. Time enough to answer all the questions will be provided, but this does not mean that you have all day. An overall time limit has been set. Divide the total time (in minutes) by the number of questions to determine the approximate time you have for each question.

5) Do not linger over difficult questions

If you come across a difficult question, mark it with a paper clip (useful to have along) and come back to it when you have been through the booklet. One caution if you do this – be sure to skip a number on your answer sheet as well. Check often to be sure that you have not lost your place and that you are marking in the row numbered the same as the question you are answering.

6) Read the questions

Be sure you know what the question asks! Many capable people are unsuccessful because they failed to *read* the questions correctly.

7) Answer all questions

Unless you have been instructed that a penalty will be deducted for incorrect answers, it is better to guess than to omit a question.

8) Speed tests

It is often better NOT to guess on speed tests. It has been found that on timed tests people are tempted to spend the last few seconds before time is called in marking answers at random – without even reading them – in the hope of picking up a few extra points. To discourage this practice, the instructions may warn you that your score will be "corrected" for guessing. That is, a penalty will be applied. The incorrect answers will be deducted from the correct ones, or some other penalty formula will be used.

9) Review your answers

If you finish before time is called, go back to the questions you guessed or omitted to give them further thought. Review other answers if you have time.

10) Return your test materials

If you are ready to leave before others have finished or time is called, take ALL your materials to the monitor and leave quietly. Never take any test material with you. The monitor can discover whose papers are not complete, and taking a test booklet may be grounds for disqualification.

VIII. EXAMINATION TECHNIQUES

1) Read the general instructions carefully. These are usually printed on the first page of the exam booklet. As a rule, these instructions refer to the timing of the examination; the fact that you should not start work until the signal and must stop work at a signal, etc. If there are any *special* instructions, such as a choice of questions to be answered, make sure that you note this instruction carefully.

2) When you are ready to start work on the examination, that is as soon as the signal has been given, read the instructions to each question booklet, underline any key words or phrases, such as *least*, *best*, *outline*, *describe* and the like. In this way you will tend to answer as requested rather than discover on reviewing your paper that you *listed without describing*, that you selected the *worst* choice rather than the *best* choice, etc.

3) If the examination is of the objective or multiple-choice type – that is, each question will also give a series of possible answers: A, B, C or D, and you are called upon to select the best answer and write the letter next to that answer on your answer paper – it is advisable to start answering each question in turn. There may be anywhere from 50 to 100 such questions in the three or four hours allotted and you can see how much time would be taken if you read through all the questions before beginning to answer any. Furthermore, if you come across a question or group of questions which you know would be difficult to answer, it would undoubtedly affect your handling of all the other questions.

4) If the examination is of the essay type and contains but a few questions, it is a moot point as to whether you should read all the questions before starting to answer any one. Of course, if you are given a choice – say five out of seven and the like – then it is essential to read all the questions so you can eliminate the two that are most difficult. If, however, you are asked to answer all the questions, there may be danger in trying to answer the easiest one first because you may find that you will spend too much time on it. The best technique is to answer the first question, then proceed to the second, etc.

5) Time your answers. Before the exam begins, write down the time it started, then add the time allowed for the examination and write down the time it must be completed, then divide the time available somewhat as follows:
   - If 3-1/2 hours are allowed, that would be 210 minutes. If you have 80 objective-type questions, that would be an average of 2-1/2 minutes per question. Allow yourself no more than 2 minutes per question, or a total of 160 minutes, which will permit about 50 minutes to review.
   - If for the time allotment of 210 minutes there are 7 essay questions to answer, that would average about 30 minutes a question. Give yourself only 25 minutes per question so that you have about 35 minutes to review.

6) The most important instruction is to *read each question* and make sure you know what is wanted. The second most important instruction is to *time yourself properly* so that you answer every question. The third most important instruction is to *answer every question.* Guess if you have to but include something for each question. Remember that you will receive no credit for a blank and will probably receive some credit if you write something in answer to an essay question. If you guess a letter – say "B" for a multiple-choice question – you may have guessed right. If you leave a blank as an answer to a multiple-choice question, the examiners may respect your feelings but it will not add a point to your score. Some exams may penalize you for wrong answers, so in such cases *only*, you may not want to guess unless you have some basis for your answer.

7) Suggestions
   a. Objective-type questions
      1. Examine the question booklet for proper sequence of pages and questions
      2. Read all instructions carefully
      3. Skip any question which seems too difficult; return to it after all other questions have been answered
      4. Apportion your time properly; do not spend too much time on any single question or group of questions

5. Note and underline key words – *all, most, fewest, least, best, worst, same, opposite,* etc.
6. Pay particular attention to negatives
7. Note unusual option, e.g., unduly long, short, complex, different or similar in content to the body of the question
8. Observe the use of "hedging" words – *probably, may, most likely,* etc.
9. Make sure that your answer is put next to the same number as the question
10. Do not second-guess unless you have good reason to believe the second answer is definitely more correct
11. Cross out original answer if you decide another answer is more accurate; do not erase until you are ready to hand your paper in
12. Answer all questions; guess unless instructed otherwise
13. Leave time for review

b. Essay questions
1. Read each question carefully
2. Determine exactly what is wanted. Underline key words or phrases.
3. Decide on outline or paragraph answer
4. Include many different points and elements unless asked to develop any one or two points or elements
5. Show impartiality by giving pros and cons unless directed to select one side only
6. Make and write down any assumptions you find necessary to answer the questions
7. Watch your English, grammar, punctuation and choice of words
8. Time your answers; don't crowd material

8) Answering the essay question

Most essay questions can be answered by framing the specific response around several key words or ideas. Here are a few such key words or ideas:

M's: manpower, materials, methods, money, management
P's: purpose, program, policy, plan, procedure, practice, problems, pitfalls, personnel, public relations

a. Six basic steps in handling problems:
1. Preliminary plan and background development
2. Collect information, data and facts
3. Analyze and interpret information, data and facts
4. Analyze and develop solutions as well as make recommendations
5. Prepare report and sell recommendations
6. Install recommendations and follow up effectiveness

b. Pitfalls to avoid
1. *Taking things for granted* – A statement of the situation does not necessarily imply that each of the elements is necessarily true; for example, a complaint may be invalid and biased so that all that can be taken for granted is that a complaint has been registered

2. *Considering only one side of a situation* – Wherever possible, indicate several alternatives and then point out the reasons you selected the best one
3. *Failing to indicate follow up* – Whenever your answer indicates action on your part, make certain that you will take proper follow-up action to see how successful your recommendations, procedures or actions turn out to be
4. *Taking too long in answering any single question* – Remember to time your answers properly

IX. AFTER THE TEST

Scoring procedures differ in detail among civil service jurisdictions although the general principles are the same. Whether the papers are hand-scored or graded by machine we have described, they are nearly always graded by number. That is, the person who marks the paper knows only the number – never the name – of the applicant. Not until all the papers have been graded will they be matched with names. If other tests, such as training and experience or oral interview ratings have been given, scores will be combined. Different parts of the examination usually have different weights. For example, the written test might count 60 percent of the final grade, and a rating of training and experience 40 percent. In many jurisdictions, veterans will have a certain number of points added to their grades.

After the final grade has been determined, the names are placed in grade order and an eligible list is established. There are various methods for resolving ties between those who get the same final grade – probably the most common is to place first the name of the person whose application was received first. Job offers are made from the eligible list in the order the names appear on it. You will be notified of your grade and your rank as soon as all these computations have been made. This will be done as rapidly as possible.

People who are found to meet the requirements in the announcement are called "eligibles." Their names are put on a list of eligible candidates. An eligible's chances of getting a job depend on how high he stands on this list and how fast agencies are filling jobs from the list.

When a job is to be filled from a list of eligibles, the agency asks for the names of people on the list of eligibles for that job. When the civil service commission receives this request, it sends to the agency the names of the three people highest on this list. Or, if the job to be filled has specialized requirements, the office sends the agency the names of the top three persons who meet these requirements from the general list.

The appointing officer makes a choice from among the three people whose names were sent to him. If the selected person accepts the appointment, the names of the others are put back on the list to be considered for future openings.

That is the rule in hiring from all kinds of eligible lists, whether they are for typist, carpenter, chemist, or something else. For every vacancy, the appointing officer has his choice of any one of the top three eligibles on the list. This explains why the person whose name is on top of the list sometimes does not get an appointment when some of the persons lower on the list do. If the appointing officer chooses the second or third eligible, the No. 1 eligible does not get a job at once, but stays on the list until he is appointed or the list is terminated.

X. HOW TO PASS THE INTERVIEW TEST

The examination for which you applied requires an oral interview test. You have already taken the written test and you are now being called for the interview test – the final part of the formal examination.

You may think that it is not possible to prepare for an interview test and that there are no procedures to follow during an interview. Our purpose is to point out some things you can do in advance that will help you and some good rules to follow and pitfalls to avoid while you are being interviewed.

What is an interview supposed to test?

The written examination is designed to test the technical knowledge and competence of the candidate; the oral is designed to evaluate intangible qualities, not readily measured otherwise, and to establish a list showing the relative fitness of each candidate – as measured against his competitors – for the position sought. Scoring is not on the basis of "right" and "wrong," but on a sliding scale of values ranging from "not passable" to "outstanding." As a matter of fact, it is possible to achieve a relatively low score without a single "incorrect" answer because of evident weakness in the qualities being measured.

Occasionally, an examination may consist entirely of an oral test – either an individual or a group oral. In such cases, information is sought concerning the technical knowledges and abilities of the candidate, since there has been no written examination for this purpose. More commonly, however, an oral test is used to supplement a written examination.

Who conducts interviews?

The composition of oral boards varies among different jurisdictions. In nearly all, a representative of the personnel department serves as chairman. One of the members of the board may be a representative of the department in which the candidate would work. In some cases, "outside experts" are used, and, frequently, a businessman or some other representative of the general public is asked to serve. Labor and management or other special groups may be represented. The aim is to secure the services of experts in the appropriate field.

However the board is composed, it is a good idea (and not at all improper or unethical) to ascertain in advance of the interview who the members are and what groups they represent. When you are introduced to them, you will have some idea of their backgrounds and interests, and at least you will not stutter and stammer over their names.

What should be done before the interview?

While knowledge about the board members is useful and takes some of the surprise element out of the interview, there is other preparation which is more substantive. It *is* possible to prepare for an oral interview in several ways:

1) Keep a copy of your application and review it carefully before the interview

This may be the only document before the oral board, and the starting point of the interview. Know what education and experience you have listed there, and the sequence and dates of all of it. Sometimes the board will ask you to review the highlights of your experience for them; you should not have to hem and haw doing it.

2) Study the class specification and the examination announcement

Usually, the oral board has one or both of these to guide them. The qualities, characteristics or knowledges required by the position sought are stated in these documents. They offer valuable clues as to the nature of the oral interview. For example, if the job involves supervisory responsibilities, the announcement will usually indicate that knowledge of modern supervisory methods and the qualifications of the candidate as a supervisor will be tested. If so, you can expect such questions, frequently in the form of a hypothetical situation which you are expected to solve. NEVER go into an oral without knowledge of the duties and responsibilities of the job you seek.

3) Think through each qualification required

Try to visualize the kind of questions you would ask if you were a board member. How well could you answer them? Try especially to appraise your own knowledge and background in each area, *measured against the job sought*, and identify any areas in which you are weak. Be critical and realistic – do not flatter yourself.

4) Do some general reading in areas in which you feel you may be weak

For example, if the job involves supervision and your past experience has NOT, some general reading in supervisory methods and practices, particularly in the field of human relations, might be useful. Do NOT study agency procedures or detailed manuals. The oral board will be testing your understanding and capacity, not your memory.

5) Get a good night's sleep and watch your general health and mental attitude

You will want a clear head at the interview. Take care of a cold or any other minor ailment, and of course, no hangovers.

What should be done on the day of the interview?

Now comes the day of the interview itself. Give yourself plenty of time to get there. Plan to arrive somewhat ahead of the scheduled time, particularly if your appointment is in the fore part of the day. If a previous candidate fails to appear, the board might be ready for you a bit early. By early afternoon an oral board is almost invariably behind schedule if there are many candidates, and you may have to wait. Take along a book or magazine to read, or your application to review, but leave any extraneous material in the waiting room when you go in for your interview. In any event, relax and compose yourself.

The matter of dress is important. The board is forming impressions about you – from your experience, your manners, your attitude, and your appearance. Give your personal appearance careful attention. Dress your best, but not your flashiest. Choose conservative, appropriate clothing, and be sure it is immaculate. This is a business interview, and your appearance should indicate that you regard it as such. Besides, being well groomed and properly dressed will help boost your confidence.

Sooner or later, someone will call your name and escort you into the interview room. *This is it.* From here on you are on your own. It is too late for any more preparation. But remember, you asked for this opportunity to prove your fitness, and you are here because your request was granted.

What happens when you go in?

The usual sequence of events will be as follows: The clerk (who is often the board stenographer) will introduce you to the chairman of the oral board, who will introduce you to the other members of the board. Acknowledge the introductions before you sit down. Do not be surprised if you find a microphone facing you or a stenotypist sitting by. Oral interviews are usually recorded in the event of an appeal or other review.

Usually the chairman of the board will open the interview by reviewing the highlights of your education and work experience from your application – primarily for the benefit of the other members of the board, as well as to get the material into the record. Do not interrupt or comment unless there is an error or significant misinterpretation; if that is the case, do not hesitate. But do not quibble about insignificant matters. Also, he will usually ask you some question about your education, experience or your present job – partly to get you to start talking and to establish the interviewing "rapport." He may start the actual questioning, or turn it over to one of the other members. Frequently, each member undertakes the questioning on a particular area, one in which he is perhaps most competent, so you can expect each member to participate in the examination. Because time is limited, you may also expect some rather abrupt switches in the direction the questioning takes, so do not be upset by it. Normally, a board member will not pursue a single line of questioning unless he discovers a particular strength or weakness.

After each member has participated, the chairman will usually ask whether any member has any further questions, then will ask you if you have anything you wish to add. Unless you are expecting this question, it may floor you. Worse, it may start you off on an extended, extemporaneous speech. The board is not usually seeking more information. The question is principally to offer you a last opportunity to present further qualifications or to indicate that you have nothing to add. So, if you feel that a significant qualification or characteristic has been overlooked, it is proper to point it out in a sentence or so. Do not compliment the board on the thoroughness of their examination – they have been sketchy, and you know it. If you wish, merely say, "No thank you, I have nothing further to add." This is a point where you can "talk yourself out" of a good impression or fail to present an important bit of information. Remember, *you close the interview yourself.*

The chairman will then say, "That is all, Mr. ______, thank you." Do not be startled; the interview is over, and quicker than you think. Thank him, gather your belongings and take your leave. Save your sigh of relief for the other side of the door.

How to put your best foot forward

Throughout this entire process, you may feel that the board individually and collectively is trying to pierce your defenses, seek out your hidden weaknesses and embarrass and confuse you. Actually, this is not true. They are obliged to make an appraisal of your qualifications for the job you are seeking, and they want to see you in your best light. Remember, they must interview all candidates and a non-cooperative candidate may become a failure in spite of their best efforts to bring out his qualifications. Here are 15 suggestions that will help you:

1) Be natural – Keep your attitude confident, not cocky

If you are not confident that you can do the job, do not expect the board to be. Do not apologize for your weaknesses, try to bring out your strong points. The board is interested in a positive, not negative, presentation. Cockiness will antagonize any board member and make him wonder if you are covering up a weakness by a false show of strength.

2) Get comfortable, but don't lounge or sprawl

Sit erectly but not stiffly. A careless posture may lead the board to conclude that you are careless in other things, or at least that you are not impressed by the importance of the occasion. Either conclusion is natural, even if incorrect. Do not fuss with your clothing, a pencil or an ashtray. Your hands may occasionally be useful to emphasize a point; do not let them become a point of distraction.

3) Do not wisecrack or make small talk

This is a serious situation, and your attitude should show that you consider it as such. Further, the time of the board is limited – they do not want to waste it, and neither should you.

4) Do not exaggerate your experience or abilities

In the first place, from information in the application or other interviews and sources, the board may know more about you than you think. Secondly, you probably will not get away with it. An experienced board is rather adept at spotting such a situation, so do not take the chance.

5) If you know a board member, do not make a point of it, yet do not hide it

Certainly you are not fooling him, and probably not the other members of the board. Do not try to take advantage of your acquaintanceship – it will probably do you little good.

6) Do not dominate the interview

Let the board do that. They will give you the clues – do not assume that you have to do all the talking. Realize that the board has a number of questions to ask you, and do not try to take up all the interview time by showing off your extensive knowledge of the answer to the first one.

7) Be attentive

You only have 20 minutes or so, and you should keep your attention at its sharpest throughout. When a member is addressing a problem or question to you, give him your undivided attention. Address your reply principally to him, but do not exclude the other board members.

8) Do not interrupt

A board member may be stating a problem for you to analyze. He will ask you a question when the time comes. Let him state the problem, and wait for the question.

9) Make sure you understand the question

Do not try to answer until you are sure what the question is. If it is not clear, restate it in your own words or ask the board member to clarify it for you. However, do not haggle about minor elements.

10) Reply promptly but not hastily

A common entry on oral board rating sheets is "candidate responded readily," or "candidate hesitated in replies." Respond as promptly and quickly as you can, but do not jump to a hasty, ill-considered answer.

11) Do not be peremptory in your answers

A brief answer is proper – but do not fire your answer back. That is a losing game from your point of view. The board member can probably ask questions much faster than you can answer them.

12) Do not try to create the answer you think the board member wants

He is interested in what kind of mind you have and how it works – not in playing games. Furthermore, he can usually spot this practice and will actually grade you down on it.

13) Do not switch sides in your reply merely to agree with a board member

Frequently, a member will take a contrary position merely to draw you out and to see if you are willing and able to defend your point of view. Do not start a debate, yet do not surrender a good position. If a position is worth taking, it is worth defending.

14) Do not be afraid to admit an error in judgment if you are shown to be wrong

The board knows that you are forced to reply without any opportunity for careful consideration. Your answer may be demonstrably wrong. If so, admit it and get on with the interview.

15) Do not dwell at length on your present job

The opening question may relate to your present assignment. Answer the question but do not go into an extended discussion. You are being examined for a *new* job, not your present one. As a matter of fact, try to phrase ALL your answers in terms of the job for which you are being examined.

Basis of Rating

Probably you will forget most of these "do's" and "don'ts" when you walk into the oral interview room. Even remembering them all will not ensure you a passing grade. Perhaps you did not have the qualifications in the first place. But remembering them will help you to put your best foot forward, without treading on the toes of the board members.

Rumor and popular opinion to the contrary notwithstanding, an oral board wants you to make the best appearance possible. They know you are under pressure – but they also want to see how you respond to it as a guide to what your reaction would be under the pressures of the job you seek. They will be influenced by the degree of poise you display, the personal traits you show and the manner in which you respond.

ABOUT THIS BOOK

This book contains tests divided into Examination Sections. Go through each test, answering every question in the margin. We have also attached a sample answer sheet at the back of the book that can be removed and used. At the end of each test look at the answer key and check your answers. On the ones you got wrong, look at the right answer choice and learn. Do not fill in the answers first. Do not memorize the questions and answers, but understand the answer and principles involved. On your test, the questions will likely be different from the samples. Questions are changed and new ones added. If you understand these past questions you should have success with any changes that arise. Tests may consist of several types of questions. We have additional books on each subject should more study be advisable or necessary for you. Finally, the more you study, the better prepared you will be. This book is intended to be the last thing you study before you walk into the examination room. Prior study of relevant texts is also recommended. NLC publishes some of these in our Fundamental Series. Knowledge and good sense are important factors in passing your exam. Good luck also helps. So now study this Passbook, absorb the material contained within and take that knowledge into the examination. Then do your best to pass that exam.

EXAMINATION SECTION

EXAMINATION SECTION
TEST 1

DIRECTIONS: Each question or incomplete statement is followed by several suggested answers or completions. Select the one that BEST answers the question or completes the statement. *PRINT THE LETTER OF THE CORRECT ANSWER IN THE SPACE AT THE RIGHT.*

1. As the supervisor of a staff of clerical employees performing various types of work, you are responsible for the accuracy and efficiency with which their work is performed.
   Of the following actions you may take to insure the accuracy of their work, the MOST practical one is for you to

   A. review each operation completed by a staff member before permitting the employee to proceed to the next operation
   B. keep a record of every error made by an employee and use this record to determine whether a careless employee should be transferred or discharged
   C. assign work in such a way that every operation is performed independently by two employees
   D. determine what errors are likely to occur and set up safeguards to prevent the occurrence of these errors

2. Assume that you are the supervisor of a small clerical unit. One of your subordinates has violated a staff regulation by failing to inform you that he will be absent on a certain day.
   Of the following, the MOST appropriate action for you to take first is to

   A. discuss this matter with your immediate superior
   B. find out the reason for his failure to obey this staff regulation
   C. determine what disciplinary action other supervisors have taken in similar cases
   D. take no action if his absence did not interfere with the work of the unit; reprimand him if it did

3. A newly appointed clerk is assigned to a unit of an agency at a time when the supervisor of the unit is very busy and has little time to devote to instructing the new employee in the work he is to perform.
   Of the following, the MOST appropriate method of training this employee is for the supervisor to

   A. instruct the new employee to observe several experienced clerks at work and question them regarding any aspect of the work he does not understand
   B. delegate the job of training this employee to an employee in the unit who is qualified to instruct him
   C. assign the new employee a simple task and inform him that more complex and varied duties will be given him when the supervisor is less busy
   D. have the employee spend his time reading the agency's annual reports and the laws, rules, and regulations governing its work

4. As a supervisor, you may find it necessary to consult with your superior before taking action on some matters.
   Of the following, the action for which it is MOST important that you obtain the prior approval of your superior is one that involves

A. assuming additional functions for your unit
B. rotating assignments among your staff members
C. initiating regular meetings of your staff
D. assigning certain members of your staff to work overtime on an emergency job

5. Suppose that a clerk who is employed in a unit under your supervision performs his work quickly but carelessly. He is about to be transferred to another unit in your department. The chief of this other unit asks you for your opinion of this employee's work habits. Of the following, the MOST appropriate reply for you to make is to

A. point out this employee's good qualities only since he may correct his bad qualities after his transfer is effected
B. say nothing good or bad about this employee, thus permitting him to start his new assignment with a clean slate
C. inform the unit chief that this clerk performed his work speedily but was careless
D. emphasize this employee's good points and minimize his bad points

6. When subordinates request his advice in solving problems encountered in their work, a certain bureau chief occasionally answers the request by first asking the subordinate what he thinks should be done.
This action by the bureau chief is, on the whole,

A. *desirable* because it stimulates subordinates to give more thought to the solution of problems encountered
B. *undesirable* because it discourages subordinates from asking questions
C. *desirable* because it discourages subordinates from asking questions
D. *undesirable* because it undermines the confidence of subordinates in the ability of their supervisor

7. Of the following factors that may be considered by a unit head in dealing with the tardy subordinate, the one which should be given LEAST consideration is the

A. frequency with which the employee is tardy
B. effect of the employee's tardiness upon the work of other employees
C. willingness of the employee to work overtime when necessary
D. cause of the employee's tardiness

8. Of the following, the action that is likely to contribute MOST to the prestige of a supervisor is for him to

A. expect all his subordinates to perform with equal efficiency any tasks assigned to them
B. observe the same rules of conduct that he expects his subordinates to observe
C. seek their advice on his personal problems and offer them his advice on their personal problems
D. be always frank and outspoken to his subordinates in pointing out their faults

9. Although an employee under your supervision frequently protests when receiving a monotonous assignment, he nevertheless performs the assigned task efficiently. His protests, however, disturb the other employees and interfere with their work.
Of the following actions you may take in handling this employee, the MOST desirable one is for you to

A. point out to him the effect of his conduct on the staff's work and request his cooperation in accepting such assignments
B. arrange to issue such assignments to him when the other members of his staff are not present
C. inform him that you will request his transfer to another unit unless he puts a halt to his unjustifiable protests
D. ask other members of the staff to tell him that he is disturbing them by his protests

10. Assume that you are the supervisor of a small clerical unit which tabulates data prepared by another unit. One of your employees calls your attention to what appears to be an erroneous figure.
Of the following, the MOST acceptable advice for you to give this employee is to tell him to

A. omit the figure containing the apparent error and continue with the tabulation
B. make whatever change in the erroneous figure that appears warranted and notify the supervisor of the unit which prepared the data that errors are being made by his staff
C. accept the questionable figure as correct and continue with the tabulation since there is no certainty that an error has been made
D. ask the supervisor of the unit that prepared the data to have the questionable figure checked for accuracy and corrected if it is erroneous

11. A clerk in an agency informs Mr. Brown, an applicant for a license issued by the agency, that the application filed by him was denied because he lacks a year and six months of required experience. Shortly after the applicant leaves the agency's office, the clerk realizes that Mr. Brown lacks only six months of required experience rather than a year and six months.
Of the following, the MOST desirable procedure to be followed in connection with this matter is that

A. a printed copy of the requirements should be sent to Mr. Brown
B. a letter explaining and correcting the error should be sent to Mr. Brown
C. no action should be taken because Mr. Brown is not qualified at the present time for the license
D. a report of this matter should be prepared and attached to Mr. Brown's application for reference if Mr. Brown should file another application

12. Mr. Stone, who has been recently placed in charge of a clerical unit staffed with ten employees, plans to institute several radical changes in the procedures of his unit.
Of the following actions he may take before adopting any of the revisions, the MOST desirable one is for Mr. Stone to

A. distribute to each staff member a memorandum describing the revised procedures and requesting the staff's cooperation in giving the revised procedures a fair trial
B. issue to each staff member a memorandum describing the proposed changes and inviting him to submit his written criticism of these proposed changes
C. issue to each staff member a memorandum describing the proposed changes and notifying him of the time and date of a staff conference to be held on the merits of the proposed changes
D. discuss the proposed changes with each staff member independently and obtain his opinion of the proposed changes

13. An assignment completed by Frank King is returned to him by his unit supervisor for certain changes. Frank King objects to making these changes.
Of the following, the MOST appropriate action for the unit supervisor to take first is to

A. permit Frank King to present his arguments against making these changes
B. inform Frank King that he is free to take the matter up with a higher authority
C. reprimand Frank King for objecting and assign another employee to make these changes
D. state briefly that his decision is final and indicate by his manner that further discussion would be useless

14. A properly conducted job analysis will reveal the qualities essential for efficient job performance.
Of the following, the MOST accurate implication of this statement is that job analysis

A. enables the supervisor to standardize procedures
B. aids the supervisor in fitting the man to the job
C. is helpful to the supervisor in scheduling work
D. assists the supervisor in estimating costs of jobs

15. All of us who are employed by a government agency are, figuratively speaking, living in glass houses.
Of the following, this quotation MOST nearly means that employees of government agencies are

A. basically secure in their positions
B. more closely supervised than are those in private industry
C. not free to exercise initiative
D. subject to constant surveillance

16. So important to good supervision is effective leadership that some supervisors who are well equipped in this respect have compensated for deficiencies in other supervisory qualities.
On the basis of this statement, the MOST accurate of the following statements is that

A. supervisory ability is the most valuable attribute a leader can have
B. effective leaders are generally deficient in other supervisory qualities
C. other supervisory qualities may be substituted for leadership ability
D. good leaders may make good supervisors even though lacking in other supervisory qualities

17. The improvement in skill and the development of proper attitudes are essential factors in the building of correct work habits.
Of the following, the MOST valid implication of this statement for a supervisor is that

A. the more skilled an employee is, the better will be his attitude toward his work
B. developing proper attitudes in subordinates toward their work is more time-consuming for the supervisor than improving their skill
C. the improvement of a worker's skill is only part of a supervisor's job
D. correct work habits are established in order to either improve the skill of workers or develop in them a proper attitude toward their work

Questions 18-21.

DIRECTIONS: Questions 18 through 21 are based upon the situation described below. Consider the facts given in this situation when answering these questions.

SITUATION: *You are the supervisor of a small unit in a large department. In order to assist your staff in handling a peak work load, ten temporary clerks have been hired for a period of two months.*

18. Of the following actions you may take before assigning specific tasks to these temporary employees, the MOST appropriate action is for you to

    A. designate one of their number as your supervisory assistant
    B. find out what clerical experience and training each one has had
    C. ask each member of this group to indicate the type of work he prefers to do
    D. escort this group throughout the department, introducing each temporary employee to all the unit heads in the department

19. The ten temporary employees have been grouped into two teams of five employees each, and the two teams have been given different assignments. After working with his group for several days, an employee in one group asks to be transferred to the other group.
    Of the following reasons for transferring this employee to the other group, the LEAST acceptable one is that

    A. there is a clash in temperament between him and some of the other members of his group
    B. he can perform the work assigned to the other group more efficiently than he can perform the work assigned to his group
    C. the work assigned to the other group is less monotonous than that assigned to his group
    D. the work assigned to his present group compels him to take frequent rest periods because of a physical disability

20. One of the temporary employees informs you that he has a suggestion for improving the method of performing the work assigned to his group.
    Of the following actions, the MOST desirable one for you to take is to

    A. ignore his suggestion since he knows little about the purpose of the assignment
    B. ask him to try out the suggestion before submitting it to you
    C. have him discuss it with his co-workers before submitting it to you
    D. listen to his suggestion and take appropriate action

21. A temporary clerk who had been decreasing the amount of work he performed and who had also been attempting to induce other temporary clerks to reduce their production was twice cautioned by you to cease these practices. On each occasion, he promised to discontinue these improper practices and to perform his work conscientiously and cooperatively. Soon thereafter, he is detected for the third time attempting to persuade the other temporary clerks to shirk their duties.
    Of the following, the MOST appropriate action for you to take is to

A. reprimand him for his improper conduct and have him transferred immediately to another unit
B. remind him that he may not be employed again as a temporary clerk if he continues his unethical practices
C. call a meeting of the temporary staff and warn them that anyone whose production falls below average will be discharged
D. report his improper practices to your immediate superior and recommend that this employee's services be terminated

22. As a supervisor in an agency, you receive a letter from the head of a civic organization requesting information which you are not permitted to divulge. In preparing your letter of reply, it is MOST desirable that you

A. begin with a pleasant phrase or statement and conclude with a brief statement denying the request
B. limit your reply to a brief statement denying the request
C. place the denial of the request between a pleasant opening phrase or statement and a cordial closing statement
D. begin with a denial of the request and conclude with a pleasant closing statement

23. Of the following, it is LEAST essential for a supervisor, in assigning work to a subordinate, to issue written instructions when the

A. supervisor will be on hand to check the work
B. instructions are to be passed on to other employees
C. assignment involves many details
D. subordinate is to be held strictly accountable for the work performed

24. The suggestion is made that all the secretaries assigned to the bureau chiefs of a certain agency can be transferred to a newly established central transcribing unit which is to be staffed with stenographers and typists. Of the following, the MOST probable effect of reassigning these secretaries would be that

A. the quality of the stenographic and typing work performed by the secretaries would deteriorate
B. the bureau chiefs would be burdened with much of the routine work that is now performed by their secretaries
C. typing and stenographic work would be performed less expeditiously and with frequent delays
D. the development of understudies for bureau chiefs would be greatly hampered

25. In a large agency where both men and women are employed as clerks, certain duties may be assigned more appropriately to women than to men.
Of the following, the assignment that is generally MOST appropriate for a woman clerk is

A. sorting and filing 3x5 index cards
B. issuing supplies from the agency's stockroom to employees presenting requisitions
C. serving at an information desk during the hours from 7:00 P.M. to 11:00 P.M. for a period of two months
D. collecting outgoing mail from the various offices of the agency and delivering incoming mail to these offices

26. A unit supervisor discovers several errors in the work performed by a subordinate. In dealing with this subordinate, it is LEAST desirable for the supervisor to

   A. give his criticism immediately rather than at a later date
   B. make it clear to the subordinate that he is criticizing the subordinate and not the subordinate's work
   C. praise, when possible, some commendable aspect of the subordinate's work before making the adverse criticism
   D. make sure that his criticism is not overheard by other employees

27. The status of the morale of a staff is usually a good indication of the quality of the leadership displayed by the supervisor of the staff.
Of the following, the BEST indication of the existence of high morale among a staff is that

   A. the employees are prompt in reporting for work
   B. the staff is always willing to subordinate personal desires to attain group objectives
   C. it is seldom necessary for the staff to work overtime
   D. the subordinates and their superior meet socially after working hours

28. The use of standard practices and procedures in large organizations is often essential in order to insure a smooth, efficient, and controlled flow of work. A strict adherence to standard practices and procedures to the extent that unnecessary delay is created is known, in general, as *red tape*.
On the basis of this statement, the MOST accurate of the following statements is that

   A. although the use of standard practices and procedures promotes efficiency, it also creates unnecessary delays and *red tape*
   B. in order to insure a smooth, efficient, and controlled plan of work, *red tape* should be eliminated by a strict adherence to standard practices and procedures
   C. *red tape* is a necessary evil which invariably creeps into any large organization which uses standard practices and procedures
   D. *red tape* exists when delay takes place as a result of a too rigid conformity with standard practices and procedures

29. The tasks of government are imposed not only by law but also by public opinion, which at any time may be made into law. Government agencies must, therefore, strive to anticipate and fulfill the needs of the public.
Of the following, the MOST valid implication of this statement is that the

   A. satisfaction of the needs of the public is one of the obligations of a government agency
   B. law prescribes what tasks government agencies should perform and public opinion determines how these tasks should be performed
   C. tasks imposed by law on a government agency have priority over those imposed by public opinion
   D. functions of a government agency should be carried out in accordance with the letter, rather than the spirit, of the law

30. The manner in which an employee performs on the job rather than his potential ability is the
true test of his value to his employer.
The one of the following which is NOT an implication of the above statement is a(n)

A. employee of great potential ability may be of little or no value to his employer
B. supervisor should observe the manner in which his subordinates perform their work
C. employee's potential ability is of no significance in determining his fitness for a specific job
D. employee should attempt to perform his work to the best of his ability

31. No routine will automatically bring itself into proper relation with changing conditions. Of the following situations, the one which MOST NEARLY exemplifies the truth of this statement is a

A. change in the rules governing the submission or reports by employees working in the field is found to be impractical and the previous procedure is reinstituted
B. long established method of filing papers in a bureau is found to be inadequate because of changes in the functions of the bureau
C. long established method of distributing orders to the staff is found to work effectively when the size of the staff is considerably increased
D. change in the rules governing hours of attendance at work proves distasteful to many employees

32. Interest is essentially an attitude of continuing attentiveness, found where activity is satisfactorily self-expressive. Whenever work is so circumscribed that the chance for self-expression or development is denied, monotony is present.
On the basis of this statement, it is MOST accurate to state that

A. tasks which are repetitive in nature do not permit self-expression and, therefore, create monotony
B. interest in one's work is increased by financial and non-financial incentives
C. jobs which are monotonous can be made self-expressive by substituting satisfactory working conditions
D. workers whose tasks afford them no opportunity for self-expression find such tasks to be monotonous

33. The first step in an organizational study is the reading of the basic documents. There is some documentary basis for any governmental organization, outlining the purposes for which it was established, conferring certain powers, and imposing certain limitations on the conferred powers. This statement indicates that in making an organization study, one should FIRST

A. review all the authoritative material in the field of government administration and organization
B. arrange the functions of the organization on a functional chart in accordance with the official documents
C. study the laws and authorities under which the organization operates
D. outline the purposes for which the organization study was originally established

34. His attitude is as provincial as an isolationist country's unwillingness to engage in any international trade whatever, on the ground that it will be required to buy something from outsiders which could possibly be produced by local talent, although not as well and not as cheaply. This statement is MOST descriptive of the attitude of the division chief in a government agency who

A. wishes to restrict promotions to supervisory positions in his division exclusively to employees in his division
B. refuses to delegate responsible tasks to subordinates qualified to perform these tasks
C. believes that informal on-the-job training of new staff members is superior to formal training methods
D. frequently makes personal issues out of matters that should be handled on an impersonal basis

35. A trainee was paid a weekly wage of $960.00 for a 40-hour work week. As a result of a new labor contract, he is paid $988.00 a week for a 38-hour work week with time-and-one-half pay for time worked in excess of 38 hours in any work week.
If he continues to work 40 hours weekly under the new contract, the amount by which his average hourly rate for a 40-hour work week under the new contract exceeds the hourly rate previously paid him lies between _________ and _________ inclusive.

A. $2.04; $2.12　　B. $2.16; $2.32　　C. $2.36; $2.52　　D. $2.56; $2.72

36. The problem of inadequate storage space arising from the large number of inactive records stored in city agencies can be solved MOST satisfactorily with the aid of

A. copy machines
B. digital archives
C. spreadsheets
D. cloud connectivity

37. To say that an employee is *erudite* means MOST NEARLY that he is

A. scholarly
B. insecure
C. efficient
D. punctual

38. The forms design section of a city agency recommended that the sizes of forms used by the agency be limited to the sizes that can be cut with the least amount of waste from either 17" x 22" or 17" x 28" sheets.
Of the following, the size that does NOT comply with this recommendation is

A. 4 1/2" x 5 1/2"
B. 3 3 /4" x 4 1/4"
C. 3 1/2" x 4 1/4"
D. 4 1/4" x 2 3/4"

39. The number of investigations conducted by an agency in 2022 was 3,600. In 2023, the number of investigations conducted was one-third more than in 2022. The number of investigations conducted in 2024 was three-fourths of the number conducted in 2023. It is anticipated that the number of investigations conducted in 2025 will be equal to the average of the three preceding years.
On the basis of this information, the MOST accurate of the following statements is that the number of investigations conducted in

A. 2022 is larger than the number anticipated for 2025
B. 2023 is smaller than the number anticipated for 2025
C. 2024 is equal to the number conducted in 2022
D. 2024 is larger than the number anticipated for 2025

40. *The office manager thought it advisable to MOLLIFY his subordinate.* The word *mollify* as used in this sentence means MOST NEARLY

A. reprimand B. caution C. calm D. question

41. *The bureau chief adopted a DILATORY policy.* The word *dilatory* as used in this sentence means MOST NEARLY

A. tending to cause delay
B. acceptable to all affected
C. severe but fair
D. prepared with great care

42. *He complained about the PAUCITY of requests.* The word *paucity* as used in this sentence means MOST NEARLY

A. great variety
B. unreasonableness
C. unexpected increase
D. scarcity

43. To say that an event is *imminent* means MOST NEARLY that it is

A. Near to hand
B. unpredictable
C. Favorable or happy
D. very significant

44. *The general manager delivered a LAUDATORY speech.* The word *laudatory* as used in this sentence means MOST NEARLY

A. clear and emphatic
B. lengthy
C. introductory
D. expressing praise

45. *We all knew of his AVERSION for performing statistical work.* The word *aversion* as used in this sentence means MOST NEARLY

A. Training
B. dislike
C. incentive
D. lack of preparation

46. *The engineer was CIRCUMSPECT in making his recommendations.* The word *circumspect* as used in this sentence means MOST NEARLY

A. hostile B. outspoken C. biased D. cautious

47. To say that certain clerical operations were *obviated* means MOST NEARLY that these operations were

A. extremely distasteful
B. easily understood
C. made unnecessary
D. very complicated

48. *The interviewer was impressed with the client's DEMEANOR.* The word *demeanor* as used in this sentence means MOST NEARLY

A. outward manner
B. plan of action
C. fluent speech
D. extensive knowledge

49. To say that the information was *gratuitous* means MOST NEARLY that it was

A. given freely
B. deeply appreciated
C. brief
D. valuable

50. *The supervisor was unaware of this EXIGENCY.*
The word *exigency* as used in this sentence means MOST NEARLY

A. unexplained absence
B. costly delay
C. pressing need
D. final action

51. *She considered the supervisor's action to be ARBITRARY.* The word *arbitrary* as used in this sentence means MOST NEARLY

A. inconsistent
B. Justifiable
C. appeasing
D. dictatorial

52. *His report on the activities of the agency was VERBOSE.*
The word *verbose* as used in this sentence means MOST NEARLY

A. vivid B. wordy C. vague D. oral

Questions 53-61.

DIRECTIONS: Questions 53 through 61 are to be answered SOLELY on the basis of the following information.

Assume that the following rules for computing service ratings are to be used experimentally in determining the service ratings of seven permanent employees. (Note that these rules are hypothetical and are NOT to be confused with the existing method of computing service ratings for employees.) The personnel record of each of these seven employees is given in Table II. You are to determine the answer to each of the questions on the basis of the rules given below for computing service ratings and the data contained in the personnel records of these seven employees.

All computations should be made as of the close of the rating period ending March 31, 2023.

RULES FOR COMPUTING SERVICE RATINGS

Service Rating
The service rating of each permanent competitive class employee shall be computed by adding the following three scores: (1) a basic score, (2) the employee's seniority score, and (3) the employee's efficiency score.

Seniority Score
An employee's seniority score shall be computed by crediting him with 1/2% per year for each year of service starting with the date of the employee's entrance as a permanent employee into the competitive class, up to a maximum of 15 years (7 1/2%). A residual fractional period of eight months or more shall be considered as a full year and credited with 1/2%. A residual fraction of from four to, but not including, eight months shall be considered as a half-year and credited with 1/4%. A residual fraction of less than four months shall receive no credit in the seniority score. For example, a person who entered the competitive class as a permanent employee on August 1, 2015 would, as of March 31, 2018, be credited with a seniority score of 1 1/2% for his two years and 8 months of service.

Efficiency Score
An employee's efficiency score shall be computed by adding the annual efficiency ratings received by him during his service in his PRESENT position. (Where there are negative efficiency ratings, such ratings shall be subtracted from the sum of the positive efficiency ratings.) An employee's annual efficiency rating shall be based on the grade he receives from his supervisor for his work performance during the annual efficiency rating period.

Basic Score
A basic score of 70% shall be given to each employee upon permanent appointment to a competitive class position.
An employee shall receive a grade of "A" for performing work of the highest quality and shall be credited with an efficiency rating of plus (+) 3%, An employee shall receive a grade of "F" for performing work of the lowest quality and shall receive an efficiency rating of minus (-) 2%. Table I, entitled "Basis for Determining Annual Efficiency Ratings," lists the six grades of work performance with their equivalent annual efficiency ratings. Table I also lists the efficiency ratings to be assigned for service in a position for less than a year during the annual efficiency rating period. The annual efficiency rating period shall run from April 1 to March 31, inclusive.

TABLE I
BASIS FOR DETERMINING ANNUAL EFFICIENCY RATINGS

		Annual Efficiency Rating for Service in a Position for:		
Quality of Work Performed	*Grade Assigned A*	*8 months to a full year*	*At least 4 months but less than 8 months*	*Less than 4 months*
Highest Quality	*A*	*+3%*	*+1½%*	*0%*
Good Quality	*B*	*+2%*	*+1%*	*0%*
Standard Quality	*C*	*+1%*	*+½%*	*0%*
Substandard Quality	*D*	*0%*	*0%*	*0%*
Poor Quality	*E*	*-1%*	*-½%*	*0%*
Lowest Quality	*F*	*-2%*	*-1%*	*0%*

Appointment or Promotion during an Efficiency Rating Period
An employee who has been appointed or promoted during an efficiency rating period shall receive for that period an efficiency rating only for work performed by him during the portion of the period that he served in the position to which he was appointed or promoted. His efficiency rating for the period shall be determined in accordance with Table I.

Sample Computation of Service Rating
John Smith entered the competitive class as a permanent employee on December 1, 2018 and was promoted to his present position as a Clerk, Grade 3 on November 1, 2021. As a Clerk, Grade 3, he received a grade of "B" for work performed during the five-month period extending from November 1, 2021 to March 31, 2022 and a grade of "C" for work performed during the full annual period extending from April 1, 2022 to March 32, 2023.
On the basis of the Rules for Computing Service Ratings, John Smith should be credited with:

70 % basic score
2 1/4% seniority score - for 4 years and 4 months of service (from 12-1-18 to 3-31-23)
2 % efficiency score - for 5 months of "B" service and a full year of "C" service
74 1/4%

TABLE II

PERSONNEL RECORD OF SEVEN PERMANENT COMPETITIVE CLASS EMPLOYEES

Employee	*Present Position*	*Date of Appointment or Promotion to Present Position*	*Date of Entry As Permanent Employee in Competitive Class*
Allen	*Clerk, Gr. 5*	*6-1-19*	*7-1-06*
Brown	*Clerk, Gr. 4*	*1-1-21*	*7-1-13*
Cole	*Clerk, Gr. 3*	*9-1-19*	*11-1-16*
Fox	*Clerk, Gr. 3*	*10-1-19*	*9-1-14*
Green	*Clerk, Gr. 2*	*12-1-17*	*12-1-17*
Hunt	*Clerk, Gr. 2*	*7-1-18*	*7-1-18*
Kane	*Steno, Gr. 3*	*11-16-20*	*3-1-17*

Grades Received Annually for Work Performed in Present Position

Employee	*4-1-17 to 3-31-18*	*4-1-18 to 3-31-19*	*4-1-19 to 3-31-20*	*4-1-20 to 3-31-21*	*4-1-21 to 3-31-22*	*4-1-22 to 3-31-23*
Allen			C*	C	B	C
Brown				C*	C	B
Cole			*A**	B	C	C
Fox			C*	C	*D*	C
Green	C*	*D*	C	*D*	C	C
Hunt		C*	C	*E*	C	C
Kane				*B**	B	C

Explanatory Notes:
** Served in present position for less than a full year during this rating period. (Note date of appointment, or promotion, to present period.)*

All seven employees have served continuously as permanent employees since their entry into the competitive class.

Questions 53-61.

DIRECTIONS: Questions 53 to 61 refer to the employees listed in Table II. You are to answer these questions SOLELY on the basis of the preceding rules for Computing Service Ratings and on the information concerning these seven employees given in Table II. You are reminded that all computations are to be made as of the close of the rating period ending March 31, 2023. Candidates may find it helpful to arrange their computations on their scratch paper in an orderly manner since the computations for one question may also be utilized in answering another question.

53. The seniority score of Allen is

A. 74% B. 8 1/2% C. 8% D. 8 1/4%

54. The seniority score of Fox exceeds that of Cole by

A. 1 1/2% B. 2% C. 1% D. 3/4 ¼

55. The seniority score of Brown is

A. Equal to Hunt's
B. twice Hunt's
C. more than Hunt's by 1 1/2%
D. less than Hunt's by 1/2%

56. Green's efficiency score is

A. twice that of Kane
B. equal to that of Kane
C. less than Kane's by 1/2%
D. less than Kane's by 1%

57. Of the following employees, the one who has the LOWEST efficiency score is

A. Brown B. Fox C. Hunt D. Kane

58. A comparison of Hunt's efficiency score with his seniority score reveals that his efficiency score is

A. less than his seniority score by 1/2%
B. less than his seniority score by 3/4%
C. equal to his seniority score
D. greater than his seniority score by 1/2%

59. Fox's service rating is

A. 72 1/2% B. 74% C. 76 1/2% D. 76 3/4%

60. Brown's service rating is

A. Less than 78%
B. 78%
C. 78 1/4%
D. more than 78 1/4%

61. Cole's service rating exceeds Kane's by

A. less than 2%
B. 2%
C. 2 1/4%
D. more than 2 1/4%

Questions 62-71.

DIRECTIONS: Each of the sentences numbered 62 to 71 may be classified under one of the following four options:
(A) faulty; contains an error in grammar only
(B) faulty; contains an error in spelling only
(C) faulty; contains an error in grammar and an error in spelling
(D) correct; contains no error in grammar or in spelling

Examine each sentence carefully to determine under which of the above four options it is best classified. Then, in the correspondingly numbered space at the right, write the letter preceding the option which is the BEST of the four listed above.

62. A recognized principle of good management is that an assignment should be given to whomever is best qualified to carry it out.

63. He considered it a privilege to be allowed to review and summarize the technical reports issued annually by your agency.

64. Because the warehouse was in an inaccessible location, deliveries of electric fixtures from the warehouse were made only in large lots.

65. Having requisitioned the office supplies, Miss Brown returned to her desk and resumed the computation of petty cash disbursements.

66. One of the advantages of this chemical solution is that records treated with it are not inflammable.

67. The complaint of this employee, in addition to the complaints of the other employees, were submitted to the grievance committee.

68. A study of the duties and responsibilities of each of the various categories of employees was conducted by an unprejudiced classification analyst.

69. Ties of friendship with this subordinate compels him to withold the censure that the subordinate deserves.

70. Neither of the agencies are affected by the decision to institute a program for rehabilitating physically handicapped men and women.

71. The chairman stated that the argument between you and he was creating an intolerable situation.

Questions 72-75.

DIRECTIONS: Each of questions 72 through 75 consists of a statement containing five words in capital letters. One of these capitalized words is not in keeping with the meaning which the statement is evidently intended to convey. The five words in capital letters in each statement are reprinted after the statement. In the space at the right, write the letter preceding the one of the five words which does MOST to spoil the true meaning of the statement.

72. The alert employee will find, EVEN in the best managed offices, violations of some of the rules of good office management. However, further study will reveal that the correction of such violations is by ALL means a SIMPLE matter, BUT requires research, time, patience, and often a high degree of MANAGERIAL ability.

A. Even B. All C. Simple D. But E. Managerial

73. The information clerk in any organization must DELEGATE tact, courtesy, and good judgment in DEALING with callers, many of whom, on the other hand, DISREGARD business ETIQUETTE in their CONTACT with the information clerk.

A. Delegate B. Dealing C. Disregard
D. Etiquette E. Contact

74. When the supervisor gives advancement or other rewards only to SUBORDINATES who have REQUESTED them, or shows a sincere INTEREST in the welfare of his staff, he is building FAVORABLE ATTITUDES.

A. Subordinates B. Requested C. Interest
E. Favorable E. Attitudes

75. An appointee to the City's civil service must be a bona fide resident of the City for at least three years immediately prior to his APPOINTMENT. An appointee who served in the Armed Forces retains as his legal address that place where he resided prior to his ENTRY into the MILITARY service, PROVIDED he has taken definite action to establish a new RESIDENCE.

A. Appointment B. Entry C. Military
D. Provided E. Residence

KEY (CORRECT ANSWERS)

1.	D	16.	D	31.	B	46.	D	61.	A
2.	B	17.	C	32.	D	47.	C	62.	A
3.	B	18.	B	33.	C	48.	A	63.	D
4.	A	19.	C	34.	A	49.	A	64.	B
5.	C	20.	D	35.	D	50.	C	65.	D
6.	A	21.	D	36.	B	51.	D	66.	B
7.	C	22.	C	37.	A	52.	8	67.	A
8.	B	23.	A	38.	B	53.	A	68.	D
9.	A	24.	B	39.	C	54.	C	69.	C
10.	D	25.	A	40.	C	55.	8	70.	C
11.	B	26.	B	41.	A	56.	C	71.	A
12.	C	27.	B	42.	D	57.	B	72.	B
13.	A	28.	D	43.	A	58.	D	73.	A
14.	B	29.	A	44.	D	59.	D	74.	B
15.	D	30.	C	45.	B	60.	B	75.	D

EXAMINATION SECTION
TEST 1

DIRECTIONS: Each question or incomplete statement is followed by several suggested answers or completions. Select the one that BEST answers the question or completes the statement. *PRINT THE LETTER OF THE CORRECT ANSWER IN THE SPACE AT THE RIGHT.*

1. As head of the filing unit in your department, you have been receiving complaints that material which should be in the files cannot be located. On investigating this matter, you find that one of your new clerks has been careless in placing material in the files. The BEST of the following actions which you might take FIRST is to 1.____

   A. admonish this clerk and tell him that he will be given a below-average service rating if his carelessness continues
   B. remind this clerk that he is a probationary employee and that his services may be terminated at the end of his probationary period if his carelessness continues
   C. call the attention of this clerk to the effects of filing and impress upon him the necessity for accuracy in filing
   D. give this clerk another assignment in the unit where accuracy is less essential

2. The GREATEST amount of improvement in the efficiency and morale of a unit will be brought about by the supervisor who 2.____

   A. reminds his employees constantly that they must follow departmental regulations
   B. frequently praises an employee in the presence of the other employees in the unit
   C. invariably gives mild reproof and constructive criticism to subordinates when he discovers that they have made a mistake
   D. assigns duties to employees in conformance with their abilities and interests as far as practicable

3. Assume that you are the supervisor of a unit which performs routine clerical work. For you to encourage your subordinates to make suggestions for increasing the efficiency of the unit is 3.____

   A. *undesirable;* employees who perform routine work may resent having additional duties and responsibilities assigned to them
   B. *desirable;* by presenting criticism of each other's work, the employees may develop a competitive spirit and in this way increase their efficiency
   C. *undesirable*; the employees may conclude that the supervisor is not capable of efficiently supervising the work of the unit
   D. *desirable*; increased interest in their assignment may be acquired by the employees, and the work of the unit may be performed more efficiently

4. The MOST accurate of the following statements regarding the chief purpose for maintaining a perpetual inventory of office supplies is that it 4.____

   A. eliminates the necessity for making a physical inventory of office supplies
   B. makes available at all times a record of the balance of office supplies on hand
   C. reduces the amount of clerical work required in distributing supplies
   D. reduces the amount of paper work involved in requisitioning supplies

5. Of the following, a centralized filing system is LEAST suitable for filing 5.____

A. material which is confidential in nature
B. routine correspondence
C. periodic reports of the divisions of the department
D. material used by several divisions of the department

6. Form letters should be used mainly when 6.____

A. an office has to reply to a great many similar inquiries
B. the type of correspondence varies widely
C. it is necessary to have letters which are well-phrased and grammatically correct
D. letters of inquiry have to be answered as soon as possible after they are received

7. Assume that you have recommended that one of your subordinates be given a below-average service rating. The subordinate disagreed with your recommendation and requests that you discuss the service rating report with him. 7.____
In taking up this matter with the employee, the BEST of the following procedures for you to follow is to

A. discuss the general standards of evaluation you have used, rather than his specific deficiencies
B. tell him that it would be too time-consuming to discuss his report with him, but inform him that objective standards were used in evaluating all employees and that the reports will be reviewed by an impartial board which will make any changes it deems necessary
C. explain the standards of evaluation you have used and discuss this subordinate's work with him in relation to these standards
D. point out to your subordinate that you are in a better position than he to compare his work with that of the other employees in your unit

8. Suppose that you are assigned to prepare a form from which certain information will be posted in a ledger. It would be MOST helpful to the person posting the information in the ledger if, in designing the form, you were to 8.____

A. use the same color paper for both the form and the ledger
B. make the form the same size as the pages of the ledger
C. have the information on the form in the same order as that used in the ledger
D. include in the form a box which is to be initialed when the data on the form have been posted in the ledger

9. A misplaced record is a lost record. 9.____
Of the following, the MOST valid implication of this statement in regard to office work is that

A. all records in an office should be filed in strict alphabetical order
B. accuracy in filing is essential
C. only one method of filing should be used throughout the office
D. files should be locked when not in use

10. John Smith is applying for a provisional appointment as a clerk in your department. He presents a letter of recommendation from a former employer stating: *John Smith was rarely late or absents he has a very pleasing manner, and never got into an argument with his fellow employees.* 10.____
The above information concerning this applicant

A. proves clearly that he produces more work than the average employee
B. indicates that he was probably attempting to conceal his inefficiency from his former employer
C. presents no conclusive evidence of his ability to do clerical work
D. indicates clearly that with additional training he will make a good supervisor

11. It is not possible to draw a hard and fast line between training courses for greater efficiency on the present job. 11.____
This statement means MOST NEARLY that

A. to be worthwhile, a training course should prepare the employee for promotion as well as for greater efficiency on the present job
B. training courses should be designed only to increase employee efficiency on the present job
C. training courses should be given only to employees who are competing for promotion
D. by attending a training course for promotion, employees may become more efficient in their present work

12. Approximate figures serve as well as exact figures to indicate trends and make comparisons. 12.____
Of the following, the MOST accurate statement on the basis of this statement is that

A. it takes less time to obtain approximate figures than exact figures
B. exact figures are rarely used as they require too much computation
C. for certain purposes, approximate figures are as revealing as exact figures
D. approximate figures can usually be used in place of exact figures

13. Suppose that you are placed in charge of a unit in your department. You find that many of the employees have been disregarding the staff regulation requiring employees to be at their desks at 9:05 A.M. 13.____
Of the following, the LEAST desirable course of action for you to take would be to

A. call a meeting of the staff and explain why it is essential that all employees be at their desks at 9:05 A.M.
B. post conspicuously on the bulletin board a notice calling the employees' attention to the frequent violation of this regulation and requesting them to observe this regulation
C. recommend an above-average service rating for all employees who consistently comply with this regulation, provided their work is satisfactory
D. summon the offenders and explain to them how their violation of this regulation results in decreasing the efficiency of the unit

14. Suppose that certain office responsibilities require you to be frequently absent from the unit you supervise. You have, therefore, decided to designate one of your staff members to act as unit head in your absence. 14.____
Of the following factors, the one which is MOST important in selecting the employee best fitted for this assignment is his

A. manner and personal appearance
B. estimated ability to perform work of a supervisory nature
C. ability to perform his present duties
D. relative seniority in the service

15. One of the assignments in the unit you supervise is the checking of a list of 500 unalphabetized names against an alphabetical 5x8 card index containing several thousand names. The clerk performing this task is to make sure that there is a card in the file for each name on the list. 15.____
The one of the following which you should suggest as the BEST procedure for the clerk to follow is for him to

A. rewrite the names on the list in alphabetical order, look for the corresponding card in the file, and place a check mark next to each name on the list for which he finds a card
B. take each name on the list in turn, look for the corresponding card in the file, and place a check mark in the corner of each card he finds
C. go through all the cards in the file in consecutive order and place a check mark next to each name on the list for which he finds a card
D. take each name on the list in turn, look for the corresponding card in the file, and place a check mark next to each name on the list for which he finds a card

16. Suppose that you are in charge of a unit which maintains a rather intricate filing system. A new file clerk has been added to your staff. 16.____
Of the following assignments that may be given to this clerk, the one which requires the LEAST amount of knowledge of the filing system is

A. placing material in the files
B. removing papers from the files
C. classifying and coding material for filing
D. keeping a record of material taken from, and returned to, the files

17. In undertaking to improve the method of performing a certain job or operation, the new office manager should first ascertain the 17.____

A. present method of performing the job
B. purpose of the job
C. number and titles of employees assigned to the job
D. methods used by other agencies to perform the same kind of job

18. The proofreading of a large number of papers has been assigned to two clerks. These clerks have been instructed to indicate all necessary corrections on a slip of paper, attach this correction slip to the papers, and send them to the typist for correction. 18.____
Of the following additional steps that might be taken before sending the papers to the xerox operator, the BEST one is that the

A. clerks should proofread each paper in its entirety after the corrections have been made on it
B. typist should make the necessary corrections and return the correction slip and the corrected papers to the clerks; the clerks should then examine the papers to see that all the requested corrections have been made properly
C. typist should make the necessary corrections, placing a check mark opposite each correction noted on the correction slip; she should then review the correction slip to make sure that no correction has been omitted
D. typist should make the necessary corrections, place a check mark opposite each correction noted on the correction slip, and return the papers and the correction slip to the clerks; the clerks should then review the correction slip to make sure that a check mark has been placed opposite each item on the correction slip

19. Suppose you are the supervisor of a unit in a department. You notice that a clerk with long service in the department is arguing with a recently appointed clerk regarding the procedure to be followed in performing a certain task. Each is convinced he is right. The argument is disturbing the other employees. 19.____
Of the following, the BEST action for you to take in dealing with this problem is to

A. call the clerks to your desk, discuss the matter with them, and then state which procedure is the correct one
B. support the employee with the longer service, for to do otherwise will impair the morale of the office
C. call the clerks to your desk and tell them to settle their differences without disturbing the others
D. order the clerks to discontinue their argument immediately and to bring the matter up at the next staff conference, where the staff will determine which procedure is the correct one

20. Assume that you devised a new procedure which you expected would result in a substantial reduction in the amount of paper used in performing the work of the unit you supervise. After trying out this new procedure in your unit for several weeks, you find that the quantity of paper saved is considerably less than you anticipated. 20.____
Of the following, the BEST action for you to take first is to

A. inform your staff that they are probably using paper unnecessarily, and that in view of the current paper shortage, you expect them to conserve paper as much as possible
B. suspend the use of this new procedure until you can discover why it has not worked out as you anticipated
C. invite your subordinates to submit suggestions as to how the procedure may be improved
D. analyze the various processes involved in the new procedure to determine whether there are any factors which you may have overlooked

21. Assume that you are the head of the bureau of information in a department. You are faced with the problem of replacing the clerk assigned to the information desk. 21.____
Of the following available employees, the one who should be given the assignment is

A. John Jones, a new clerk who specialized in English at college and recently received a Master of Arts degree; at present, he has no permanent assignment
B. Mary Smith, an excellent stenographer who has had much experience as secretary to one of the bureau heads; she is intelligent, pleasant in manner, and learns quickly
C. Richard Roe, a clerk who has been rated as *tactful, dependable,* and *resourceful* by the various bureau heads who have prepared his service rating reports during the four years that he has been in the department
D. Jane Doe, who is a diligent typist when she works alone but who disturbs the other typists by her constant stream of chatter when she works near them

22. The one of the following which is the MOST accurate statement regarding routine operations in an office is that 22.____

A. routine assignments should not last more than two or three days each week
B. methods for performing routine work should be standardized as much as is practicable
C. routine work performed by one employee should be checked by another employee
D. changes in the procedures of a unit should not affect the existing routine operations of the unit

23. Modern management realizes the importance of sound personnel practices in business administration. It has found that production is largely dependent upon the effective utilization of an employee's interests, capabilities, and skills. 23.____
Of the following, the MOST logical implication of the above statement is that

A. there should be one bureau in each business organization to take charge of both production and personnel administration
B. production cannot be increased without the utilization of a sound personnel policy
C. production will increase if the number of persons assigned to work in a business organization is increased
D. maximum efficiency in an organization cannot be achieved without proper placement of employees

24. One of the stenographers under your supervision has completed all of her assignments, and there is no additional typing to be done. 24.____
It would be LEAST desirable for you to suggest that she

A. straighten up the supply cabinet to improve its appearance
B. check the files for material that is surplus or outdated
C. read the daily newspaper to keep up with current events
D. practice shorthand or typing to improve her speed

25. Of the following, the BEST way for a supervisor to determine when further on-the-job training in a particular work area is needed is by 25.____

A. evaluating the employees' work performance
B. asking the employees
C. determining the ratio of idle time to total work time
D. classifying the jobs in the work area

Questions 26-30.

DIRECTIONS: Each of Questions 26 through 30 consists of a statement containing five words in capital letters. One of these words in capital letters is not in keeping with the meaning which the statement is evidently intended to carry. The five words in capital letters in each statement are reprinted after the statement. In the space at the right, write the letter preceding the one of the five words which does most to spoil the true meaning of the statement.

26. Within each major DIVISION in a properly set-up public or private organization, provision is made so that each NECESSARY activity is CARED for and lines of AUTHORITY and responsibility are clear-cut and INFINITE. 26.____

A. division B. necessary C. cared
D. authority E. infinite

27. In public service, the scale of salaries paid must be INCIDENTAL to the services rendered, with due CONSIDERATION for the attraction of the desired MANPOWER and for the MAINTENANCE of a standard of living COMMENSURATE with the work to be performed. 27.____

A. incidental B. consideration C. manpower
D. maintenance E. commensurate

28. An understanding of the AIMS of an organization by the staff will AID greatly in increasing the DEMAND of the correspondence work of the office, and will to a large extent DETERMINE the NATURE of the correspondence. 28.____

A. aims B. aid C. demand
D. determine E. nature

29. BECAUSE the Civil Service Commission strongly feels that the MERIT system is a key factor in the MAINTENANCE of democratic government, it has adopted as one of its major DEFENSES the progressive democratization of its own PROCEDURES in dealing with candidates for positions in the public service. 29.____

A. Because B. merit C. maintenance
D. defenses E. procedures

30. Retirement and pensions systems are ESSENTIAL not only to provide employees with a means of support in the future, but also to prevent longevity and CHARITABLE considerations from UPSETTING the PROMOTIONAL opportunities for RETIRED members of the career service. 30.____

A. essential B. charitable C. upsetting
D. promotional E. retired

31. Suppose that the amount of money spent for supplies in 2005 for a division of a department was $15,650. This represented an increase of 12% over the amount spent for supplies for this division in 2004. The amount of money spent for supplies for this division in 2004 was MOST NEARLY 31.____

A. $13,973 B. $13,772 C. $14,346 D. $13,872

32. Suppose that a group of five clerks have been assigned to insert 24,000 letters into envelopes. The clerks perform this work at the following rates of speed: Clerk A, 1100 letters an hour; Clerk B, 1450 letters an hour; Clerk C, 1200 letters an hour; Clerk D, 1300 letters an hour; Clerk E, 1250 letters an hour. At the end of two hours of work, Clerks C and D are assigned to another task. Fron the time that Clerks C and D were taken off the assignment, the number of hours required for the remaining clerks to complete this assignment is 32.____

A. less than 3 hours
B. 3 hours
C. more than 3 hours, but less than 4 hours
D. more than 4 hours

33. The employees were SKEPTICAL about the usefulness of the new procedure. The word *skeptical,* as used in this sentence, means MOST NEARLY 33.____

A. enthusiastic B. indifferent
C. doubtful D. misinformed

34. He presented ABSTRUSE reasons in defense of his proposal. The word *abstruse,* as used in this sentence, means MOST NEARLY 34.____

A. unnecessary under the circumstances
B. apparently without merit or value
C. hard to be understood
D. obviously sound

35. A program of AUSTERITY is in effect in many countries. The word *austerity,* as used in this sentence, means MOST NEARLY 35.____

A. rigorous self-restraint B. military censorship
C. rugged individualism D. self-indulgence

36. The terms of the contract were ABROGATED at the last meeting of the board. The *word abrogated,* as used in this sentence, means MOST NEARLY 36.____

A. discussed B. summarized
C. agreed upon D. annulled

37. The enforcement of STRINGENT regulations is a difficult task. The word *stringent,* as used in this sentence, means MOST NEARLY 37.____

A. unreasonable B. strict
C. unpopular D. obscure

38. You should not DISPARAGE the value of his suggestions. The word *disparage,* as used in this sentence, means MOST NEARLY 38.____

A. ignore B. exaggerate
C. belittle D. reveal

39. The employee's conduct was considered REPREHENSIBLE by his superior. The word *reprehensible,* as used in this sentence, means MOST NEARLY 39.____

A. worthy of reward or honor
B. in accordance with rules and regulations
C. detrimental to efficiency and morale
D. deserving of censure or rebuke

40. He said he would EMULATE the persistence of his co-workers. The word *emulate,* as used in this sentence, means MOST NEARLY 40.____

A. strive to equal
B. acknowledge
C. encourage
D. attach no significance to

41. The revised regulations on discipline contained several MITIGATING provisions. The word *mitigating,* as used in this sentence, means MOST NEARLY 41.____

A. making more effective
B. containing contradictions
C. rendering less harsh
D. producing much criticism

42. The arrival of the inspector at the office on that day was FORTUITOUS. The word *fortuitous,* as used in this sentence, means MOST NEARLY 42.____

A. accidental
B. unfortunate
C. prearranged
D. desirable

43. A clerk who comes across the abbreviation *et.al.* should know that it stands for 43.____

A. for example
B. and others
C. disposition pending
D. and every month thereafter

Questions 44-50.

DIRECTIONS: Questions 44 through 50 are to be answered SOLELY on the basis of the following information.

Assume that the following regulations were established in your department to compute vacation allowances for services rendered by its employees during the period from June 1, 2007 through May 31, 2008. You are to determine the answer to each of the questions on the basis of these regulations.

VACATION REGULATIONS
(For the Period June 1, 2007 - May 31, 2008)

The vacation allowance for this period is to be taken after May 31, 2008.

Standard Vacation Allowance

Permanent per annum employees shall be granted 25 days vacation for a full year's service in such status. Employees who have served less than a full year in a permanent per annum status shall receive an allowance of 2 days for each month of such service.

Per diem employees shall be granted 1 1/2 days vacation for each month of service in such status.

Temporary employees shall be granted one day of vacation for each month of service in such status.

No vacation credit shall accrue to employees for the time they are on leave of absence.

Additional Allowance for Overtime

One day of vacation allowance shall be granted for each seven hours of accrued overtime. Where there is a balance of less than 7 hours of accrued overtime, one-half day of vacation shall be granted for each 3 1/2 hours of such overtime. In no case shall the additional vacation allowed for accrued overtime exceed 6 days.

Deductions for Excessive Sick Leave

Sick leave allowance for all employees, regardless of length of service, shall be 12 days for the year. Sick leave taken in excess of 12 days shall be deducted from vacation allowance. Any unused sick leave balance will be canceled on May 31, 2008.

Deductions for Excessive Lateness

Deductions for excessive lateness shall be made from vacation allowance in accordance with the following schedule:

No. of Times Late	Deduction from Vacation Allowance
0-50	no deduction
51-60	1/2 day
61-70	1 day
71-80	1 1/2 days
81-90	2 days
91-100	2 1/2 days
101-120	4 days
121-140	6 days
141 or over	penalty to be determined by Secretary of Department

Unused Vacation

Unused vacation allowance earned during the previous year shall be added to the current vacation allowance, up to a maximum of twelve days.

Note that the vacation allowances are for services rendered during the year ending May 31, 2008, and that computations for all employees are to be made as of that date.

44. Employee A served as a temporary employee from June 1, 2007 through January 31, 2008, and as a permanent per annum employee from February 1, 2008 through May 31, 2008. During the year, he accumulated 45 1/2 hours of overtime and was late 65 times. His vacation allowance should be ______ days. 44.____

A. 16 B. 15 C. 21 1/2 D. 21

45. Employee B was newly appointed to the department as a per diem employee on September 1, 2007. During the year, he took 15 days of sick leave and was late 48 times. His vacation allowance should be ______ days. 45.____

A. less than 10
B. 10 1/2
C. 15
D. 12 1/2

46. Employee C has been a permanent per annum employee throughout the year. He had 15 days of vacation due him from the previous year. During the year, he was late 85 times, he took 10 days of sick leave, and he accumulated 38 1/2 hours of overtime. His vacation allowance should be ______ days. 46.____

A. 38 1/2
B. 42 1/2
C. 40 1/2
D. more than 43

47. Employee D was newly appointed to the department as a permanent per annum employee on July 1, 2007. He was on leave of absence from December 1, 2007 through February 28, 2008. During the year, he took 6 days of sick leave, he was late 70 times, and he accumulated 21 hours of overtime. His vacation allowance should be ______ days. 47.____

A. 24
B. 18
C. 17 1/2
D. 19 1/2

48. Employee E served as a per diem employee from June 1, 2007 through July 31, 2007, and as a permanent per annum employee from August 1, 2007 to May 31, 2008. He had 6 days of vacation due him from the previous year. During the year, he took 13 days of sick leave, he accumulated 70 hours of overtime, and he was late 132 times. His vacation allowance should be ______ days. 48.____

A. less than 29
B. 29
C. 30
D. more than 30

49. The maximum total vacation allowance which a permanent per annum employee can have due him by May 31, 2008 is ______ days. 49.____

A. 43
B. 25
C. 31
D. 37

50. An employee who has served as a temporary employee for 6 months and as a permanent per annum employee for 6 months will earn exactly 50.____

A. two-thirds as much vacation as an employee who has been on a permanent per annum basis for the whole year
B. as much vacation as an employee who has been on a per diem basis for the whole year
C. as much vacation as an employee who has been on a per diem basis for 4 months and on a permanent per annum basis for 8 months
D. as much vacation as an employee who has been on a per diem basis for 8 months and on a permanent per annum basis for 5 months

Questions 51-60.

DIRECTIONS: Each of Questions 51 through 60 may be classified under one of the following four categories:

A. faulty because of incorrect grammar or sentence structure
B. faulty because of incorrect punctuation
C. faulty because of incorrect spelling
D. correct

Examine each sentence carefully to determine under which of the above four options it is best classified. Then, in the space at the right, write the letter preceding the option which is the BEST of the four suggested above. Each incorrect sentence contains but one type of error. Consider a sentence to be correct if it contains none of the types of errors mentioned, even though there may be other correct ways of expressing the same thought.

51. Although the department's supply of scratch pads and stationery have diminished considerably, the allotment for our division has not been reduced. 51.____

52. You have not told us whom you wish to designate as your secretary. 52.____

53. Upon reading the minutes of the last meeting, the new proposal was taken up for consideration. 53.____

54. Before beginning the discussion, we locked the door as a precautionery measure. 54.____

55. The supervisor remarked, "Only those clerks, who perform routine work, are permitted to take a rest period." 55.____

56. Not only will this duplicating machine make accurate copies, but it will also produce a quantity of work equal to fifteen transcribing typists. 56.____

57. "Mr. Jones," said the supervisor, "we regret our inability to grant you an extention of your leave of absence." 57.____

58. Although the employees find the work monotonous and fatigueing, they rarely complain. 58.____

59. We completed the tabulation of the receipts on time despite the fact that Miss Smith our fastest operator was absent for over a week. 59.____

60. The reaction of the employees who attended the meeting, as well as the reaction of those who did not attend, indicates clearly that the schedule is satisfactory to everyone concerned. 60.____

KEY (CORRECT ANSWERS)

1.	C	16.	D	31.	A	46.	C
2.	D	17.	B	32.	B	47.	B
3.	D	18.	B	33.	C	48.	A
4.	B	19.	A	34.	C	49.	A
5.	A	20.	D	35.	A	50.	B
6.	A	21.	C	36.	D	51.	A
7.	C	22.	B	37.	B	52.	D
8.	C	23.	D	38.	C	53.	A
9.	B	24.	C	39.	D	54.	C
10.	C	25.	A	40.	A	55.	B
11.	D	26.	E	41.	C	56.	A
12.	C	27.	A	42.	A	57.	C
13.	C	28.	C	43.	B	58.	C
14.	B	29.	D	44.	D	59.	B
15.	D	30.	E	45.	B	60.	D

EXAMINATION SECTION
TEST 1

DIRECTIONS: Each question or incomplete statement is followed by several suggested answers or completions. Select the one that BEST answers the question or completes the statement. *PRINT THE LETTER OF THE CORRECT ANSWER IN THE SPACE AT THE RIGHT.*

Questions 1-2.

DIRECTIONS: Questions 1 and 2 are to be answered on the basis of the following conditions.

Assume that you work for Department A, which occupies several floors in one building. There is a reception office on each floor. All visitors (persons not employed in the department) are required to go to the reception office on the same floor as the office of the person they want to see. They sign a register, their presence is announced by the receptionist, and they wait in the *reception room for the person they are visiting.*

1. As you are walking in the corridor of your department on your way to a meeting in Room 314, a visitor approaches you and asks you to direct her to Room 312. She says that she is delivering some papers to Mr. Crane in that office. The MOST APPROPRIATE action for you to take is to

   A. offer to deliver the papers to Mr. Crane since you will be passing his office
   B. suggest that she come with you since you will be passing Room 312
   C. direct her to the reception office where Mr. Crane will be contacted for her
   D. take her to the reception office and contact Mr. Crane for her

2. You are acting as receptionist in the reception office on the second floor. A man enters, stating that he is an accountant from another department and that he has an appointment with Mr. Prince, who is located in Room 102 on the first floor. The BEST action for you to take is to

   A. phone the reception office on the first floor and ask the receptionist to contact Mr. Prince
   B. advise the man to go to the reception office on the first floor where he will be further assisted
   C. contact Mr. Prince for him and ask that he come to your office where his visitor is waiting
   D. send him directly to Room 102 where he can see Mr. Prince

3. One of the employees whom you supervise complains to you that you give her more work than the other employees and that she cannot finish these assignments by the time you expect them to be completed.
   Of the following, the FIRST action you should then take is to

   A. tell the employee that you expect more work from her because the other employees do not have her capabilities
   B. assure the employee that you always divide the work equally among your subordinates

C. review the employee's recent assignments in order to determine whether her complaint is justified
D. ask the employee if there are any personal problems which are interfering with the completion of the assignments

4. Assume that a staff regulation exists which requires an employee to inform his supervisor if the employee will be absent on a particular day.
If an employee fails to follow this regulation, the FIRST action his supervisor should take is to

A. inform his own supervisor of the situation and ask for further instructions
B. ask the employee to explain his failure to follow the regulation
C. tell the employee that another breach of the regulation will lead to disciplinary action
D. reprimand the employee for failing to follow the regulation

5. An employee tells his supervisor that he submitted an idea to the employees' suggestion program by mail over two months ago and still has not received an indication that the suggestion is being considered. The employee states that when one of his co-workers sent in a suggestion, he received a response within one week. The employee then asks his supervisor what he should do.
Which of the following is the BEST response for the supervisor to make?

A. "Next time you have a suggestion, see me about it first and I will make sure that it is properly handled."
B. "I'll try to find out whether your suggestion was received by the program and whether a response was sent."
C. "Your suggestion probably wasn't that good so there's no sense in pursuing the matter any further."
D. "Let's get together and submit the suggestion jointly so that it will carry more weight."

6. Assume that you have been trying to teach a newly appointed employee the filing procedures used in your office. The employee seems to be having difficulty learning the procedures even though you consider them relatively simple and you originally learned them in less time than you have already spent trying to teach the new employee.
Before you spend any time trying to teach him any new filing procedures, which of the following actions should you take FIRST?

A. Try to teach him some other aspect of your office's work.
B. Tell him that you had little difficulty learning the procedures and ask him why he finds them so hard to learn.
C. Review with him those procedures you have tried to teach him and determine whether he understands them.
D. Report to your supervisor that the new employee is unsuited for the work performed in your office.

7. There is a rule in your office that all employees must sign in and out for lunch. You notice that a new employee who is under your direct supervision has not signed in or out for lunch for the past three days. Of the following, the MOST effective action to take is to

A. immediately report this matter to your supervisor
B. note this infraction of rules on the employee's personnel record
C. remind the employee that she must sign in and out for lunch every day
D. send around a memorandum to all employees in the office telling them they must sign in and out for lunch every day

Questions 8-15.

DIRECTIONS: Questions 8 through 15 each show in Column I names written on four cards (fettered w, x, y, z) which have to be filed. You are to choose the option (lettered A, B, C, or D) in Column II which BEST represents the proper order of filing according to the rules and sample question given below. The cards are to be filed according to the following Rules for Alphabetical Filing.

RULES FOR ALPHABETICAL FILING

Names of individuals

1. *The names of individuals are filed in strict alphabetical order, first according to the last name, then according to first name or initial, and finally according to middle name or initial. For example: George Allen precedes Edward Bell and Leonard Reston precedes Lucille Reston.*

2. *When last names are the same, for example, A. Green and Agnes Green, the one with the initial comes before the one with the name written out when the first initials are identical.*

3. *When first and last names are the same, a name without a middle initial comes before one with a middle initial. For example: Ralph Simon comes before both Ralph A. Simon and Ralph Adam Simon.*

4. *When first and last names are the same, a name with a middle initial comes before one with a middle name beginning with the same initial. For example: Sam P. Rogers comes before Sam Paul Rogers.*

5. *Prefixes such as De , 0', Mac, Mc, and Van are filed as written and are treated as part of the names to which they are connected. For example: Gladys McTeaque is filed before Frances Meadows.*

6. *Abbreviated names are treated as if they were spelled out. For example: Chas. is filed as Charles and Thos. is filed as Thomas.*

7. *Titles and designations such as Dr., Mr., and Prof, are ignored in filing.*

Names of Organizations

1. *The names of business organizations are filed according to the order in which each word in the name appears. When an organization name bears the name of a person, it is filed according to the rules for filing names of people as given above. Vivian Quinn Boutique would, therefore, come before Security Locks Inc. because Quinn comes before Security.*

2. *When numerals occur in a name, they are treated as if they were spelled out. For example: 4th Street Thrift Shop is filed as Fourth Street Thrift Shop.*

3. *When the following words are part of the name of an organization, they are ignored: on, he, of, and.*

SAMPLE

	Column I	Column II	The correct way to file the cards is:
w.	Jane Earl	A. w, y, z, x	y. James Earl
x.	James A. Earle	B. y, w, z, x	w. Jane Earl
y.	James Earl	C. x, y, w, z	z. J. Earle
z.	J. Earle	D. x, w, y, z	x. James A. Earle

The correct filing order is shown by the letters, y, w, z, x (in that sequence). Since, in Column II, B appears in front of the letters, y, w, z, x (in that sequence), B is the correct answer to the sample question.

Now answer the following questions using that same procedure.

		Column I	Column II
8.	w.	James Rothschild	A. x, z, w, y
	x.	Julius B. Rothchild	B. x, w, z, y
	y.	B. Rothstein	C. z, y, w, x
	z.	Brian Joel Rothenstein	D. z, w, x, y
9.	w.	George S. Wise	A. w, y, z, x
	x.	S.G. Wise	B. x, w, y, z
	y.	Geo. Stuart Wise	C. y, x, w, z
	z.	Prof. Diana Wise	D. z, w, y, x
10.	w.	10th Street Bus Terminal	A. x, z, w, y
	x.	Buckingham Travel Agency	B. y, x, w, z
	y.	The Buckingham Theater	C. w, z, y, x
	z.	Burt Tompkins Studio	D. x, w, y, z
11.	w.	National Council of American Importers	A. w, y, x, z
	x.	National Chain Co. of Providence	B. x, z, w, y
	y.	National Council on Alcoholism	C. z, x, w, y
	z.	National Chain Co.	D. z, x, y, w
12.	w.	Dr. Herbert Alvary	A. w, y, x, z
	x.	Mr. Victor Alvarado	B. z, w, x, y
	y.	Alvar Industries	C. y, z, x, w
	z.	V. Alvarado	D. w, z, x, y

Column I			Column II
13.	w.	Joan MacBride	A. w, x, z, y
	x.	Wm. Mackey	B. w, y, z, x
	y.	Roslyn McKenzie	C. w, z, x, y
	z.	Winifred Mackey	D. w, y, x, z

Column I			Column II
14.	w.	3 Way Trucking Co.	A. y, x, z, w
	x.	3rd Street Bakery	B. y, z, w, x
	y.	380 Realty Corp.	C. x, y, z, w
	z.	Three Lions Pub	D. x, y, w, z
15.	w.	Miss Rose Leonard	A. z, w, x, y
	x.	Rev. Leonard Lucas	B. w, z, y, x
	y.	Sylvia Leonard Linen Shop	C. w, x, z, y
	z.	Rose S. Leonard	D. z, w, y, x

Questions 16-19.

DIRECTIONS: Answer Questions 16 through 19 ONLY on the basis of the information given in the following passage.

Work measurement concerns accomplishment or productivity. It has to do with results; it does not deal with the amount of energy used up, although in many cases this may be in direct proportion to the work output. Work measurement not only helps a manager to distribute work loads fairly, but it also enables him to define work success in actual units, evaluate employee performance, and determine where corrective help is needed. Work measurement is accomplished by measuring the amount produced, measuring the time spent to produce it, and relating the two. To illustrate, it is common to speak of so many orders processed within a given time. The number of orders processed becomes meaningful when related to the amount of time taken.

Much of the work in an office can be measured fairly accurately and inexpensively. The extent of wo.rk measurement possible in any given case will depend upon the particular type of office tasks performed, but usually from two-thirds to three-fourths of all work in an office can be measured. It is true that difficulty in work measurement is encountered, for example, when the office work is irregular and not repeated often, or when the work is primarily mental rather than manual. These are problems, but they are used as excuses for doing no work measurement far more frequently than is justified.

16. According to the above passage, which of the following BEST illustrates the type of information obtained as a result of work measurement? A

    A. clerk takes one hour to file 150 folders
    B. typist types five letters
    C. stenographer works harder typing from shorthand notes than she does typing from a typed draft
    D. clerk keeps track of employees' time by computing sick leave, annual leave, and overtime leave

17. The above passage does NOT indicate that work measurement can be used to help a supervisor to determine

    A. why an employee is performing poorly on the job
    B. who are the fast and slow workers in the unit
    C. how the work in the unit should be divided up
    D. how long it should take to perform a certain task

18. According to the above passage, the kind of work that would be MOST difficult to measure would be such work as

    A. sorting mail
    B. designing a form for a new procedure
    C. photocopying various materials
    D. answering inquiries with form letters

19. The excuses mentioned in the above passage for failure to perform work measurement can be BEST summarized as the

    A. repetitive nature of office work
    B. costs involved in carrying out accurate work measurement
    C. inability to properly use the results obtained from work measurement
    D. difficulty involved in measuring certain types of work

Questions 20-24.

DIRECTIONS: In each of Questions 20 through 24, there is a sentence containing one underlined word. Choose the word (bettered A, B, C, or D) which means MOST NEARLY the same as the underlined word as it is used in the sentence.

20. Mr. Warren could not attend the luncheon because he had a prior appointment.

    A. conflicting B. official
    C. previous D. important

21. The time allowed to complete the task was not adequate.

    A. long B. enough C. excessive D. required

22. The investigation unit began an extensive search for the information.

    A. complicated B. superficial
    C. thorough D. leisurely

23. The secretary answered the telephone in a courteous manner.

    A. businesslike B. friendly
    C. formal D. polite

24. The recipient of the money checked the total amount.

    A. receiver B. carrier C. borrower D. giver

25. You receive a telephone call from an employee in another agency requesting information about a project being carried out by a division other than your own. You know little about the work being done, but you would like to help the caller.
Of the following, the BEST action for you to take is to

    A. ask the caller exactly what he would like to know and then tell him all you know about the work being done
    B. ask the caller to tell you exactly what he would like to know so that you can get the information while he waits
    C. tell the caller that you will have the call transferred to the division working on the project
    D. request that the caller write to you so that you can send him the necessary information

---

KEY (CORRECT ANSWERS)

1. C
2. B
3. C
4. B
5. B
6. C
7. C
8. A
9. D
10. B
11. D
12. C
13. A
14. C
15. B
16. A
17. A
18. B
19. D
20. C
21. B
22. C
23. D
24. A
25. C

TEST 2

DIRECTIONS: Each question or incomplete statement is followed by several suggested answers or completions. Select the one that BEST answers the question or completes the statement. *PRINT THE LETTER OF THE CORRECT ANSWER IN THE SPACE AT THE RIGHT.*

1. Which of the following actions by a supervisor is LEAST likely to result in an increase in morale or productivity?

   A. Delegating additional responsibility but not authority to his subordinates
   B. Spending more time than his subordinates in planning and organizing the office's work
   C. Giving positive rather than negative orders to his subordinates
   D. Keeping his subordinates informed about changes in rules or policies which affect their work

Questions 2-8.

DIRECTIONS: Questions 2 through 8 are based SOLELY on the information and the form given below.

The following form is a Weekly Summary of New Employees and lists all employees appointed to Department F in the week indicated. In addition to the starting date and name, the form includes each new employee's time card number, title, status, work location and supervisor 's name.

DEPARTMENT F

Weekly Summary of New Employees — Week Starting March 25

Starting Date	*Name Last, First*	*Time Card No.*	*Title*	*Status*	*Work Location*	*Supervisor*
3/25	*Astaire, Hannah*	*361*	*Typist*	*Prov.*	*Rm. 312*	*Merrill, Judy*
3/25	*Silber, Arthur*	*545*	*Clerk*	*Perm.*	*Rm. 532*	*Rizzo, Joe*
3/26	*Vecchio, Robert*	*620*	*Accountant*	*Perm.*	*Rm. 620*	*Harper, Ruth*
3/26	*Goldberg, Sally*	*373*	*Stenographer*	*Prov.*	*Rm. 308*	*Merrill, Judy*
3/26	*Yee, Bruce*	*555*	*Accountant*	*Perm.*	*Rm. 530*	*Rizzo, Joe*
3/27	*Dunning, Betty*	*469*	*Typist*	*Perm.*	*Rm. 411*	*Miller, Tony*
3/28	*Goldman, Sara*	*576*	*Stenographer*	*Prov.*	*Rm. 532*	*Rizzo, Joe*
3/29	*Vesquez, Roy*	*624*	*Accountant*	*Perm.*	*Rm. 622*	*Harper, Ruth*
3/29	*Browning, David*	*464*	*Typist*	*Perm.*	*Rm. 411*	*Miller, Tony*

2. On which one of the following dates did two employees *in the same title* begin work?

   A. 3/25 B. 3/26 C. 3/27 D. 3/29

3. To which one of the following supervisors was ONE typist assigned?

   A. Judy Merrill
   B. Tony Miller
   C. Ruth Harper
   D. Joe Rizzo

4. Which one of the following supervisors was assigned the GREATEST number of new employees during the week of March 25?

   A. Ruth Harper
   B. Judy Merrill
   C. Tony Miller
   D. Joe Rizzo

5. Which one of the following employees was assigned *three days after another employee* to the same job location?

   A. Sara Goldman
   B. David Browning
   C. Bruce Yee
   D. Roy Vesquez

6. The title in which BOTH provisional and permanent appointments were made is

   A. accountant B. clerk C. stenographer D. typist

7. The employee who started work on the SAME day and have the SAME status but DIFFERENT titles are

   A. Arthur Silber and Hannah Astaire
   B. Robert Vecchio and Bruce Yee
   C. Sally Goldberg and Sara Goldman
   D. Roy Vesquez and David Browning

8. On the basis of the information given on the form, which one of the following conclusions regarding time card numbers appears to be CORRECT?

   A. The first digit of the time card number is coded according to the assigned title.
   B. The middle digit of the time card number is coded according to the assigned title.
   C. The first digit of the time card number is coded according to the employees' floor locations.
   D. Time card numbers are randomly assigned.

9. Assume that a caller arrives at your desk and states that she is your supervisor's daughter and that she would like to see her father. You have been under the impression that your supervisor has only a two-year-old son.
   Of the following, the BEST way to deal with this visitor is to

   A. offer her a seat and advise your supervisor of the visitor
   B. tell her to go right into her father's office
   C. ask her for some proof to show that she is your supervisor's daughter
   D. escort her into your supervisor's office and ask him if the visitor is his daughter

10. Assume that you answer the telephone and the caller says that he is a police officer and asks for personal information about one of your co-workers.
    Of the following, the BEST course of action for you to take is to

A. give the caller the information he has requested
B. ask the caller for the telephone number of the phone he is using, call him back, and then give him the information
C. refuse to give him any information and offer to transfer the call to your supervisor
D. ask the caller for his name and badge number before giving him the information

Questions 11-16.

DIRECTIONS: Questions 11 through 16 each consist of a sentence which may or may not be an example of good English usage. Consider grammar, punctuation, spelling, capitalization, awkwardness, etc. Examine each sentence, and then choose the correct statement about it from the four choices below it. If the English usage in the sentence given is better than it would be with any of the changes suggested in Options B, C, or D, choose Option A. Do not choose an option that will change the meaning of the sentence.

11. The recruiting officer said, *"There are many different goverment jobs available."*

A. This is an example of acceptable writing.
B. The word *There* should not be capitalized.
C. The word *goverment* should be spelled *government.*
D. The comma after the word *said* should be removed.

12. He can recommend a mechanic whose work is reliable.

A. This is an example of acceptable writing.
B. The word *reliable* should be spelled *relyable.*
C. The word *whose* should be spelled *who's.*
D. The word *mechanic* should be spelled *mecanic.*

13. She typed quickly; like someone who had not a moment to lose.

A. This is an example of acceptable writing.
B. The word *not* should be removed.
C. The semicolon should be changed to a comma.
D. The word *quickly* should be placed before instead of after the word *typed.*

14. She insisted that she had to much work to do.

A. This is an example of acceptable writing.
B. The word *insisted* should be spelled *incisted.*
C. The word *to* used in front of *much* should be spelled loo.
D. The word *do* should be changed to be *done.*

15. He excepted praise from his supervisor for a job well done.

A. This is an example of acceptable writing.
B. The word *excepted* should be spelled *accepted.*
C. The order of the words *well done* should be changed to *done well.*
D. There should be a comma after the word *supervisor*

16. What appears to be intentional errors in grammar occur several times in the passage.

    A. This is an example of acceptable writing.
    B. The word occur should be spelled occurr.
    C. The word appears should be changed to appear.
    D. The phrase several times should be changed to from time to time.

17. The daily compensation to be paid to each consultant hired in a certain agency is computed by dividing his professional earnings in the previous year by 250. The maximum daily compensation they can receive is $200 each. Four consultants who were hired to work on a special project had the following professional earnings in the previous year: $37,500, $44,000, $46,500, and $61,100.
What will be the TOTAL DAILY COST to the agency for these four consultants?

    A. $932 B. $824 C. $756 D. $712

18. In a typing and stenographic pool consisting of 30 employees, 2/5 of them are typists, 1/3 of them are senior typists and senior stenographers, and the rest are stenographers. If there are 5 more stenographers than senior stenographers, how many senior stenographers are in the typing and stenographic pool?

    A. 3 B. S C. 8 D. 10

19. There are 3330 copies of a three-page report to be collated. One clerk starts collating at 9:00 A.M. and is joined 15 minutes later by two other clerks. It takes 15 minutes for each of these clerks to collate 90 copies of the report.
At what time should the job be completed if ALL three clerks continue working at the SAME rate without breaks?

    A. 12:00 Noon B. 12:15 P.M. C. 1:00 P.M. D. 1:15 P.M.

20. By the end of last year, membership in the blood credit program in a certain agency had increased from the year before by 500, bringing the total to 2500.
If the membership increased by the same percentage this year, the TOTAL number of members in the blood credit program for this agency by the end of this year should be

    A. 2625 B. 3000 C. 3125 D. 3250

21. During this year, an agency suggestion program put into practice suggestions from 24 employees, thereby saving the agency 40 times the amount of money it paid in awards. If 1/3 of the employees were awarded $50 each, 1/2 of the employees were awarded $25 each, and the rest were awarded $10 each, how much money did the agency SAVE by using the suggestions?

    A. $18,760 B. $29,600 C. $32,400 D. $46,740

22. Which of the following actions should a supervisor generally find MOST effective as a method of determining whether subordinates need additional training in performing their work?

    A. Compiling a list of absences and latenesses of subordinates
    B. Observing the manner in which his subordinates carry out their various tasks
    C. Reviewing the grievances submitted by subordinates
    D. Reminding his subordinates to consult him if they experience difficulty in completing an assignment

23. Of the following types of letters, the MOST difficult to trace if lost after mailing is the _______ letter.

A. special delivery
B. registered
C. insured
D. certified

24. Suppose that you are looking over a few incoming letters that have been put in your mail basket. You see that one has a return address on the envelope but not on the letter itself. Of the following, the BEST way to make sure there is a correct record of the return address is to

A. return the letter to the sender and ask him to fill in his address on his own letter
B. put the letter back into the envelope and close the opening with a paper clip
C. copy the address onto a 3"x5" index card and throw away the envelope
D. copy the address onto the letter and staple the envelope to the letter

25. Although most incoming mail that you receive in an office will pertain to business matters, there are times when a letter may be delivered for your supervisor that is marked *Personal.*
Of the following, the BEST way 1or you to handle this type of mail is to

A. open the letter but do not read it, and route it along with the other mail
B. read the letter to see if it really is personal
C. have the letter forwarded unopened to your supervisor's home address
D. deliver the letter to your supervisor's desk unopened

KEY (CORRECT ANSWERS)

1. A
2. B
3. A
4. D
5. A
6. D
7. D
8. C
9. A
10. C
11. C
12. A
13. C
14. C
15. B
16. C
17. D
18. A
19. B
20. C
21. B
22. B
23. D
24. D
25. D

EXAMINATION SECTION
TEST 1

DIRECTIONS: Each question or incomplete statement is followed by several suggested answers or completions. Select the one that BEST answers the question or completes the statement. *PRINT THE LETTER OF THE CORRECT ANSWER IN THE SPACE AT THE RIGHT.*

1. The MOST important reason for a supervisor to encourage his staff to make suggestions for improving the work of the unit is that such suggestions may 1.____

   A. indicate who is the most efficient employee in the unit
   B. increase the productivity of the unit
   C. raise the morale of the employees who make the suggestions
   D. reduce the amount of supervision necessary to perform the work of the unit

2. The PRIMARY purpose of a probationary period for a new employee is to 2.____

   A. thoroughly train the new employee in his job duties
   B. permit the new employee to become adjusted to his duties
   C. determine the fitness of the new employee for the job
   D. acquaint the new employee fully with the objectives of his agency

3. A unit supervisor finds that he is spending too much time on routine tasks, and not enough time on coordinating the work of his employees. 3.____
   It would be MOST advisable for this supervisor to

   A. delegate the task of work coordination to a capable subordinate
   B. eliminate some of the routine tasks that the unit is required to perform
   C. assign some of the routine tasks to his subordinates
   D. postpone the performance of routine tasks until he has achieved proper coordination of his employees' work

4. Of the following, the MOST important reason for having an office manual in looseleaf form rather than in permanent binding is that the looseleaf form 4.____

   A. facilitates the addition of new material and the removal of obsolete material
   B. permits several people to use different sections of the manual at the same time
   C. is less expensive to prepare than permanent binding
   D. is more durable than permanent binding

5. In his first discussion with an employee newly appointed to the title of Clerk in an agency, the LEAST important of the following topics for a supervisor of a clerical unit to include is the 5.____

   A. duties the subordinate is expected to perform on the job
   B. functions of the unit
   C. methods of determining standards of clerical performance
   D. nature and duration of the training the subordinate will receive on the job

6. Assume that you have been assigned to organize the files so that all the records now located in the various units in your bureau will be centrally located in a separate files unit. In setting up this system of centrally located files, you should be concerned LEAST with making certain that 6.____

   A. the material stored in the files has been checked for accuracy of content
   B. the filing system will be flexible enough to allow for possible future expansion
   C. material stored in the files can be located readily when needed
   D. the filing system will be readily understood by employees assigned to maintaining the files

7. A supervisor of a unit in a city department has just been told by a subordinate, Mr. Jones, that another employee, Mr. Smith, deliberately disobeyed an important rule of the department by taking home some confidential departmental material. Of the following courses of action, it would be MOST advisable for the supervisor first to 7.____

   A. discuss the matter privately with both Mr. Jones and Mr. Smith at the same time
   B. call a meeting of the entire unit and discuss the matter generally without mentioning any employee by name
   C. arrange to supervise Mr. Smith's activities more closely
   D. discuss the matter privately with Mr. Smith

8. A clerk who has the choice of sending a business letter either by certified mail or by registered mail should realize that 8.____

   A. it is less expensive to send letters by certified mail than by registered mail
   B. it is safer to send letters by certified mail than by registered mail
   C. letters sent by certified mail reach their destinations faster than those sent by registered mail
   D. the person to whom a certified letter is sent is not asked to acknowledge receipt of the letter

9. If the management of a public agency wishes to retain the elasticity of youth among employees who have been with the agency for a long time, it must furnish variety and novelty of work. To carry out the above recommendation, the BEST course of action for an agency to take is to 9.____

   A. encourage older employees to retire at the minimum retirement age
   B. vary its employees' assignments from time to time
   C. assign the routine tasks to newer and younger employees
   D. provide its employees with varied recreational activities

10. The one of the following actions which would be MOST efficient and economical for a supervisor to take to minimize the effect of seasonal fluctuations in the work load of his unit is to 10.____

   A. increase his permanent staff until it is large enough to handle the work of the busy season
   B. request the purchase of time and labor saving equipment to be used primarily during the busy season

C. lower, temporarily, the standards for quality of work performance during peak loads
D. schedule for the slow season work that it is not essential to perform during the busy season

11. A clerk in an agency should realize that each letter he sends out in response to a letter of inquiry from the public represents an expenditure of time and money by his agency. 11.____
The one of the following which is the MOST valid implication of this statement is that such a clerk should

A. use the telephone to answer letters of inquiry directly and promptly
B. answer mail inquiries with lengthy letters to eliminate the need for further correspondence
C. prevent the accumulation of a large number of similar inquiries by answering each of these letters promptly
D. use simple, concise language in answer to letters of inquiry

12. The forms and methods of discipline used in public agencies are as varied as the offenses which prompt disciplinary action, and range in severity from a frown of disapproval to dismissal from the service and even to prosecution in the courts. 12.____
On the basis of this sentence, the MOST accurate of the following statements is that

A. the severity of disciplinary measures varies directly with the seriousness of the offenses
B. dismissal from the service is the most severe action that can be taken by a public agency
C. public agencies use a variety of disciplinary measures to cope with offenses
D. public agencies sometimes administer excessive punishments

13. A well-planned training program can assist new employees to acquire the information they need to work effectively. Of the following, the information that a newly-appointed clerk would need LEAST in order to perform his work effectively is knowledge of the 13.____

A. acceptable ways of taking and recording telephone messages
B. techniques of evaluating the effectiveness of office forms used in the agency
C. methods of filing papers used in his bureau
D. proper manner of handling visitors to the agency

14. A supervisor of a unit who is not specific when making assignments creates a dangerous source of friction, misunderstanding, and inefficiency. 14.____
The MOST valid implication of this statement is that

A. supervisors are usually unaware that they are creating sources of friction
B. it is often difficult to remove sources of friction and misunderstanding
C. a competent supervisor attempts to find a solution to each problem facing him
D. employees will perform more efficiently if their duties are defined clearly

15. The employees' interest in the subject matter of a training course must be fully aroused if they are to derive the maximum benefits from the training. 15.____
Of the following, the LEAST effective method of arousing such interest is to

A. state to the employees that the subject matter of the training course will be of interest to mature, responsible workers
B. point out to the employees that the training course may help them to win promotion

C. explain to the employees how the training course will help them to perform their work better
D. relate the training course to the employees' interests and previous experiences

16. The control of clerical work in a public agency appears impossible if the clerical work is regarded merely as a series of duties unrelated to the functions of the agency. However, this control becomes feasible when it is realized that clerical work links and coordinates the functions of the agency. 16.____
On the basis of this statement, the MOST accurate of the following statements is that the

A. complexity of clerical work may not be fully understood by those assigned to control it
B. clerical work can be readily controlled if it is coordinated by other work of the agency
C. number of clerical tasks may be reduced by regarding coordination as the function of clerical work
D. purposes of clerical work must be understood to make possible its proper control

17. Assume that as supervisor of a unit you are to prepare a vacation schedule for the employees in your unit. 17.____
Of the following, the factor which is LEAST important for you to consider in setting up this schedule is

A. the vacation preferences of each employee in the unit
B. the anticipated work load in the unit during the vacation period
C. how well each employee has performed his work
D. how essential a specific employee's services will be during the vacation period

18. In order to promote efficiency and economy in an agency, it is advisable for the management to systematize and standardize procedures and relationships insofar as this can be done; however, excessive routinizing which does not permit individual contributions or achievements should be avoided. 18.____
On the basis of this statement, it is MOST accurate to state that

A. systematized procedures should be designed mainly to encourage individual achievements
B. standardized procedures should allow for individual accomplishments
C. systematization of procedures may not be possible in organizations which have a large variety of functions
D. individual employees of an organization must fully accept standardized procedures if the procedures are to be effective

19. Trained employees work most efficiently and with a minimum expenditure of time and energy. Suitable equipment and definite, well-developed procedures are effective only when employees know how to use the equipment and procedures. This statement means MOST NEARLY that 19.____

A. employees can be trained most efficiently when suitable equipment and definite procedures are used
B. training of employees is a costly but worthwhile investment

C. suitable equipment and definite procedures are of greatest value when employees have been properly trained to use them
D. the cost of suitable equipment and definite procedures is negligible when the saving in time and energy that they bring is considered

20. Assume that your supervisor has asked you to present to him comprehensive, periodic reports on the progress that your unit is making in meeting its work goals. 20.____
For you to give your superior oral reports rather than written ones is

A. *desirable*; it will be easier for him to transmit your oral report to his superiors
B. *undesirable*; the oral reports will provide no permanent record to which he may refer
C. *undesirable;* there will be less opportunity for you to discuss the oral reports with him than the written ones
D. *desirable;* the oral reports will require little time and effort to prepare

21. Assume that an employee under your supervision complains to you that your evaluation of his work is too low. 21.____
The MOST appropriate action for you to take FIRST is to

A. explain how you arrived at the evaluation of his work
B. encourage him to improve the quality of his work by pointing out specifically how he can do so
C. suggest that he appeal to an impartial higher authority if he disagrees with your evaluation
D. point out to him specific instances in which his work has been unsatisfactory

22. The nature of the experience and education that are made a prerequisite to employment determines in large degree the training job to be done after employment begins. 22.____
On the basis of this statement, it is MOST accurate to state that

A. the more comprehensive the experience and education required for employment the more extensive the training that is usually given after appointment
B. the training that is given to employees depends upon the experience and education required of them before appointment
C. employees who possess the experience and education required for employment should need little additional training after appointment
D. the nature of the work that employees are expected to perform determines the training that they will need

23. Assume that you are preparing a report evaluating the work of a clerk who was transferred to your unit from another unit in the agency about a year ago. 23.____
Of the following, the method that would probably be MOST helpful to you in making this evaluation is to

A. consult the evaluations this employee received from his former supervisors
B. observe this employee at his work for a week shortly before you prepare the report
C. examine the employee's production records and compare them with the standards set for the position
D. obtain tactfully from his fellow employees their frank opinions of his work

24. Of the following, the CHIEF value of a flow-of-work chart to the management of an organization is its usefulness in 24.____

    A. locating the causes of delay in carrying out an operation
    B. training new employees in the performance of their duties
    C. determining the effectiveness of the employees in the organization
    D. determining the accuracy of its organization chart

25. Assume that a procedure for handling certain office forms has just been extensively revised. As supervisor of a small unit, you are to instruct your subordinates in the use of the new procedure, which is rather complicated. 25.____
Of the following, it would be LEAST helpful to your subordinates for you to

    A. compare the revised procedure with the one it has replaced
    B. state that you believe the revised procedure to be better than the one it has replaced
    C. tell them that they will probably find it difficult to learn the new procedure
    D. give only a general outline of the revised procedure at first and then follow with more detailed instructions

26. A supervisor may make assignments to his subordinates in the form of a command, a request, or a call for volunteers. It is LEAST desirable for a supervisor to make an assignment in the form of a command when 26.____

    A. a serious emergency has risen
    B. an employee objects to carrying out an assignment
    C. the assignment must be completed immediately
    D. the assignment is an unpleasant one

27. For an office supervisor to confer periodically with his subordinates in order to anticipate job problems which are likely to arise is desirable MAINLY because 27.____

    A. there will be fewer problems for which hasty decisions will have to be made
    B. some problems which are anticipated may not arise
    C. his subordinates will learn to refer the problems arising in the unit to him
    D. constant anticipation of future problems tends to raise additional problems

28. A methods improvement program might be called a war against habit. 28.____
The MOST accurate implication of this statement is that

    A. routine handling of routine office assignments should be discouraged
    B. standardization of office procedures may encourage employees to form inefficient work habits
    C. employees tend to continue the use of existing procedures, even when such procedures are inefficient
    D. procedures should be changed constantly to prevent them from becoming habits

29. An office supervisor may give either a written or an oral order to his subordinates when making an assignment. 29.____
Of the following, it would be MOST appropriate for a supervisor to issue an order in writing when

    A. a large number of two-page reports must be stapled together before the end of the day
    B. the assignment is to be completed within two hours after it is issued to his subordinates

C. his subordinates have completed an identical assignment the day before
D. several entries must be made on a form at varying intervals of time by different clerks

30. A supervisor should always remember that the instruction or training of new employees is most effective if it is given when and where it is needed. 30.____
On the basis of this statement, it is MOST appropriate to conclude that

A. the new employee should be trained to handle any aspect of his work at the time he starts his job
B. the new employee should be given the training essential to get him started and additional training when he requires it
C. an employee who has received excessive training will be just as ineffective as one who has received inadequate training
D. a new employee is trained most effectively by his own supervisor

31. Some employees see an agency training program as a threat. Of the following, the MOST likely reason for such an employee attitude toward training is that the employees involved feel that 31.____

A. some trainers are incompetent
B. training rarely solves real work-a-day problems
C. training may attempt to change comfortable behavior patterns
D. training sessions are boring

32. Of the following, the CHIEF characteristic which distinguishes a good supervisor from a poor supervisor is the good supervisor's 32.____

A. ability to favorably impress others
B. unwillingness to accept monotony or routine
C. ability to deal constructively with problem situations
D. strong drive to overcome opposition

33. Of the following, the MAIN disadvantage of on-the-job training is that, generally, 33.____

A. special equipment may be needed
B. production may be slowed down
C. the instructor must maintain an individual relationship with the trainee
D. the on-the-job instructor must be better qualified than the classroom instructor

34. All of the following are correct methods for a supervisor to use in connection with employee discipline EXCEPT: 34.____

A. Trying not to be too lenient or too harsh
B. Informing employees of the rules and the penalties for violations of the rules
C. Imposing discipline immediately after the violation is discovered
D. Making sure, when you apply discipline, that the employee understands that you do not want to do it

35. Of the following, the MAIN reason for a supervisor to establish standard procedures for his unit is to 35.____

A. increase the motivation of his subordinates
B. make it easier for the subordinates to submit to authority

C. reduce the number of times that his subordinates have to consult him
D. reduce the number of mistakes that his subordinates will make

36. When delegating responsibility for an assignment to a subordinate, it is MOST important that you 36.____

A. retain all authority necessary to complete the assignment
B. make yourself generally available for consultation with the subordinate
C. inform your superiors that you are no longer responsible for the assignment
D. decrease the number of subordinates whom you have to supervise

37. You, as a unit head, have been asked to submit budget estimates of staff, equipment, and supplies in terms of programs for your unit for the coming fiscal year. 37.____
In addition to their use in planning, such unit budget estimates can be BEST used to

A. reveal excessive costs in operations
B. justify increases in the debt limit
C. analyze employee salary adjustments
D. predict the success of future programs

38. Because higher status is important to many employees, they will often make an effort to achieve it as an end in itself. 38.____
Of the following, the BEST course of action for the supervisor to take on the basis of the preceding statement is to

A. attach higher status to that behavior of subordinates which is directed toward reaching the goals of the organization
B. avoid showing sympathy toward subordinates' wishes for increased wages, improved working conditions, or other benefits
C. foster interpersonal competitiveness among subordinates so that personal friendliness is replaced by the desire to protect individual status
D. reprimand subordinates whenever their work is in some way unsatisfactory in order to adjust their status accordingly

39. Assume that a large office in a certain organization operates long hours and is thus on two shifts with a slight overlap. Those employees, including supervisors, who are most productive are given their choice of shifts. The earlier shift is considered preferable by most employees. 39.____
As a result of this method of assignment, which of the following is MOST likely to result?

A. Most non-supervisory employees will be assigned to the late shift; most supervisors will be assigned to the early shift.
B. Most supervisors will be assigned to the late shift; most non-supervisory employees will be assigned to the early shift.
C. The early shift will be more productive than the late shift.
D. The late shift will be more productive than the early shift.

40. Assume that a supervisor of a unit in which the employees are of average friendliness tells a newly hired employee on her first day that her co-workers are very friendly. The other employees hear his remarks to the new employee. Which of the following is the MOST likely result of this action of the supervisor? The 40.____

A. newly hired employee will tend to feel less friendly than if the supervisor had said nothing
B. newly hired employee will tend to believe that her co-workers are very friendly
C. other employees will tend to feel less friendly toward one another
D. other employees will tend to see the newly hired employee as insincerely friendly

41. A recent study of employee absenteeism showed that, although unscheduled absence for part of a week is relatively high for young employees, unscheduled absence for a full week is low. However, although full-week unscheduled absence is least frequent for the youngest employees, the frequency of such absence increases as the age of employees increases. 41.____
Which of the following statements is the MOST logical explanation for the greater full-week absenteeism among older employees?

A. Older employees are more likely to be males.
B. Older employees are more likely to have more relatively serious illnesses.
C. Younger employees are more likely to take longer vacations.
D. Younger employees are more likely to be newly hired.

42. An employee can be motivated to fulfill his needs as he sees them. He is not motivated by what others think he ought to have, but what he himself wants. 42.____
Which of the following statements follows MOST logically from the foregoing viewpoint?

A. A person's different traits may be separately classified, but they are all part of one system comprising a whole person.
B. Every job, however simple, entitles the person who does it to proper respect and recognition of his unique aspirations and abilities.
C. No matter what equipment and facilities an organization has, they cannot be put to use except by people who have been motivated.
D. To an observer, a person's needs may be unrealistic, but they are still controlling.

43. Assume that you are a supervisor of a unit which is about to start work on an urgent job. One of your subordinates starts to talk to you about the urgent job but seems not to be saying what is really on his mind. 43.____
What is the BEST thing for you to say under these circumstances?

A. I'm not sure I understand. Can you explain that?
B. Please come to the point. We haven't got all day.
C. What is it? Can't you see I'm busy?
D. Haven't you got work to do? What do you want?

44. Assume that you have recently been assigned to a new subordinate. You have explained to this subordinate how to fill out certain forms which will constitute the major portion of her job. After the first day, you find that she has filled out the forms correctly but has not completed as many as most other workers normally complete in a day. 44.____
Of the following, the MOST appropriate action for you to take is to

A. tell the subordinate how many forms she is expected to complete
B. instruct the subordinate in the correct method of filling out the forms
C. monitor the subordinate's production to see if she improves
D. reassign the job of filling out the forms to a more experienced worker in the unit

45. One of the problems commonly met by the supervisor is the *touchy* employee who imagines slights when none is intended. 45.____
Of the following, the BEST way to deal with such an employee is to

A. ignore him until he sees the error of his behavior
B. frequently reassure him of his value as a person
C. advise him that oversensitive people rarely get promoted
D. issue written instructions to him to avoid misinterpretation

46. The understanding supervisor should recognize that a certain amount of anxiety is common to all newly hired employees. 46.____
If you are a supervisor of a unit and a newly-hired employee has been assigned to you, you can usually assume that the LEAST likely worry that the new employee has is worry about

A. the job and the standards required in the job
B. his acceptance by the other people in your unit
C. the difficulty of advancing to top positions in the agency
D. your fairness in evaluating his work

47. In assigning work to subordinates, it is often desirable for you to tell them the overall or ultimate objective of the assignment. 47.____
Of the following, the BEST reason for telling them the objective is that it will

A. assure them that you know what you are doing
B. eliminate most of the possible complaints about the assignment
C. give them confidence in their ability to do the assignment
D. help them to make decisions consistent with the objective

48. Assume that the regular 8-hour working day of a laborer is from 8 A.M. to 5 P.M., with an hour off for lunch. He earns a regular hourly rate of pay for these 8 hours and is paid at the rate of time-and-a-half for each hour worked after his regular working day. 48.____
If, on a certain day, he works from 8 A.M. to 6 P.M., with an hour off for lunch, and earns $99.76, his regular hourly rate of pay is

A. $8.50 B. $9.00 C. $10.50 D. $11.50

49. Two clerical units, X and Y, each having a different number of clerks, are assigned to file registration cards. It takes Unit X, which contains 8 clerks, 21 days to file the same number of cards that Unit Y can file, in 28 days. It is also a fact that Unit X can file 174,528 cards in 72 days. 49.____
Assuming that all the clerks in both units work at the same rate of speed, the number of cards which can be filed by Unit Y in 144 days, if 4 more clerks are added to the staff of Unit Y, is MOST NEARLY

A. 349,000 B. 436,000 C. 523,000 D. 669,000

50. Each side of a square room which is being used as an office measures 66 feet. The floor of the room is divided by six traffic aisles, each aisle being six feet wide. Three of the aisles run parallel to the east and west sides of the room and the other three run parallel to the north and south sides of the room, so that the remaining floor space is divided into 16 equal sections.
If all of the floor space which is not being used for traffic aisles is occupied by desk and chair sets, and each set takes up 24 square feet of floor space, the number of desk and chair sets in the room is 50.____

A. 80 B. 64 C. 36 D. 96

KEY (CORRECT ANSWERS)

1. B	11. D	21. A	31. C	41. B
2. C	12. C	22. B	32. C	42. D
3. C	13. B	23. C	33. B	43. A
4. A	14. D	24. A	34. D	44. C
5. C	15. A	25. C	35. C	45. B
6. A	16. B	26. D	36. B	46. C
7. D	17. C	27. A	37. A	47. D
8. A	18. B	28. C	38. A	48. C
9. B	19. C	29. D	39. C	49. B
10. D	20. B	30. B	40. B	50. D

TEST 2

DIRECTIONS: Each question or incomplete statement is followed by several suggested answers or completions. Select the one that BEST answers the question or completes the statement. *PRINT THE LETTER OF THE CORRECT ANSWER IN THE SPACE AT THE RIGHT.*

Questions 1-6.

DIRECTIONS: Each of Questions 1 through 6 consists of statements which contains one word that is incorrectly used because it is not in keeping with the meaning that the statement is evidently intended to convey. For each of these questions, you are to select the incorrectly used word and substitute for it one of the words lettered A, B, C, D, or E, which helps BEST to convey the meaning of the quotation. In the space at the right, write the letter preceding the word which should be substituted for the incorrectly used word.

1. The determination of the value of the employees in an organization is fundamental not only as a guide to the administration of salary schedules, promotion, demotion, and transfer, but also as a means of keeping the working force on its toes and of checking the originality of selection methods. 1.____

   A. effectiveness
   B. initiation
   C. increasing
   D. system
   E. none of these

2. No training course can operate to full advantage without job descriptions which indicate training requirements so that those parts of the job requiring the most training can be carefully analyzed before the training course is completed. 2.____

   A. improved
   B. started
   C. least
   D. meet
   E. predict

3. The criticism that supervisors are discriminatory in their treatment of subordinates is to some extent untrue, for the subjective nature of many supervisory decisions makes it probable that many employees who have not progressed will attribute their lack of success to supervisory favoritism. 3.____

   A. knowledge
   B. unavoidable
   C. detrimental
   D. deny
   E. indifferent

4. Some demands of employees will, if satisfied, result in a decrease in production. Some supervisors largely ignore such demands on the part of their subordinates, and instead, concentrate on the direction and production of work; others yield to such requests and thereby emphasize the production goals and objectives set by higher levels of authority. 4.____

   A. responsibility
   B. increase
   C. neglect
   D. value
   E. morale

5. It is generally accepted that when a supervisor is at least as well informed about the work of his unit as are his subordinates, he will fail to win their approval, which is essential to him if he is to supervise the unit effectively. 5.____

   A. unimportant
   B. preferable
   C. unless
   D. attention
   E. poorly

6. The laws of almost every state permit certain classes of persons to vote despite their absence from home at election time. Sometimes this privilege is given only to members of the armed forces of the United States, though more commonly it is extended to all voters whose occupations make absence preventable. 6.____

A. prohibition B. sanction C. intangible
D. avoidable E. necessary

Questions 7-25.

DIRECTIONS: Each of Questions 7 through 25 consists of a word in capitals followed by four suggested meanings of the word. Print in the space at the right the number preceding the word which means MOST NEARLY the same as the word in capitals.

7. ALLEVIATE 7.____

A. soothe B. make difficult
C. introduce gradually D. complicate

8. OSTENSIBLE 8.____

A. intelligent B. successful
C. necessary D. apparent

9. REDUNDANT 9.____

A. excessive B. sufficient
C. logical D. unpopular

10. TANTAMOUNT 10.____

A. superior B. opposed
C. equivalent D. disturbing

11. EXPUNGE 11.____

A. leap over B. erase
C. exploit D. concede fully

12. VESTIGE 12.____

A. ancestor B. basis C. choice D. remnant

13. CONTENTION 13.____

A. modification B. controversy
C. cooperation D. sight

14. PROSCRIBE 14.____

A. recommend B. avoid C. provide D. prohibit

15. URBANE 15.____

A. polite B. adjacent to a city
C. modern D. common

16. INADVERTENT 16.____

A. unknown
B. public
C. deliberate
D. unintentional

17. EVINCE 17.____

A. enlarge
B. conceal
C. display
D. evade

18. SIMULATE 18.____

A. attempt
B. imitate
C. elude
D. arouse

19. PRECLUDE 19.____

A. prevent
B. contribute generously
C. simplify
D. prepare gradually

20. REMISS 20.____

A. careless
B. absent
C. guilty
D. thorough

21. CONTRIVE 21.____

A. contract
B. restrict
C. scheme
D. contribute

22. MALIGN 22.____

A. mislead deliberately
B. slander
C. flatter excessively
D. disturb

23. CONTINGENT 23.____

A. loose
B. intentional
C. dependent
D. forceful

24. SPORADIC 24.____

A. quick
B. alert
C. destroyed
D. scattered

25. COALESCE 25.____

A. unite
B. reveal
C. abate
D. freeze

Questions 26-33.

DIRECTIONS: Each of Questions 26 through 33 consists of three sentences lettered A, B, and C. In each of these questions, one of the sentences may contain an error in grammar, sentence structure, or punctuation, or all three sentences may be correct. If one of the sentences in a question contains an error in grammar, sentence structure, or punctuation, write in the space at the right, the letter preceding the sentence which contains the error. If all three sentences are correct, write the letter D.

26. 26.____

A. Mr. Smith appears to be less competent than I in performing these duties.
B. The supervisor spoke to the employee, who had made the error, but did not reprimand him.
C. When he found the book lying on the table, he immediately notified the owner.

27. A. Being locked in the desk, we were certain that the papers would not be taken. 27.____
B. It wasn't I who dictated the telegram; I believe it was Eleanor.
C. You should interview whoever comes to the office today.

28. A. The clerk was instructed to set the machine on the table before summoning the manager. 28.____
B. He said that he was not familiar with those kind of activities.
C. A box of pencils, in addition to erasers and blotters, was included in the shipment of supplies.

29. A. The supervisor remarked, "Assigning an employee to the proper type of work is not always easy." 29.____
B. The employer found that each of the applicants were qualified to perform the duties of the position.
C. Any competent student is permitted to take this course if he obtains the consent of the instructor.

30. A. The prize was awarded to the employee whom the judges believed to be most deserving. 30.____
B. Since the instructor believes this book is the better of the two, he is recommending it for use in the school.
C. It was obvious to the employees that the completion of the task by the scheduled date would require their working overtime.

31. A. These reports have been typed by employees who were trained by a capable supervisor. 31.____
B. This employee is as old, if not older, than any other employee in the department.
C. Running rapidly down the street, the manager soon reached the office.

32. A. It is believed, that if these terms are accepted, the building can be constructed at a reasonable cost. 32.____
B. The typists are seated in the large office; the stenographers, in the small office.
C. Either the operators or the machines are at fault.

33. A. Mr. Jones, who is the head of the agency, will come today to discuss the plans for the new training program. 33.____
B. The reason the report is not finished is that the supply of paper is exhausted.
C. It is now obvious that neither of the two employees is able to handle this type of assignment.

Questions 34-40.

DIRECTIONS: Each of Questions 34 through 40 consists of four words. In each question, one of the words may be spelled incorrectly or all four words may be spelled correctly. If one of the words in a question is spelled incorrectly, print in the space at the right the letter preceding the word which is spelled incorrectly. If all four words are spelled correctly, print the letter E.

34. A. guarantee B. committment 34.____
C. mitigate D. publicly

35. A. prerogative B. apprise 35.____
C. extrordinary D. continual

36. A. arrogant B. handicapped 36.____
C. judicious D. perennial

37. A. permissable B. deceive 37.____
C. innumerable D. retrieve

38. A. notable B. allegiance 38.____
C. reimburse D. illegal

39. A. interceed B. benefited 39.____
C. analogous D. altogether

40. A. seizure B. irrelevant 40.____
C. inordinate D. dissapproved

Questions 41-50.

DIRECTIONS: Questions 41 through 50 are based on the Production Record table shown on the following page for the Information Unit in Agency X for the work week ended Friday, December 6. The table shows, for each employee, the quantity of each type of work performed and the percentage of the work week spent in performing each type of work.

NOTE: Assume that each employee works 7 hours a day and 5 days a week, making a total of 35 hours for the work week.

PRODUCTION RECORD - INFORMATION UNIT IN AGENCY X
(For the work week ended Friday, December 6)

	Number of			
	Papers Filed	Sheets Proofread	Visitors Received	Envelopes Addressed
Miss Agar	3120	33	178	752
Mr . Brun	1565	59	252	724
Miss Case	2142	62	214	426
Mr. Dale	4259	29	144	1132
Miss Earl	2054	58	212	878
Mr. Farr	1610	69	245	621
Miss Glen	2390	57	230	790
Mr . Hope	3425	32	176	805
Miss Iver	3736	56	148	650
Mr. Joad	3212	55	181	495

Percentage of Work Week Spent On

	Filing Papers	Proof-reading	Receiving Visitors	Addressing Envelopes	Performing Miscellaneous Work
Miss Agar	30%	9%	34%	11%	16%
Mr . Brun	13%	15%	52%	10%	10%
Miss Case	23%	18%	38%	6%	15%
Mr. Dale	50%	7%	17%	16%	10%
Miss Earl	24%	14%	37%	14%	11%
Mr. Farr	16%	19%	48%	8%	9%
Miss Glen	27%	12%	42%	12%	7%
Mr . Hope	38%	8%	32%	13%	9%
Miss Iver	43%	13%	24%	9%	11%
Mr. Joad	33%	11%	36%	7%	13%

41. For the week, the average amount of time which the employees spent in proofreading was MOST NEARLY ______ hours. 41.____

A. 3.1 B. 3.6 C. 4.4 D. 5.1

42. The average number of visitors received daily by an employee was MOST NEARLY 42.____

A. 40 B. 57 C. 198 D. 395

43. Of the following employees, the one who addressed envelopes at the FASTEST rate was 43.____

A. Miss Agar
B. Mr. Brun
C. Miss Case
D. Mr. Dale

44. Mr. Farr's rate of filing papers was MOST NEARLY ______ pages per minute. 44.____

A. 2 B. 1.7 C. 5 D. 12

45. The average number of hours that Mr. Brun spent daily on receiving visitors exceeded the average number of hours that Miss Iver spent daily on the same type of work by MOST NEARLY ______ hours. 45.____

A. 2 B. 3 C. 4 D. 5

46. Miss Earl worked at a faster rate than Miss Glen in 46.____

A. filing papers
B. proofreading sheets
C. receiving visitors
D. addressing envelopes

47. Mr. Joad's rate of filing papers ______ Miss Iver's rate of filing papers by approximately ______%. 47.____

A. was less than; 10
B. exceeded; 33
C. C. was less than; 16
D. exceeded; 12

48. Assume that in the following week, Miss Case is instructed to increase the percentage of her time spent in filing papers to 35%. 48.____
If she continued to file papers at the same rate as she did for the week ended December 6, the number of additional papers that she filed the following week was MOST NEARLY

A. 3260 B. 5400 C. 250 D. 1120

49. Assume that in the following week, Mr. Hope increased his weekly total of envelopes addressed to 1092. 49.____
If he continued to spend the same amount of time on this assignment as he did for the week ended December 6, the increase in his rate of addressing envelopes the following week was MOST NEARLY ______ envelopes per hour.

A. 15 B. 65 C. 155 D. 240

50. Assume that in the following week, Miss Agar and Mr. Dale spent 3 and 9 hours less, respectively, on filing papers than they had spent for the week ended December 6, without changing their rates of work. 50.____
The total number of papers filed during the following week by both Miss Agar and Mr. Dale was MOST NEARLY

A. 4235 B. 4295 C. 4315 D. 4370

KEY (CORRECT ANSWERS)

1.	A	11.	B	21.	C	31.	B	41.	C
2.	B	12.	D	22.	B	32.	A	42.	A
3.	B	13.	B	23.	C	33.	D	43.	B
4.	C	14.	D	24.	D	34.	B	44.	C
5.	C	15.	A	25.	A	35.	C	45.	A
6.	E	16.	D	26.	B	36.	E	46.	C
7.	A	17.	C	27.	A	37.	A	47.	D
8.	D	18.	B	28.	B	38.	E	48.	D
9.	A	19.	A	29.	B	39.	A	49.	B
10.	C	20.	A	30.	D	40.	D	50.	B

EXAMINATION SECTION

TEST 1

DIRECTIONS: Each question or incomplete statement is followed by several suggested answers or completions. Select the one that BEST answers the question or completes the statement. *PRINT THE LETTER OF THE CORRECT ANSWER IN THE SPACE AT THE RIGHT.*

1. Good procedure in handling complaints from the public may be divided into the following four principal stages: 1.____
   I. Investigation of the complaint
   II. Receipt of the complaint
   III. Assignment of responsibility for investigation and correction
   IV. Notification of correction

   The ORDER in which these stages ordinarily come is:
   A. III, II, I, IV B. II, III, I, IV C. II, III, IV, I D. II, IV, III, I

2. The department may expect the MOST severe public criticism if 2.____
   A. it asks for an increase in its annual budget
   B. it purchases new and costly street cleaning equipment
   C. sanitation officers and men are reclassified to higher salary grades
   D. there is delay in cleaning streets of snow

3. The MOST important function of public relations in the department should be to 3.____
   A. develop cooperation on the part of the public in keeping streets clean
   B. get stricter penalties enacted for health code violations
   C. recruit candidates for entrance positions who ca be developed into supervisors
   D. train career personnel so that they can advance in the department

4. The one of the following which has MOST frequently elicited unfavorable public comment has been 4.____
   A. dirty sidewalks or streets B. dumping on lot
   C. failure to curb dogs D. overflowing garbage cans

5. It has been suggested that, as a public relations measure, sections hold *open house* for the public. 5.____
   The MOST effective time for this would be
   A. during the summer when children are not in school and can accompany their parents
   B. during the winter when show is likely to fall and the public can see snow removal preparations
   C. immediately after a heavy snow storm when department snow removal operations are in full progress
   D. when street sanitation is receiving general attention as during *Keep City Clean* week

6. When a public agency conducts a public relations program, it is MOST likely to find that each recipient of its message will 6.____
   A. disagree with the basic purpose of the message if the officials are not well known to him
   B. accept the message if it is presented by someone perceived as having a definite intention to persuade
   C. ignore the message unless it is presented in a literate and clever manner
   D. give greater attention to certain portions of the message as a result of his individual and cultural differences

7. Following are three statements about public relations and communications: 7.____
   I. A person who seeks to influence public opinion can speed up a trend
   II. Mass communications is the exposure of a mass audience to an idea
   III. All media are equally effective in reaching opinion leaders
   Which of the following choices CORRECTLY classifies the above statements into those which are correct and those which are not?
   A. I and II are correct, but III is not.
   B. II and III are correct, but I is not.
   C. I and III are correct, but II is not.
   D III is correct, but I and II are not.

8. Public relations experts say that MAXIMUM effect for a message results from 8.____
   A. concentrating in one medium
   B. ignoring mass media and concentrating on *opinion makers*
   C. presenting only those factors which support a given position
   D. using a combination of two or more of the available media

9. To assure credibility and avoid hostility, the public relations man MUST 9.____
   A. make certain his message is truthful, not evasive or exaggerated
   B. make sure his message contains some dire consequence if ignored
   C. repeat the message often enough so that it cannot be ignored
   D. try to reach as many people and groups as possible

10. The public relations man MUST be prepared to assume that members of his audience 10.____
    A. may have developed attitudes toward his proposals—favorable, neutral, or unfavorable
    B. will be immediately hostile
    C. will consider his proposals with an open mind
    D. will invariably need an introduction to his subject

11. The one of the following statements that is CORRECT is: 11.____
    A. When a stupid question is asked of you by the public, it should be disregarded
    B. If you insist on formality between you and the public, the public will not be able to ask stupid questions that cannot be answered
    C. The public should be treated courteously, regardless of how stupid their questions may be
    D. You should explain to the public how stupid their questions are

12. With regard to public relations, the MOST important item which should be emphasized in an employee training program is that 12.____
    A. each inspector is a public relations agent
    B an inspector should give the public all the information it asks for
    C. it is better to make mistakes and give erroneous information than to tell the public that you do not know the correct answer to their problem
    D. public relations is so specialized a field that only persons specially trained in it should consider it

13. Members of the public frequently ask about departmental procedures. Of the following, it is BEST to 13.____
    A. advise the public to put the question in writing so that he can get a proper formal reply
    B. refuse to answer because this is a confidential matter
    C. explain the procedure as briefly as possible
    D. attempt to avoid the issue by discussing other matters

14. The effectiveness of a public relations program in a public agency such as the authority is BEST indicated by the 14.____
    A. amount of mass media publicity favorable to the policies of the authority
    B. morale of those employees who directly serve the patrons of the authority
    C. public's understanding and support of the authority's program and policies
    D. number of complaint received by the authority from patrons using its facilities

15. In an attempt to improve public opinion about a certain idea, the BEST course of action for an agency to take would be to present the 15.____
    A. clearest statements of the idea even though the language is somewhat technical
    B. idea as the result of long-term studies
    C. idea in association with something familiar to most people
    D. idea as the viewpoint of the majority leaders

16. The fundamental factor in any agency's community relations program is 16.____
    A. an outline of the objectives
    B. relations with the media
    C. the everyday actions of the employees
    D. a well-planned supervisory program

17. The FUNDAMENTAL factor in the success of a community relations program is 17.____
    A. true commitment by the community
    B. true commitment by the administration
    C. a well-planned, systematic approach
    D. the actions of individuals in their contacts with the public

18. The statement below which is LEAST correct is: 18.____
    A. Because of selection standards, the supervisor frequently encounters problems resulting from subordinates' inability to express themselves in the language of the profession.
    B. Distortion of the meaning of a communication is usually brought about by a failure to use language that has a precise meaning to others.
    C. The term *filtering* is the distortion or dilution of content of a communication that occurs as information is passed from individual to individual.
    D. The complexity of the *communications net* will directly affect.

19. Consider the following three statements that may or may not be CORRECT: 19.____
    I. In order to prevent the stifling of communications flow, supervisors should insist that employees use the formal communications network.
    II. Two-way communications are faster and more accurate than one-way communications.
    III. There is a direct correlation between the effectiveness of communications and the total setting in which they occur.

    The choice below which MOST accurately describes the above statement is:
    A. All three are correct.
    B. All three are incorrect.
    C. More than one statement is correct.
    D. Only one of the statements is correct.

20. The statement below which is MOST inaccurate is: 20.____
    A. The supervisor's most important tool in learning whether or not he is communicating well is feedback.
    B. Follow-up is essential if useful feedback is to be obtained.
    C. Subordinates are entitled, as a matter of right, to explanations from management concerning the reasons for orders or directives.
    D. A skilled supervisor is often able to use the grapevine to good advantage.

21. *Since concurrence by those affected is not sought, this kind of communication can be issued with relative ease.* 21.____

    The kind of communication being referred to in this quotation is
    A. autocratic B. democratic C. directive D. free-rein

22. The statement below which is LEAST correct is: 22.___
    A. Clarity is more important in oral communicating than in written since the readers of a written communication can read it over again.
    B. Excessive use of abbreviations in written communications should be avoided.
    C. Short sentences with simple words are preferred over complex sentences and difficult words in a written communication.
    D. The *newspaper* style of writing ordinarily simplifies expression and facilitates understanding.

23. Which one of the following is the MOST important factor for the department to consider in building a good public image? 23.____
    A. A good working relationship with the news media
    B. An efficient community relations program
    C. An efficient system for handling citizen complaints
    D. The proper maintenance of facilities and equipment
    E. The behavior of individuals in their contacts with the public.

24. It has been said that the ability to communicate clearly and concisely is the MOST important single skill of the supervisor. 24.____
    Consider the following statements:
    I. The adage, *Actions speak louder than words*, has NO application in superior/subordinate communications since good communications are accomplished with words.
    II. The environment in which a communication takes place will *rarely* determine its effect.
    III. Words are symbolic representations which must be associated with past experience or else they are meaningless.
    The choice below which MOST accurately describes the above statements is:
    A. I, II, and III are correct.
    B. I and II are correct, but III is not.
    C. I and III are correct, but II is not.
    D. III is correct, but I and II are not.
    E. I, II, and III are incorrect.

25. According to expert opinion, the effectiveness of an organization is very dependent upon good upward, downward, and lateral communications. Lateral communications are most important to the activity of coordinating the efforts of organizational units. Before real communication can take place at any level, barriers to communication must be recognized, understood, and removed. 25.____
    Consider the following three statements:
    I. The *principal* barrier to good communications is a failure to establish empathy between sender and receiver.
    II. The difference in status or rank between the sender and receiver of a communication may be a communications barrier.
    III. Communications are easier if they travel upward from subordinate to superior
    The choice below which MOST accurately describes the above statements is:
    A. I, II and III are incorrect.
    B. I and II are incorrect.
    C. I, II, and III are correct.
    D. I and II are correct.
    E. I and III are incorrect.

KEY (CORRECT ANSWERS)

1. B
2. D
3. A
4. A
5. D

6. D
7. A
8. D
9. A
10. A

11. C
12. A
13. C
14. C
15. C

16. C
17. D
18. A
19. D
20. C

21. A
22. A
23. E
24. D
25. E

EXAMINATION SECTION

TEST 1

DIRECTIONS: Each question or incomplete statement is followed by several suggested answers or completions. Select the one that BEST answers the question or completes the statement. *PRINT THE LETTER OF THE CORRECT ANSWER IN THE SPACE AT THE RIGHT.*

1. In public agencies, communications should be based PRIMARILY on a 1.____
   A. two-way flow from the top down and from the bottom up, most of which should be given in writing to avoid ambiguity
   B. multi-direction flow among all levels and with outside persons
   C. rapid, internal one-way flow from the top down
   D. two-way flow of information, most of which should be given orally for purposes of clarity

2. In some organizations, changes in policy or procedures are often communicated by word of mouth from supervisors to employees with no prior discussion or exchange of viewpoints with employees. 2.____
   This procedure often produces employee dissatisfaction CHIEFLY because
   A. information is mostly unusable since a considerable amount of time is required to transmit information
   B. lower-level supervisors tend to be excessively concerned with minor details
   C. management has failed to seek employees' advice before making changes
   D. valuable staff time is lost between decision-making and the implementation of decisions

3. For good letter writing, you should try to visualize the person to whom you are writing, especially if you know him. 3.____
   Of the following rules, it is LEAST helpful in such visualization to think of
   A. the person's likes and dislikes, his concerns, and his needs
   B. what you would be likely to say if speaking in person
   C. what you would expect to be asked if speaking in person
   D. your official position in order to be certain that your words are proper

4. One approach to good informal letter writing is to make letters and conversational. 4.____
   All of the following practices will usually help to do this EXCEPT:
   A. If possible, use a style which is similar to the style used when speaking
   B. Substitute phrases for single words (e.g., *at the present time for now*)
   C. Use contractions of words (e.g., *you're* for *you are*)
   D. Use ordinary vocabulary when possible

5. All of the following rules will aid in producing clarity in report-writing EXCEPT: 5.____
   A. Give specific details or examples, if possible
   B. Keep related words close together in each sentence
   C. Present information in sequential order
   D. Put several thoughts or ideas in each paragraph

6. The one of the following statements about public relations which is MOST accurate is that 6.____
   A. in the long run, appearance gains better results than performance
   B. objectivity is decreased if outside public relations consultants are employed
   C. public relations is the responsibility of every employee
   D. public relations should be based on a formal publicity program

7. The form of communication which is usually considered to be MOST personally directed to the intended recipient is the 7.____
   A. brochure B. film C. letter D. radio

8. In general, a document that presents an organization's views or opinions on a particular topic is MOST accurately known as a 8.____
   A. tear sheet B. position paper
   C. flyer D. journal

9. Assume that you have been asked to speak before an organization of persons who oppose a newly announced program in which you are involved. You feel tense about talking to this group. 9.____
   Which of the following rules generally would be MOST useful in gaining rapport when speaking before the audience?
   A. Impress them with your experience
   B. Stress all areas of disagreement
   C. Talk to the group as to one person
   D. Use formal grammar and language

10. An organization must have an effective public relations program since, at its best, public relations is a bridge to change. 10.____
    All of the following statements about communication and human behavior have validity EXCEPT:
    A. People are more likely to talk about controversial matters with like-minded people than with those holding other views
    B. The earlier an experience, the more powerful its effect since it influences how later experiences will be interpreted
    C. In periods of social tension, official sources gain increased believability
    D. Those who are already interested in a topic are the ones who are most open to receive new communications about it

11. An employee should be encouraged to talk easily and frankly when he is dealing with his supervisor. 11.____
In order to encourage such free communication, it would be MOST appropriate for a supervisor to behave in a(n)
    A. sincere manner; assure the employee that you will deal with him honestly and openly
    B. official manner; you are a supervisor and must always act formally with subordinates
    C. investigative manner; you must probe and question to get to a basis of trust
    D. unemotional manner; the employee's emotions and background should play no part in your dealings with him

12. Research findings show that an increase in free communication within an agency GENERALLY results in which one of the following? 12.____
    A. Improved morale and productivity
    B. Increased promotional opportunities
    C. An increase in authority
    D. A spirit of honesty

13. Assume that you are a supervisor and your superiors have given you a new-type procedure to be followed. 13.____
Before passing this information on to your subordinates, the one of the following actions that you should take FIRST is to
    A. ask your superiors to send out a memorandum to the entire staff
    B. clarify the procedure in your own mind
    C. set up a training course to provide instruction on the new procedure
    D. write a memorandum to your subordinates

14. Communication is necessary for an organization to be effective. 14.____
The one of the following which is LEAST important for most communication systems is that
    A. messages are sent quickly and directly to the person who needs them to operate
    B. information should be conveyed understandably and accurately
    C. the method used to transmit information should be kept secret so that security can be maintained
    D. senders of messages must know how their messages are received and acted upon

15. Which one of the following is the CHIEF advantage of listening willingly to subordinates and encouraging them to talk freely and honestly? 15.____
It
    A. reveals to supervisors the degree to which ideas that are passed down are accepted by subordinates
    B. reduces the participation of subordinates in the operation of the department
    C. encourages subordinates to try for promotion
    D. enables supervisors to learn more readily what the *grapevine* is saying

16. A supervisor may be informed through either oral or written reports. 16.____
Which one of the following is an ADVANTAGE of using oral reports?
   A. There is no need for a formal record of the report.
   B. An exact duplicate of the report is not easily transmitted to others.
   C. A good oral report requires little time for preparation.
   D. An oral report involves two-way communication between a subordinate and his supervisor.

17. Of the following, the MOST important reason why supervisors should communicate effectively with the public is to 17.____
   A. improve the public's understanding of information that is important for them to know
   B. establish a friendly relationship
   C. obtain information about the kinds of people who come to the agency
   D. convince the public that services are adequate

18. Supervisors should generally NOT use phrases like *too hard*, *too easy*, and *a lot* PRINCIPALLY because such phrases 18.____
   A. may be offensive to some minority groups
   B. are too informal
   C. mean different things to different people
   D. are difficult to remember

19. The ability to communicate clearly and concisely is an important element in effective leadership. 19.____
Which of the following statements about oral and written communication is GENERALLY true?
   A. Oral communication is more time-consuming.
   B. Written communication is more likely to be misinterpreted.
   C. Oral communication is useful only in emergencies.
   D. Written communication is useful mainly when giving information to fewer than twenty people.

20. Rumors can often have harmful and disruptive effects on an organization. 20.____
Which one of the following is the BEST way to prevent rumors from becoming a problem?
   A. Refuse to act on rumors, thereby making them less believable.
   B. Increase the amount of information passed along by the *grapevine*.
   C. Distribute as much factual information as possible.
   D. Provide training in report writing.

21. Suppose that a subordinate asks you about a rumor he has heard. The rumor deals with a subject which your superiors consider *confidential*. 21.____
Which of the following BEST describes how you should answer the subordinate? Tell

A. the subordinate that you don't make the rules and that he should speak to higher ranking officials
B. the subordinate that you will ask your superior for information
C. him only that you cannot comment on the matter
D. him the rumor is not true

22. Supervisors often find it difficult to *get their message across* when instructing newly appointed employees in their various duties. 22.____
The MAIN reason for this is generally that the
A. duties of the employees have increased
B. supervisor is often so expert in his area that he fails to see it from the learner's point of view
C. supervisor adapts his instruction to the slowest learner in the group
D. new employees are younger, less concerned with job security and more interested in fringe benefits

23. Assume that you are discussing a job problem with an employee under your supervision. During the discussion, you see that the man's eyes are turning away from you and that he is not paying attention. 23.____
In order to get the man's attention, you should FIRST
A. ask him to look you in the eye
B. talk to him about sports
C. tell him he is being very rude
D. change your tone of voice

24. As a supervisor, you may find it necessary to conduct meetings with your subordinates. 24.____
Of the following, which would be MOST helpful in assuring that a meeting accomplishes the purpose for which it was called?
A. Give notice of the conclusions you would like to reach at the start of the meeting.
B. Delay the start of the meeting until everyone is present.
C. Write down points to be discussed in proper sequence.
D. Make sure everyone is clear on whatever conclusions have been reached and on what must be done after the meeting.

25. Every supervisor will occasionally be called upon to deliver a reprimand to a subordinate. If done properly, this can greatly help an employee improve his performance. 25.____
Which one of the following is NOT a good practice to follow when giving a reprimand?
A. Maintain your composure and temper
B. Reprimand a subordinate in the presence of other employees so they can learn the same lesson
C. Try to understand why the employee was not able to perform satisfactorily
D. Let your knowledge of the man involved determine the exact nature of the reprimand

KEY (CORRECT ANSWERS)

1. C
2. B
3. D
4. B
5. D

6. C
7. C
8. B
9. C
10. C

11. A
12. A
13. B
14. C
15. A

16. D
17. A
18. C
19. B
20. C

21. B
22. B
23. D
24. D
25. B

TEST 2

DIRECTIONS: Each question or incomplete statement is followed by several suggested answers or completions. Select the one that BEST answers the question or completes the statement. *PRINT THE LETTER OF THE CORRECT ANSWER IN THE SPACE AT THE RIGHT.*

1. Usually one thinks of communication as a single step, essentially that of transmitting an idea. 1.____
   Actually, however, this is only part of a total process, the FIRST step of which should be
   A. the prompt dissemination of the idea to those who may be affected by it
   B. motivating those affected to take the required action
   C. clarifying the idea in one's own mind
   D. deciding to whom the idea is to be communicated

2. Research studies on patterns of informal communication have concluded that most individuals in a group tend to be passive recipients of news, while a few make it their business to spread it around in an organization. 2.____
   With this conclusion in mind, it would be MOST correct for the supervisor to attempt to identify these few individuals and
   A. give them the complete facts on important matters in advance of others
   B. inform the other subordinates of the identity of these few individuals so that their influence may be minimized
   C. keep them straight on the facts on important matters
   D. warn them to cease passing along any information to others

3. The one of the following which is the PRINCIPAL advantage of making an oral report is that it 3.____
   A. affords an immediate opportunity for two-way communication between the subordinate and superior
   B. is an easy method for the superior to use in transmitting information to others of equal rank
   C. saves the time of all concerned
   D. permits more precise pinpointing of praise or blame by means of follow-up questions by the superior

4. An agency may sometimes undertake a public relations program of a defensive nature. 4.____
   With reference to the use of defensive public relations, it would be MOST correct to state that it
   A. is bound to be ineffective since defensive statements, even though supported by factual data, can never hope to even partly overcome the effects of prior unfavorable attacks
   B. proves that the agency has failed to establish good relationships with newspapers, radio stations, or other means of publicity

C. shows that the upper echelons of the agency have failed to develop sound public relations procedures and techniques
D. is sometimes required to aid morale by protecting the agency from unjustified criticism and misunderstanding of policies or procedures

5. Of the following factors which contribute to possible undesirable public attitudes towards an agency, the one which is MOST susceptible to being changed by the efforts of the individual employee in an organization is that 5.____
A. enforcement of unpopular regulations as offended many individuals
B. the organization itself has an unsatisfactory reputation
C. the public is not interested in agency matters
D. there are many errors in judgment committed by individual subordinates

6. It is not enough for an agency's services to be of a high quality; attention must also be given to the acceptability of these services to the general public. This statement is GENERALLY 6.____
A. *false*; a superior quality of service automatically wins public support
B. *true*; the agency cannot generally progress beyond the understanding and support of the public
C. *false*; the acceptance by the public of agency services determines their quality
D. *true*; the agency is generally unable to engage in any effective enforcement activity without public support

7. Sustained agency participation in a program sponsored by a community organization is MOST justified when 7.____
A. the achievement of agency objectives in some area depends partly on the activity of this organization
B. the community organization is attempting to widen the base of participation in all community affairs
C. the agency is uncertain as to what the community wants
D. the agency is uncertain as to what the community wants

8. Of the following, the LEAST likely way in which a records system may serve a supervisor is in 8.____
A. developing a sympathetic and cooperative public attitude toward the agency
B. improving the quality of supervision by permitting a check on the accomplishment of subordinates
C. permit a precise prediction of the exact incidences in specific categories for the following year
D. helping to take the guesswork out of the distribution of the agency

9. Assuming that the *grapevine* in any organization is virtually indestructible, the one of the following which it is MOST important for management to understand is: 9.____
   A. What is being spread by means of the *grapevine* and the reason for spreading it
   B. What is being spread by means of the *grapevine* and how it is being spread
   C. Who is involved in spreading the information that is on the *grapevine*
   D. Why those who are involved in spreading the information are doing so

10. When the supervisor writes a report concerning an investigation to which he has been assigned, it should be LEAST intended to provide 10.____
    A. a permanent official record of relevant information gathered
    B. a summary of case findings limited to facts which tend to indicate the guilt of a suspect
    C. a statement of the facts on which higher authorities may base a corrective or disciplinary action
    D. other investigators with information so that they may continue with other phases of the investigation

11. In survey work, questionnaires rather than interviews are sometimes used. The one of the following which is a DISADVANTAGE of the questionnaire method as compared with the interview is the 11.____
    A. difficulty of accurately interpreting the results
    B. problem of maintaining anonymity of the participant
    C. fact that it is relatively uneconomical
    D. requirement of special training for the distribution of questionnaires

12. in his contacts with the public, an employee should attempt to create a good climate of support for his agency. This statement is GENERALLY 12.____
    A. *false*; such attempts are clearly beyond the scope of his responsibility
    B. *true*; employees of an agency who come in contact with the public have the opportunity to affect public relations
    C. *false*; such activity should be restricted to supervisors trained in public relations techniques
    D. *true*; the future expansion of the agency depends to a great extent on continued public support of the agency

13. The repeated use by a supervisor of a call for volunteers to get a job done is objectionable MAINLY because it 13.____
    A. may create a feeling of animosity between the volunteers and the non-volunteers
    B. may indicate that the supervisor is avoiding responsibility for making assignments which will be most productive
    C. is an indication that the supervisor is not familiar with the individual capabilities of his men
    D. is unfair to men who, for valid reasons, do not, or cannot volunteer

14. Of the following statements concerning subordinates' expressions to a supervisor of their opinions and feelings concerning work situations, the one which is MOST correct is that 14.____
    A. by listening and responding to such expressions the supervisor encourages the development of complaints
    B. the lack of such expressions should indicate to the supervisor that there is a high level of job satisfaction
    C. the more the supervisor listens to and responds to such expressions, the more he demonstrates lack of supervisory ability
    D. by listening and responding to such expressions, the supervisor will enable many subordinates to understand and solve their own problems on the job

15. In attempting to motivate employees, rewards are considered preferable to punishment PRIMARILY because 15.____
    A. punishment seldom has any effect on human behavior
    B. punishment usually results in decreased production
    C. supervisors find it difficult to punish
    D. rewards are more likely to result in willing cooperation

16. In an attempt to combat the low morale in his organization, a high level supervisor publicized an *open-door policy* to allow employees who wished to do so to come to him with their complaints. 16.____
    Which of the following is LEAST likely to account for the fact that no employee came in with a complaint?
    A. Employees are generally reluctant to go over the heads of their immediate supervisor.
    B. The employees did not feel that management would help them.
    C. The low morale was not due to complaints associated with the job.
    D. The employees felt that they had more to lose than to gain.

17. It is MOST desirable to use written instructions rather than oral instructions for a particular job when 17.____
    A. a mistake on the job will not be serious
    B. the job can be completed in a short time
    C. there is no need to explain the job minutely
    D. the job involves many details

18. If you receive a telephone call regarding a matter which your office does not handle, you should FIRST 18.____
    A. give the caller the telephone number of the proper office so that he can dial again
    B. offer to transfer the caller to the proper office
    C. suggest that the caller re-dial since he probably dialed incorrectly
    D. tell the caller he has reached the wrong office and then hang up

19. When you answer the telephone, the MOST important reason for identifying yourself and your organization is to 19.____
    A. give the caller time to collect his or her thoughts
    B. impress the caller with your courtesy
    C. inform the caller that he or she has reached the right number
    D. set a business-like tone at the beginning of the conversation

20. As soon as you pick up the phone, a very angry caller begins immediately to complain about city agencies and *red tape*. He says that he has been shifted to two or three different offices. It turs out that he is seeking information which is not immediately available to you. You believe, you know, however, where it can be found. 20.____
    Which of the following actions is the BEST one for you to take?
    A. To eliminate all confusion, suggest that the caller write the agency stating explicitly what he wants.
    B. Apologize by telling the caller how busy city agencies now are, but also tell him directly that you do not have the information he needs.
    C. Ask for the caller's telephone number and assure him you will call back after you have checked further.
    D. Give the caller the name and telephone number of the person who might be able to help, but explain that you are not positive he will get results/

21. Which of the following approaches usually provides the BEST communication in the objectives and values of a new program which is to be introduced? 21.____
    A. A general written description of the program by the program manager for review by those who share responsibility
    B. An effective verbal presentation by the program manager to those affected
    C. Development of the plan and operational approach in carrying out the program by the program manager assisted by his key subordinates
    D. Development of the plan by the program manager's supervisor

22. What is the BEST approach for introducing change? 22.____
    A
    A. combination of written and also verbal communication to all personnel affected by the change
    B. general bulletin to all personnel
    C. meeting pointing out all the values of the new approach
    D. written directive to key personnel

23. Of the following, committees are BEST used for 23.____
    A. advising the head of the organization
    B. improving functional work
    C. making executive decisions
    D. making specific planning decisions

24. An effective discussion leader is one who 24.____
    A. announces the problem and his preconceived solution at the start of the discussion
    B. guides and directs the discussion according to pre-arranged outline
    C. interrupts or corrects confused participants to save time
    D. permits anyone to say anything at any time

25. The human relations movement in management theory is basically concerned with 25.____
    A. counteracting employee unrest
    B. eliminating the *time and motion* man
    C. interrelationships among individuals in organizations
    D. the psychology of the worker

KEY (CORRECT ANSWERS)

1. C
2. C
3. A
4. D
5. D

6. B
7. A
8. C
9. A
10. B

11. A
12. B
13. B
14. D
15. D

16. C
17. D
18. B
19. C
20. C

21. C
22. A
23. A
24. B
25. C

COMMUNICATION

EXAMINATION SECTION
TEST 1

DIRECTIONS: Each question or incomplete statement is followed by several suggested answers or completions. Select the one that BEST answers the question or completes the statement. *PRINT THE LETTER OF THE CORRECT ANSWER IN THE SPACE AT THE RIGHT.*

1. In some agencies the counsel to the agency head is given the right to bypass the chain of command and issue orders directly to the staff concerning matters that involve certain specific processes and practices. 1.____
This situation MOST nearly illustrates the principle of _____ authority.
   A. the acceptance theory of
   B. multiple-linear
   C. splintered
   D. functional

2. It is commonly understood that communication is an important part of the administrative process. 2.____
Which of the following is NOT a valid principle of the communication process in administration?
   A. The channels of communication should be spontaneous.
   B. The lines of communication should be as direct and as short as possible.
   C. Communications should be authenticated.
   D. The persons serving in communications centers should be competent.

3. Of the following, the one factor which is generally considered LEAST essential to successful committee operations is 3.____
   A. stating a clear definition of the authority and scope of the committee
   B. selecting the committee chairman carefully
   C. limiting the size of the committee to four persons
   D. limiting the subject matter to that which can be handled in group discussion

4. Of the following, the failure by line managers to accept and appreciate the benefits and limitations of a new program or system VERY FREQUENTLY can be traced to the 4.____
   A. budgetary problems involved
   B. resultant need to reduce staff
   C. lack of controls it engenders
   D. failure of top management to support its implementation

5. If a manager were thinking about using a committee of subordinates to solve an operating problem, which of the following would generally NOT be an advantage of such use of the committee approach? 5.____
   A. Improved coordination
   B. Low cost
   C. Increased motivation
   D. Integrated judgment

6. Every supervisor has many occasions to lead a conference or participate in a conference of some sort. 6.____
Of the following statements that pertain to conferences and conference leadership, which is generally considered to be MOST valid?
   A. Since World War II, the trend has been toward fewer shared decisions and more conferences.
   B. The most important part of a conference leader's job is to direct discussion.
   C. In providing opportunities for group interaction, management should avoid consideration of its past management philosophy.
   D. A good administrator cannot lead a good conference if he is a poor public speaker.

7. Of the following, it is usually LEAST desirable for a conference leader to 7.____
   A. call the name of a person after asking a question
   B. summarize proceedings periodically
   C. make a practice of repeating questions
   D. ask a question without indicating who is to reply

8. Assume that, in a certain organization, a situation has developed in which there is little difference in status or authority between individuals. 8.____
Which of the following would be the MOST likely result with regard to communication in this organization?
   A. Both the accuracy and flow of communication will be improved.
   B. Both the accuracy and flow of communication will substantially decrease.
   C. Employees will seek more formal lines of communication.
   D. Neither the flow nor the accuracy of communication will be improved over the former hierarchical structure.

9. The main function of many agency administrative officers is "information management." Information that is received by an administrative officer may be classified as active or passive, depending upon whether or not it requires the recipient to take some action. 9.____
Of the following, the item received which is clearly the MOST active information is
   A. an appointment of a new staff member
   B. a payment voucher for a new desk
   C. a press release concerning a past event
   D. the minutes of a staff meeting

10. Of the following, the one LEAST considered to be a communication barrier is 10.____
   A. group feedback
   B. charged words
   C. selective perception
   D. symbolic meanings

11. Management studies support the hypothesis that, in spite of the tendency of employees to censor the information communicated to their supervisor, subordinates are more likely to communicate problem-oriented information UPWARD when they have a 11.____
   A. long period of service in the organization
   B. high degree of trust in the supervisor
   C. high educational level
   D. low status on the organizational ladder

12. Electronic data processing equipment can produce more information faster than can be generated by any other means. 12.____
In view of this, the MOST important problem faced by management at present is to
   A. keep computers fully occupied
   B. find enough computer personnel
   C. assimilate and properly evaluate the information
   D. obtain funds to establish appropriate information systems

13. A well-designed management information system essentially provides each executive and manager the information he needs for 13.____
   A. determining computer time requirements
   B. planning and measuring results
   C. drawing a new organization chart
   D. developing a new office layout

14. It is generally agreed that management policies should be periodically reappraised and restated in accordance with current conditions. 14.____
Of the following, the approach which would be MOST effective in determining whether a policy should be revised is to
   A. conduct interviews with staff members at all levels in order to ascertain the relationship between the policy and actual practice
   B. make proposed revisions in the policy and apply it to current problems
   C. make up hypothetical situations using both the old policy and a revised version in order to make comparisons
   D. call a meeting of top level staff in order to discuss ways of revising the policy

15. Your superior has asked you to notify division employees of an important change in one of the operating procedures described in the division manual. Every employee presently has a copy of this manual. 15.____
Which of the following is normally the MOST practical way to get the employees to understand such a change?
   A. Notify each employee individually of the change and answer any questions he might have
   B. Send a written notice to key personnel, directing them to inform the people under them

C. Call a general meeting, distribute a corrected page for the manual, and discuss the change
D. Send a memo to employees describing the change in general terms and asking them to make the necessary corrections in their copies of the manual

16. Assume that the work in your department involves the use of any technical terms. 16.____
In such a situation, when you are answering inquiries from the general public, it would usually be BEST to
A. use simple language and avoid the technical terms
B. employ the technical terms whenever possible
C. bandy technical terms freely, but explain each term in parentheses
D. apologize if you are forced to use a technical term

17. Suppose that you receive a telephone call from someone identifying himself as an employee in another city department who asks to be given information which your own department regards as confidential. 17.____
Which of the following is the BEST way of handling such a request?
A. Give the information requested, since your caller as official standing
B. Grant the request, provided the caller gives you a signed receipt
C. Refuse the request, because you have no way of knowing whether the caller is really who he claims to be
D. Explain that the information is confidential and inform the caller of the channels he must go through to have the information released to him

18. Studies show that office employees place high importance on the social and human aspects of the organization. What office employees like best about their jobs is the kind of people with whom they work. So strive hard to group people who are most likely to get along well together. 18.____
Based on this information, it is MOST reasonable to assume that office workers are most pleased to work in a group which
A. is congenial
B. has high productivity
C. allows individual creativity
D. is unlike other groups

19. A certain supervisor does not compliment members of his staff when they come up with good ideas. He feels that coming up with good ideas is part of the job and does not merit special attention. 19.____
This supervisor's practice is
A. *poor*, because recognition for good ideas is a good motivator
B. *poor*, because the staff will suspect that the supervisor has no good ideas of his own
C. *good*, because it is reasonable to assume that employees will tell their supervisor of ways to improve office practice
D. *good*, because the other members of the staff are not made to seem inferior by comparison

20. Some employees of a department have sent an anonymous letter containing many complaints to the department head. 20.____
Of the following, what is this MOST likely to show about the department?
    A. It is probably a good place to work.
    B. Communications are probably poor.
    C. The complaints are probably unjustified.
    D. These employees are probably untrustworthy.

21. Which of the following actions would usually be MOST appropriate for a supervisor to take after receiving an instruction sheet from his superior explaining a new procedure which is to be followed? 21.____
    A. Put the instruction sheet aside temporarily until he determines what is wrong with the old procedure.
    B. Call his superior and ask whether the procedure is one he must implement immediately.
    C. Write a memorandum to the superior asking for more details.
    D. Try the new procedure and advise the superior of any problems or possible improvements.

22. Of the following, which one is considered the PRIMARY advantage of using a committee to resolved a problem in an organization? 22.____
    A. No one person will be held accountable for the decision since a group of people was involved.
    B. People with different backgrounds give attention to the problem.
    C. The decision will take considerable time so there is unlikely to be a decision that will later be regretted.
    D. One person cannot dominate the decision-making process.

23. Employees in a certain office come to their supervisor with all their complaints about the office and the work. Almost every employee has had at least one minor complaint at some time. 23.____
The situation with respect to complaints in this office may BEST be described as probably
    A. *good*; employees who complain care about their jobs and work hard
    B. *good*; grievances brought out into the open can be corrected
    C. *bad*; only serious complaints should be discussed
    D. *bad*; it indicates the staff does not have confidence in the administration

24. The administrator who allows his staff to suggest ways to do their work will usually find that 24.____
    A. this practice contributes to high productivity
    B. the administrator's ideas produce greater output
    C. clerical employees suggest inefficient work methods
    D. subordinate employees resent performing a management function

25. The MAIN purpose for a supervisor's questioning the employees at a conference he is holding is to 25.____
    A. stress those areas of information covered but not understood by the participants
    B. encourage participants to think through the problem under discussion
    C. catch those subordinates who are not paying attention
    D. permit the more knowledgeable participants to display their grasp of the problems being discussed

KEY (CORRECT ANSWERS)

1.	D	11.	B
2.	A	12.	C
3.	C	13.	B
4.	D	14.	A
5.	B	15.	C
6.	B	16.	A
7.	C	17.	D
8.	D	18.	A
9.	A	19.	A
10.	A	20.	B

21.	D
22.	B
23.	B
24.	A
25.	B

TEST 2

DIRECTIONS: Each question or incomplete statement is followed by several suggested answers or completions. Select the one that BEST answers the question or completes the statement. *PRINT THE LETTER OF THE CORRECT ANSWER IN THE SPACE AT THE RIGHT.*

1. For a superior to use *consultative supervision* with his subordinates effectively, it is ESSENTIAL that he 1.____
   A. accept the fact that his formal authority will be weakened by the procedure
   B. admit that he does not know more than all his men together and that his ideas are not always best
   C. utilize a committee system so that the procedure is orderly
   D. make sure that all subordinates are consulted so that no one feels left out

2. The *grapevine* is an informal means of communication in an organization. The attitude of a supervisor with respect to the grapevine should be to 2.____
   A. ignore it since it deals mainly with rumors and sensational information
   B. regard it as a serious danger which should be eliminated
   C. accept it as a real line of communication which should be listened to
   D. utilize it for most purposes instead of the official line of communication

3. The supervisor of an office that must deal with the public should realize that planning in this type of work situation 3.____
   A. is useless because he does not know how many people will request service or what service they will request
   B. must be done at a higher level but that he should be ready to implement the results of such planning
   C. is useful primarily for those activities that are not concerned with public contact
   D. is useful for all the activities of the office, including those that relate to public contact

4. Assume that it is your job to receive incoming telephone calls. Those calls which you cannot handle yourself have to be transferred to the appropriate office. 4.____
   If you receive an outside call for an extension line which is busy, the one of the following which you should do FIRST is to
   A. interrupt the person speaking on the extension and tell him a call is waiting
   B. tell the caller the line is busy and let him know every thirty seconds whether or not it is free
   C. leave the caller on "hold" until the extension is free
   D. tell the caller the line is busy and ask him if he wishes to wait

5. Your superior has subscribed to several publications directly related to your division's work, and he has asked you to see to it that the publications are circulated among the supervisory personnel in the division. There are eight supervisors involved. 5.____
The BEST method of insuring that all eight see these publications is to
   A. place the publication in the division's general reference library as soon as it arrives
   B. inform each supervisor whenever a publication arrives and remind all of them that they are responsible for reading it
   C. prepare a standard slip that can be stapled to each publication, listing the eight supervisors and saying, "Please read, initial your name, and pass along"
   D. send a memo to the eight supervisors saying that they may wish to purchase individual subscriptions in their own names if they are interested in seeing each issue

6. Your superior has telephoned a number of key officials in your agency to ask whether they can meet at a certain time next month. He has found that they can all make it, and he has asked you to confirm the meeting. 6.____
Which of the following is the BEST way to confirm such a meeting?
   A. Note the meeting on your superior's calendar.
   B. Post a notice of the meeting on the agency bulletin board.
   C. Call the officials on the day of the meeting to remind them of the meeting.
   D. Write a memo to each official involved, repeating the time and place of the meeting.

7. Assume that a new city regulation requires that certain kinds of private organizations file information forms with your department. You have been asked to write the short explanatory message that will be printed on the front cover of the pamphlet containing the forms and instructions. 7.____
Which of the following would be the MOST appropriate way of beginning this message?
   A. Get the readers' attention by emphasizing immediately that there are legal penalties for organizations that fail to file before a certain date.
   B. Briefly state the nature of the enclosed forms and the types of organizations that must file.
   C. Say that your department is very sorry to have to put organizations to such an inconvenience.
   D. Quote the entire regulation adopted by the city, even if it is quite long and is expressed din complicated legal language.

8. Suppose that you have been told to make up the vacation schedule for the 18 employees in a particular unit. In order for the unit to operate effectively, only a few employees can be on vacation at the same time. 8.____
Which of the following is the MOST advisable approach in making up the schedule?
   A. Draw up a schedule assigning vacations in alphabetical order
   B. Find out when the supervisors want to take their vacations, and randomly assign whatever periods are left to the non-supervisory personnel

C. Assign the most desirable times to employees of longest standing and the least desirable times to the newest employees
D. Have all employees state their own preference, and then work out any conflicts in consultation with the people involved

9. Assume that you have been asked to prepare job descriptions for various positions in your department. 9.____
Which of the following are the basic points that should be covered in a *job description*?
A. General duties and responsibilities of the position, with examples of day-to-day tasks
B. Comments on the performances of present employees
C. Estimates of the number of openings that may be available in each category during the coming year
D. Instructions for carrying out the specific tasks assigned to your department

10. Of the following, the biggest DISADVANTAGE in allowing a free flow of communications in an agency is that such a free flow 10.____
A. decreases creativity
B. increases the use of the *grapevine*
C. lengthens the chain of command
D. reduces the executive's power to direct the flow of information

11. A downward flow of authority in an organization is one example of _____ communication. 11.____
A. horizontal B. informal C. circular D. vertical

12. Of the following, the one that would MOST likely block effective communication is 12.____
A. concentration only on the issues at hand
B. lack of interest or commitment
C. use of written reports
D. use of charts and graphs

13. An ADVANTAGE of the *lecture* as a teaching tool is that it 13.____
A. enables a person to present his ideas to a large number of people
B. allows the audience to retain a maximum of the information given
C. holds the attention of the audience for the longest time
D. enables the audience member to easily recall the main points

14. An ADVANTAGE of the *small-group* discussion as a teaching tool is that 14.____
A. it always focuses attention on one person as the leader
B. it places collective responsibility on the group as a whole
C. its members gain experience by summarizing the ideas of others
D. each member of the group acts as a member of a team

15. The one of the following that is an ADVANTAGE of a *large-group* discussion, when compared to a small-group discussion, is that the large-group discussion 15.____
    A. moves along more quickly than a small-group discussion
    B. allows its participants to feel more at ease, and speak out more freely
    C. gives the whole group a chance to exchange ideas on a certain subject at the same occasion
    D. allows its members to feel a greater sense of personal responsibility

KEY (CORRECT ANSWERS)

1.	D	6.	D	11.	D
2.	C	7.	B	12.	B
3.	D	8.	D	13.	A
4.	D	9.	A	14.	D
5.	C	10.	D	15.	C

READING COMPREHENSION
UNDERSTANDING AND INTERPRETING WRITTEN MATERIAL

EXAMINATION SECTION

This exam section includes some passages and questions related to functions of the first computerized offices, which consisted of typewriters and other such manual office equipment.

TEST 1

DIRECTIONS: Each question or incomplete statement is followed by several suggested answers or completions. Select the one that BEST answers the question or completes the statement. *PRINT THE LETTER OF THE CORRECT ANSWER IN THE SPACE AT THE RIGHT.*

Questions 1-2.

DIRECTIONS: Questions 1 and 2 are to be answered SOLELY on the basis of the following passage.

The employees in a unit or division of a government agency may be referred to as a work group. Within a government agency which has existed for some time, the work groups will have evolved traditions of their own. The persons in these work groups acquire these traditions as part of the process of work adjustment within their groups. Usually, a work group in a large organization will contain *oldtimers*, *newcomers*, and *in-betweeners*. Like the supervisor of a group, who is not necessarily an oldtimer or the oldest member, oldtimers usually have great influence. They can recall events unknown to others and are a storehouse of information and advice about current problems in the light of past experience. They pass along the traditions of the group to the others who, in turn, become oldtimers themselves. Thus, the traditions of the group which have been honored and revered by long acceptance are continued.

1. According to the above passage, the traditions of a work group within a government agency are developed 1.____
   - A. at the time the group is established
   - B. over a considerable period of time
   - C. in order to give recognition to oldtimers
   - D. for the group before it is established

2. According to the above passage, the oldtimers within a work group 2.____
   - A. are the means by which long accepted practices and customs are perpetuated
   - B. would best be able to settle current problems that arise
   - C. are honored because of the changes they have made in the traditions
   - D. have demonstrated that they have learned to do their work well

Questions 3-4.

DIRECTIONS: Questions 3 and 4 are to be answered SOLELY on the following passage.

In public agencies, the success of a person assigned to perform first-line supervisory duties depends in large part upon the personal relations between him and his subordinate employees. The goal of supervising effort is something more than to obtain compliance with procedures established by some central office. The major objective is work accomplishment. In order for this goal to be attained, employees must want to attain it and must exercise initiative in their work. Only if employees are generally satisfied with the type of supervision which exists in an organization will they put forth their best efforts.

3. According to the above passage, in order for employees to try to do their work as well as they can, it is essential that 3.____
   A. they participate in determining their working conditions and rates of pay
   B. their supervisors support the employees' viewpoints in meetings with higher management
   C. they are content with the supervisory practices which are being used
   D. their supervisors make the changes in working procedures that the employees request

4. It can be inferred from the above passage that the goals of a unit in a public agency will not be reached unless the employees in the unit 4.____
   A. wish to reach them and are given the opportunity to make individual contributions to the work
   B. understand the relationship between the goals of the unit and goals of the agency
   C. have satisfactory personal relationships with employees of other units in the agency
   D. carefully follow the directions issued by higher authorities

Questions 5-9.

DIRECTIONS: Questions 5 through 9 are to be answered SOLELY on the basis of the following passage.

In an employee thinks he can save money, time, or material for the city or has an idea about how to do something better than it is being done, he shouldn't keep it to himself. He should send his ideas to the Employees' Suggestion Program, using the special form which is kept on hand in all departments. An employee may send in as many ideas as he wishes. To make sure that each idea is judged fairly, the name of the suggester is not made known until an award is made. The awards are certificate of merit or cash prizes ranging from $10 to $500.

5. According to the above passage, an employee who knows how to do a job in a better way should 5.____
   A. be sure it saves enough time to be worthwhile
   B. get paid the money he saves for the city
   C. keep it to himself to avoid being accused of causing a speed-up
   D. send his idea to the Employees' Suggestion Program

6. In order to send his idea to the Employees' Suggestion Program, an employee should 6.____
   A. ask the Department of Personnel for a special form
   B. get the special form in his own department
   C. mail the idea using Special Delivery
   D. send it on plain, white letter-size paper

7. An employee may send to the Employees' Suggestion Program 7.____
   A. as many ideas as he can think of
   B. no more than one idea each week
   C. no more than ten ideas in a month
   D. only one idea on each part of the job

8. The reason the name of an employee who makes a suggestion is not made known at first is to 8.____
   A. give the employee a larger award
   B. help the judges give more awards
   C. insure fairness in judging
   D. only one idea on each part of the job

9. An employee whose suggestion receives an award may be given a 9.____
   A. bonus once a year
   B. certificate for $10
   C. cash prize of up to $500
   D. salary increase of $500

Questions 10-12.

DIRECTIONS: Questions 10 through 12 are to be answered SOLELY on the basis of the following passage.

According to the rules of the Department of Personnel, the work of every permanent city employee is reviewed and rated by his supervisor at least once a year. The civil service rating system gives the employee and his supervisor a chance to talk about the progress made during the past year as well as about those parts of the job in which the employee needs to do better. In order to receive a pay increase each year, the employee must have a satisfactory service rating. Service ratings also count toward an employee's final mark on a promotion examination.

10. According to the above passage, a permanent city employee is rated AT LEAST once 10.____
    A. before his work is reviewed
    B. every six months
    C. yearly by his supervisor
    D. yearly by the Department of Personnel

11. According to the above passage, under the rating system the supervisor and the employee can discuss how 11.____
    A. much more work needs to be done next year
    B. the employee did his work last year
    C. the work can be made easier next year
    D. the work of the Department can be increased

12. According to the above passage, a permanent city employee will NOT receive a yearly pay increase 12.____
    A. if he received a pay increase the year before
    B. if he used his service rating for his mark on a promotion examination
    C. if his service rating is unsatisfactory
    D. unless he got some kind of a service rating

Questions 13-16.

DIRECTIONS: Questions 13 through 16 are to be answered SOLELY on the basis of the following passage.

It is an accepted fact that the rank and file employee can frequently advance worthwhile suggestions toward increasing efficiency. For this reason, an Employees' Suggestion System has been developed and put into operation. Suitable means have been provided at each departmental location for the confidential submission of suggestions. Numerous suggestions have been received thus far and, after study, about five percent of the ideas submitted are being translated into action. It is planned to set up, eventually, monetary awards for all worthwhile suggestions.

13. According to the above passage, a MAJOR reason why an Employees' Suggestion System was established is that 13.____
    A. an organized program of improvement is better than a haphazard one
    B. employees can often give good suggestions to increase efficiency
    C. once a fact is accepted, it is better to act on it than to do nothing
    D. the suggestions of rank and file employees were being neglected

14. According to the above passage, under the Employees' Suggestion System, 14.____
    A. a file of worthwhile suggestions will eventually be set up at each departmental location
    B. it is possible for employees to turn in suggestions without fellow employees knowing of it
    C. means have been provided for the regular and frequent collection of suggestions submitted
    D. provision has been made for the judging of worthwhile suggestions by an Employees' Suggestion Committee

15. According to the above passage, it is reasonable to assume that 15.____
    A. all suggestions must be turned in at a central office
    B. employees who make worthwhile suggestions will be promoted
    C. not all the prizes offered will be monetary ones
    D. prizes of money will be given for the best suggestions

16. According to the above passage, of the many suggestions made, 16.____
    A. all are first tested
    B. a small part are put into use
    C. most are very worthwhile
    D. samples are studied

Questions 17-20.

DIRECTIONS: Questions 17 through 20 are to be answered SOLELY on the basis of the following passage.

Employees may be granted leaves of absence without pay at the discretion of the Personnel Officer. Such a leave without pay shall begin on the first working day on which the employee does not report for duty and shall continue to the first day on which the employee returns to duty. The Personnel Division may vary the dates of the leave for the record so as to conform with payroll periods, but in no case shall an employee be off the payroll for a different number of calendar days than would have been the case if the actual dates mentioned above had been used. An employee who has vacation or overtime to his credit, which is available for normal use, may take time off immediately prior to beginning a leave of absence without pay, chargeable against all or part of such vacation or overtime.

17. According to the above passage, the Personnel Officer must 17.____
    A. decide if a leave of absence without pay should be granted
    B. require that a leave end on the last working day of a payroll period
    C. see to it that a leave of absence to conform with a payroll period
    D. vary the dates of a leave of absence to conform with a payroll period

18. According to the above passage, the exact dates of a leave of absence without pay may be varied provided that the 18.____
    A. calendar days an employee is off the payroll equal the actual leave granted
    B. leave conforms to an even number of payroll periods
    C. leave when granted made provision for variance to simplify payroll records
    D. Personnel Officer approves the variation

19. According to the above passage, a leave of absence without pay must extend from the 19.____
    A. first day of a calendar period to the first day the employee resumes work
    B. first day of a payroll period to the last calendar day of the leave
    C. first working day missed to the first day on which the employee resumes work
    D. last day on which an employee works through the first day he returns to work

20. According to the above passage, an employee may take extra time off just before the start of a leave of absence without pay if 20.____
    A. he charges this extra time against his leave
    B. he has a favorable balance of vacation or overtime which has been frozen
    C. the vacation or overtime that he would normally use for a leave without pay has not been charged in this way before
    D. there is time to his credit which he may use

Question 21.

DIRECTIONS: Question 21 is to be answered SOLELY on the basis of the following passage.

In considering those things which are motivators and incentives to work, it might be just as erroneous not to give sufficient weight to money as an incentive as it is to give too much weight. It is not a problem of establishing a rank-order of importance, but one of knowing that motivation is a blend or mixture rather than a pure element. It is simple to say that cultural factors count more than financial considerations, but this leads only to the conclusion that our society is financial-oriented.

21. Based on the above passage, in our society, cultural and social motivations to work are 21.____
   A. things which cannot be avoided
   B. melded to financial incentives
   C. of less consideration than high pay
   D. not balanced equally with economic or financial considerations

Question 22.

DIRECTIONS: Question 22 is to be answered SOLELY on the basis of the following passage.

A general principle of training and learning with respect to people is that they learn more readily if they receive *feedback*. Essential to maintaining proper motivational levels is knowledge of results which indicate level of progress. Feedback also assists the learning process by identifying mistakes. If this kind of information were not given to the learner, then improper or inappropriate job performance may be instilled.

22. Based on the above passage, which of the following is MOST accurate? 22.____
   A. Learning will not take place without feedback.
   B. In the absence of feedback, improper or inappropriate job performance will be learned.
   C. To properly motivate a learner, the learner must have his progress made known to him.
   D. Trainees should be told exactly what to do if they are to learn properly

Questions 23

DIRECTIONS: Question 23 is to be answered SOLELY on the basis of the following passage.

In a democracy, the obligation of public officials is twofold. They must not only do an efficient and satisfactory job of administration, but also they must persuade the public that it is an efficient and satisfactory job. It is a burden which, if properly assumed, will make democracy work and perpetuate reform government.

23. The above passage means that 23.____
   A. public officials should try to please everybody

B. public opinion is instrumental if determining the policy of public officials
C. satisfactory performance of the job of administration will eliminate opposition to its work
D. frank and open procedure in a public agency will aid in maintaining progressive government

Question 24.

DIRECTIONS: Question 24 is to be answered SOLELY on the basis of the following passage.

Upon retirement for service, a member shall receive a retirement allowance which shall consist of an annuity which shall be the actuarial equivalent of his accumulated deductions at the time of his retirement and a pension, in addition to his annuity, which shall be equal to one service-fraction of his final compensation, multiplied by the number of years of service since he last became a member credited to him, and a pension which is the actuarial equivalent of the reserve-for-increased-take-home-pay to which he may then be entitled, if any.

24. According to the above passage, a retirement allowance shall consist of a(n) 24.____
A. annuity, plus a pension, plus an actuarial equivalent
B. annuity, plus a pension, plus reserve-for-increased-take-home-pay, if any
C. annuity, plus reserve-for-increased-take-home-pay, if any, plus final compensation
D. pension, plus reserve-for-increased-take-home-pay, if any, plus accumulated deductions

Question 25.

DIRECTIONS: Question 25 is to be answered SOLELY on the basis of the following passage.

Membership in the retirement system shall cease upon the occurrence of any one of the following conditions: when the time out of service of any member who has total service of less than 25 years, shall aggregate more than 5 years; when the time out of service of any member who has total service of 25 years or more, shall aggregate more than 10 years; when any member shall have withdrawn more than 50% of his accumulated deductions; or when any member shall have withdrawn the cash benefit provided by Section B3.35.0 of the Administrative Code.

25. According to the information in the above passage, membership in the retirement system shall cease when an employee 25.____
A. with 17 years of service has been on a leave of absence for 3 years
B. withdraws 50% of his accumulated deductions
C. with 28 years of service has been out of service for 10 years
D. withdraws his cash benefits

KEY (CORRECT ANSWERS)

1. B
2. A
3. C
4. A
5. D

6. B
7. A
8. C
9. B
10. C

11. B
12. C
13. B
14. B
15. D

16. B
17. A
18. A
19. C
20. D

21. B
22. C
23. D
24. B
25. D

TEST 2

DIRECTIONS: Each question or incomplete statement is followed by several suggested answers or completions. Select the one that BEST answers the question or completes the statement. *PRINT THE LETTER OF THE CORRECT ANSWER IN THE SPACE AT THE RIGHT.*

Questions 1-6.

DIRECTIONS: Questions 1 through 6 are to be answered SOLELY on the basis of the following passage.

Since almost every office has some contact with data-processed records, a stenographer should have some understanding of the basic operations of data processing. Data processing systems now handle a vast majority of all office paperwork. On coded forms and other specialized media, data are recorded before being fed into the computer for processing. The data written on the source document is converted in highly advanced ways in order to make the information accessible to the user. After data has been converted, it must be verified to guarantee absolute accuracy. In this manner, data becomes a permanent record which can be read by computers that compare, store, compute, and otherwise process data at high speeds.

One key person in a computer installation is a programmer, the man or woman who puts business and scientific problems into special symbolic languages that can be read by the computer. Jobs done by the computer range all the way from payroll operations to chemical process control, but most computer applications are directed toward management data. Most programmers employed by business come to their positions with college degrees; the rest are promoted to their positions from within the organization on the basis of demonstrated ability without regard to education.

1. Of the following, the BEST title for the above passage is 1.____
   A. The Stenographer As Data Processor
   B. The Relation of Data Input to Stenography
   C. Understanding Data Processing
   D. Permanent Office Records

2. According to the above passage, a stenographer should understand the basic operations of data processing because 2.____
   A. almost every office today has contact with data processed by computer
   B. any office worker may be asked to verify the accuracy of data
   C. most offices are involved in the production of permanent records
   D. data may be converted into computer language by specialized media

3. According to the above passage, data accuracy is reviewed during the ______ stage. 3._____
   A. processing
   B. verification
   C. programming
   D. stenographic

4. According to the above passage, computers are used MOST often to handle 4.____
   A. management data
   B. problems of higher education
   C. the control of chemical processes
   D. payroll operations

5. Computer programming is taught in many colleges and business schools. The above passage implies that programmers in industry 5.____
   A. must have professional training
   B. need professional training to advance
   C. must have at least a college education to do adequate programming tasks
   D. do not necessarily need college education to do programming work

6. According to the above passage, data to be processed by computer should be 6.____
   A. recent B. basic C. complete D. verified

Questions 7-10.

DIRECTIONS: Questions 7 through 10 are to be answered SOLELY on the basis of the following passage.

There is nothing that will take the place of good sense on the part of the stenographer. You may be perfect in transcribing exactly what the dictator says and your speed may be adequate, but without an understanding of the dictator's intent as well as his words, you are likely to be a mediocre secretary.

A serious error that is made when taking dictation is putting down something that does not make sense. Most people who dictate material would rather be asked to repeat and explain than to receive transcribed material which has errors due to inattention or doubt. Many dictators request that their grammar be corrected by their secretaries, but unless specifically asked to do so, secretaries should not do it without first checking with the dictator. Secretaries should be aware that, in some cases, dictators may use incorrect grammar or slang expressions to create a particular effect.

Some people dictate commas, periods, and paragraphs, while others expect the stenographer to know when, where, and how to punctuate. A well-trained secretary should be able to indicate the proper punctuation by listening to the pauses and tones of the dictator's voice.

A stenographer who has taken dictation from the same person for a period of time should be able to understand him under most conditions. By increasing her tack, alertness, and efficiency, a secretary can become more competent.

7. According to the above passage, which of the following statements concerning the dictation of punctuation is CORRECT? 7.____
   A. Dictator may use incorrect punctuation to create a desired style.
   B. Dictator should indicate all punctuation.

C. Stenographer should know how to punctuate based on the pauses and tones of the dictator.
D. Stenographer should not type any punctuation if it has not been dictated to her.

8. According to the above passage, how should secretaries handle grammatical errors in a dictation? 8.____
Secretaries should
A. *not correct* grammatical errors unless the dictator is aware that this is being done
B. *correct* grammatical errors by having the dictator repeat the line with proper pauses
C. *correct* grammatical errors if they have checked the correctness in a grammar book
D. *correct* grammatical errors based on their own good sense

9. If a stenographer is confused about the method of spacing and indenting of a report which has just been dictated to her, she GENERALLY should 9.____
A. do the best she can
B. ask the dictator to explain what she should do
C. try to improve her ability to understand dictated material
D. accept the fact that her stenographic ability is not adequate

10. In the last line of the first paragraph, the word *mediocre* means MOST NEARLY 10.____
A. superior B. respected C. disregarded D. second-rate

Questions 11-12.

DIRECTIONS: Questions 11 and 12 are to be answered SOLELY on the basis of the following passage.

The number of legible carbon copies required to be produced determines the weight of the carbon paper to be used. When only one copy is made, heavy carbon paper is satisfactory. Most typists, however, use medium-weight carbon paper and find it serviceable for up to three or four copies. If five or more copies are to be made, it is wise to use light carbon paper. On the other hand, the finish of carbon paper to be used depends largely on the stroke of the typist and, in lesser degree, on the number of copies to be made and on whether the typewriter has pica or elite type. A soft-finish carbon paper should be used if the typist's touch is light or if a noiseless machine is used. It is desirable for the average typist to use medium-finish carbon paper for ordinary work, when only a few carbon copies are required. Elite type requires a harder carbon finish than pica type for the same number of copies.

11. According to the above passage, the lighter the carbon paper used, the 11.____
A. softer the finish of the carbon paper will be
B. greater the number of legible carbon copies that can be made
C. greater the number of times the carbon paper can be used
D. lighter the typist's touch should be

12. According to the above passage, the MOST important factor which determines whether the finish of carbon paper to be used in typing should be hard, medium, or soft is 12.____
    A. the touch of the typist
    B. the number of carbon copies required
    C. whether the type in the typewriter is pica or elite
    D. whether a machine with pica type will produce the same number of carbon copies as a machine with elite type

Questions 13-16.

DIRECTIONS: Questions 13 through 16 are to be answered SOLELY on the basis of the following passage.

Looking back at past developments in office work, advances were made at higher speeds and at greater efficiency thanks largely to the typewriter. The typewriter was a substitute for handwriting and, in the hands of a skilled typist, not only turned out letters and other documents at least three times faster than a penman, but turned out the greater volume more uniformly and legibly. With the use of carbon paper and onionskin paper, identical copies could be made at the same time.

The typewriter, besides its effect on the conduct of business and government, had a very important effect on the position of women. The typewriter did much to bring women into business and government, and in a short time span, women far outnumbered men as typists. Many women used the keys of the typewriter to climb the ladder to professional managerial positions.

The typewriter, as its name implies, employs type to make an ink impression on paper. For many years, the manual typewriter was the standard machine used. Eventually, the electric typewriter became dominant, leading to innovations in and widespread use of completely automatic electronic typewriters.

The mechanism of the office manual typewriter includes a set of keys arranged systematically in rows; a semicircular frame of type, connected to the keys by levers; the carriage, or paper carrier; a rubber roller, called a platen, against which the type strikes; and an inked ribbon which makes the impression of the type character when the key strikes it.

13. The above passage mentions a number of good features of the combination of a skilled typist and a typewriter. 13.____
    Of the following the feature which is NOT mentioned in the passage is
    A. speed B. reliability C. uniformity D. legibility

14. According to the above passage, a skilled typist can 14.____
    A. turn out at least five carbon copies of typed matter
    B. type at least three times faster than a penman can write
    C. type more than 80 words in a minute
    D. readily move into a managerial position

15. According to the above passage, which of the following is NOT part of the mechanism of a manual typewriter? 15.____
    A. Carbon paper
    B. Platen
    C. Paper carrier
    D. Inked ribbon

16. According to the above passage, the typewriter helped 16.____
    A. men more than women in business
    B. women in career advancement into management
    C. men and women equally, but women have taken better advantage of it
    D. more women than men, because men generally dislike routine typing work

Questions 17-21.

DIRECTIONS: Questions 17 through 21 are to be answered SOLELY on the basis of the following passage.

The recipient gains an impression of a typewritten letter before he begins to read the message. Factors which provide for a good first impression include margins and spacing that are visually pleasing, formal parts of the letter which are correctly placed according to the style of the letter, copy which is free of obvious erasures and over-strikes, and transcript that is even and clear. The problem for the typist is that of how to produce that first, positive impression of her work.

There are several general rules which a typist can follow when she wishes to prepare a properly spaced letter on a sheet of letterhead. Ordinarily, the width of a letter should not be less than four inches nor more than six inches. The side margins should also have a desirable relation to the bottom margin and the space between the letterhead and the body of the letter. Usually the most appealing arrangement is when the side margins are even and the bottom margin is slightly wider than the side margins. In some offices, however, standard line length is used for all business letter, and the secretary then varies the spacing between the date line and the inside address according to the length of the letter.

17. The BEST title for the above passage would be 17.____
    A. Writing Office Letters
    B. Making Good First Impressions
    C. Judging Well-Typed Letters
    D. Good Placing and Spacing for Office Letters

18. According to the above passage, which of the following might be considered the way in which people very quickly judge the quality of work which has been typed? By 18.____
    A. measuring the margins to see if they are correct
    B. looking at the spacing and cleanliness of the typescript
    C. scanning the body of the letter for meaning
    D. reading the date line and address for errors

19. What, according to the above passage, would be definitely UNDESIRABLE as the average line length of a typed letter? 19.____
    A. 4" B. 6" C. 5" D. 7"

20. According to the above passage, when the line length is kept standard, the secretary 20.____
    A. does not have to vary the spacing at all since this also is standard
    B. adjusts the spacing between the date line and inside address for different lengths of letters
    C. uses the longest line as a guidance for spacing between the date line and inside address
    D. varies the number of spaces between the lines

21. According to the above passage, side margins are MOST pleasing when they 21.____
    A. are even and somewhat smaller than the bottom margin
    B. are slightly wider than the bottom margin
    C. vary with the length of the letter
    D. are figured independently from the letterhead and the body of the letter

Questions 22-25.

DIRECTIONS: Questions 22 through 25 are to be answered SOLELY on the basis of the following passage.

Typed pages can reflect the simplicity of modern art in a machine age. Lightness and evenness can be achieved by proper layout and balance of typed lines and white space. Instead of solid, cramped masses of uneven, crowded typing, there should be a pleasing balance up and down as well as horizontal.

To have real balance, your page must have a center. The eyes see the center of the sheet slightly above the real center. This is the way both you and the reader see it. Try imagining a line down the center of the page that divides the paper in equal halves. On either side of your paper, white space and blocks of typing need to be similar in size and shape. Although left and right margins should be equal, top and bottom margins need not be as exact. It looks better to hold a bottom border wider than a top margin, so that your typing rests upon a cushion of white space. To add interest to the appearance of the page, try making one paragraph between one-half and two-thirds the size of an adjacent paragraph.

Thus, by taking full advantage of your typewriter, the pages that you type will not only be accurate but will also be attractive.

22. It can be inferred from the above passage that the basic importance of proper balancing on a typed page is that proper balancing 22.____
    A. makes a typed page a work of modern art
    B. provides exercise in proper positioning of a typewriter
    C. increases the amount of typed copy on the paper
    D. draws greater attention and interest to the page

23. A reader will tend to see the center of a typed page 23.____
    A. somewhat higher than the true center
    B. somewhat lower than the true center
    C. on either side of the true center
    D. about two-thirds of an inch above the true center

24. Which of the following suggestions is NOT given by the above passage? 24.____
    A. Bottom margins may be wider than top borders.
    B. Keep all paragraphs approximately the same size.
    C. Divide your page with an imaginary line down the middle.
    D. Side margins should be equalized.

25. Of the following, the BEST title for the above passage is 25.____
    A. Increasing the Accuracy of the Typed Page
    B. Determination of Margins for Typed Copy
    C. Layout and Balance of the Typed Page
    D. How to Take Full Advantage of the Typewriter

KEY (CORRECT ANSWERS)

1.	C	11.	B
2.	A	12.	A
3.	B	13.	B
4.	A	14.	B
5.	D	15.	A
6.	D	16.	B
7.	C	17.	D
8.	A	18.	B
9.	B	19.	D
10.	D	20.	B

21.	A
22.	D
23.	A
24.	B
25.	C

TEST 3

DIRECTIONS: Each question or incomplete statement is followed by several suggested answers or completions. Select the one that BEST answers the question or completes the statement. *PRINT THE LETTER OF THE CORRECT ANSWER IN THE SPACE AT THE RIGHT.*

Questions 1-5.

DIRECTIONS: Questions 1 through 5 are to be answered SOLELY on the basis of the following passage.

A written report is a communication of information from one person to another. It is an account of some matter especially investigated, however routine that matter may be. The ultimate basis of any good written report is facts, which become known through observation and verification. Good written reports may seem to be no more than general ideas and opinions. However, in such cases, the facts leading too these opinions were gathered, verified, and reported earlier, and the opinions are dependent upon these facts. Good style, proper form, and emphasis cannot make a good written report out of unreliable information and bad judgment; but on the other hand, solid investigation and brilliant thinking are not likely to become very useful until they are effectively communicated to others. If a person's work calls for written reports, then his work is often no better than his written reports.

1. Based on the information in the above passage, it can be concluded that opinions expressed in a report should be 1.____
   A. based on facts which are gathered and reported
   B. emphasized repeatedly when they result from a special investigation
   C. kept to a minimum
   D. separated from the body of the report

2. In the above passage, the one of the following which is mentioned as a way of establishing facts is 2.____
   A. authority
   B. reporting
   C. communication
   D. verification

3. According to the above passage, the characteristic shared by ALL written reports is that they are 3.____
   A. accounts of routine matters
   B. transmissions of information
   C. reliable and logical
   D. written in proper form

4. Which of the following conclusions can logically be drawn from the information given in the above passage? 4.____
   A. Brilliant thinking can make up for unreliable information in a report.
   B. One method of judging an individual's work is the quality of the written reports he is required to submit.
   C. Proper form and emphasis can make a good report out of unreliable information.
   D. Good written reports that seem to be no more than general ideas should be rewritten.

5. Which of the following suggested titles would be MOST appropriate for the above passage? 5.____
   A. Gathering and Organizing Facts
   B. Techniques of Observation
   C. Nature and Purpose of Reports
   D. Reports and Opinions: Differences and Similarities

Questions 6-8.

DIRECTIONS: Questions 6 through 8 are to be answered SOLELY on the basis of the following passage.

The most important unit of the mimeograph machine is a perforated metal drum over which is stretched a cloth ink pad. A reservoir inside the drum contains the ink which flows through the perforations and saturates the ink pad. To operate the machine, the operator first removes from the machine the protective sheet, which keeps the ink from drying while the machine is not in use. He then hooks the stencil face down on the drum, draws the stencil smoothly over the drum, and fastens the stencil at the bottom. The speed with which the drum turns determines the blackness of the copies printed. Slow turning gives heavy, black copies; fast turning gives light, clear-cut reproductions. If reproductions are run on other than porous paper, slip-sheeting is necessary to prevent smearing. Often, the printed copy fails to drop readily as it comes from the machine. This may be due to static electricity. To remedy this difficulty, the operator fastens a strip of tinsel from side to side near the impression roller so that the printed copy just touches the soft stems of the tinsel as it is ejected from the machine, thus grounding the static electricity to the frame of the machine.

6. According to the above passage, 6.____
   A. turning the drum fast produces light copies
   B. stencils should be placed face up on the drum
   C. ink pads should be changed daily
   D. slip-sheeting is necessary when porous paper is being used

7. According to the above passage, when a mimeograph machine is not in use, the 7.____
   A. ink should be drained from the drum
   B. ink pad should be removed
   C. machine should be covered with a protective sheet
   D. counter should be set at zero

8. According to the above passage, static electricity is grounded to the frame of the mimeograph machine by means of 8.____
   A. a slip-sheeting device
   B. a strip of tinsel
   C. an impression roller
   D. hooks located at the top of the drum

Questions 9-10.

DIRECTIONS: Questions 9 and 10 are to be answered SOLELY on the basis of the following passage.

The proofreading of material typed from copy is performed more accurately and more speedily when two persons perform this work as a team. The person who did not do the typing should read aloud the original copy while the person who did the typing should check the reading against the typed copy. The reader should speak very slowly and repeat the figures, using a different grouping of number when repeating the figures. For example, in reading 1967, the reader may say *one-nine-six-seven* on first reading the figure and *nineteen-sixty-seven* on repeating the figure. The reader should read all punctuation marks, taking nothing for granted. Since mistakes can occur anywhere, everything typed should be proofread. To avoid confusion, the proofreading team should use the standard proofreading marks, which are given in most dictionaries.

9. According to the above passage, the 9.____
   A. person who holds the typed copy is called the reader
   B. two members of a proofreading team should take turns in reading the typed copy aloud
   C. typed copy should be checked by the person who did the typing
   D. person who did not do the typing should read aloud from the typed copy

10. According to the above passage, 10.____
   A. it is unnecessary to read the period at the end of a sentence
   B. typographical errors should be noted on the original copy
   C. each person should develop his own set of proofreading marks
   D. figures should be read twice

Questions 11-16.

DIRECTIONS: Questions 11 through 16 are to be answered SOLELY on the basis of the following passage.

Basic to every office is the need for proper lighting. Inadequate lighting is a familiar cause of fatigue and serves to create a somewhat dismal atmosphere in the office. One requirement of proper lighting is that it be of an appropriate intensity. Intensity is measured in foot-candles. According to the Illuminating Engineering Society of New York, for casual seeing tasks such as in reception rooms, inactive file rooms, and other service areas, it is recommending that the amount of light be 30 foot-candle. For ordinary seeing tasks such as reading, work in active file rooms, and in mailrooms, the recommended lighting is 100 foot-candles. For very difficult seeing tasks such as accounting, transcribing, and business machine use, the recommended lighting is 150 foot-candles.

Lighting intensity is only one requirement. Shadows and glare are to be avoided. For example, the larger the proportion of a ceiling filled with lighting units, the more glare-free and comfortable the lighting will be. Natural lighting from window is not too dependable because on dark wintry days, windows yield little usable light, and on sunny afternoons, the glare from windows may be very distracting. Desks should not face the windows. Finally, the main lighting source ought to be overhead and to the left of the user.

11. According to the above passage, insufficient light in the office may cause 11.____
    A. glare B. tiredness C. shadows D. distraction

12. Based on the above passage, which of the following must be considered when planning lighting arrangements? The 12.____
    A. amount of natural light present
    B. amount of work to be done
    C. level of difficulty of work to be done
    D. type of activity to be carried out

13. It can be inferred from the above passage that a well-coordinated lighting scheme is LIKELY to result in 13.____
    A. greater employee productivity
    B. elimination of light reflection
    C. lower lighting cost
    D. more use of natural light

14. Of the following, the BEST title for the above passage is 14.____
    A. Characteristics of Light
    B. Light Measurement Devices
    C. Factors to Consider When Planning Lighting Systems
    D. comfort vs. Cost When Devising Lighting Arrangements

15. According to the above passage, a foot-candle is a measurement of the 15.____
    A. number of bulbs used
    B. strength of the light
    C. contrast between glare and shadow
    D. proportion of the ceiling filled with lighting units

16. According to the above passage, the number of foot-candles of light that would be needed to copy figures onto a payroll is _____ foot-candles. 16.____
    A. less than 30 B. 100 C. 30 D. 140

Questions 17-23.

DIRECTIONS: Questions 17 through 23 are to be answered SOLELY on the basis of the following passage.

<u>FEE SCHEDULE</u>

1. A candidate for any baccalaureate degree is not required to pay tuition fees for undergraduate courses until he exceeds 128 credits. Candidates exceeding 128 credits in undergraduate courses are charged at the rate of $100 a credit for each credit of undergraduate course work in excess of 128. Candidates for a baccalaureate degree who are taking graduate courses must pay the same fee as any other student taking graduate courses.

B. Non-degree students and college graduates are charged tuition fees for courses, whether undergraduate or graduate, at the rate of $180 a credit. For such students, there is an additional charge of $150 for each class hour per week in excess of the number of course credits. For example, if a three-credit course meets five hours a week, there is an additional charge for the extra two hours. Graduate courses are shown with a (G) before the course number.

C. All students are required to pay the laboratory fees indicated after the number of credits given for that course.

D. All students must pay a $250 general fee each semester.

E. Candidates for a baccalaureate degree are charged a $150 medical insurance fee for each semester. All other students are charged a $100 medical insurance fee each semester.

17. Miss Burton is not a candidate for a degree. She registers for the following courses in the spring semester: Economics 12, 4 hours a week, 3 credits; History (G 23, 4 hours a week, 3 credits; English 1, 2 hours a week, 2 credits. The TOTAL amount in fees that Miss Burton must pay is 17.____
   A. less than $2,000
   B. at least $2,000 but less than $2,100
   C. at least $2,100 but less than $2,200
   D. $2,200 or over

18. Miss Gray is not a candidate for a degree. She registers for the following courses in the fall semester: History 3, 3 hours a week, 3 credits; English 5, 3 hours a week, 2 credits; Physics 5, 6 hours a week, 3 credits, laboratory fee $60; Mathematics 7, 4 hours a week, 3 credits. The TOTAL amount in fees that Miss Gray must pay is 18.____
   A. less than $3,150
   B. at least $3,150 but less than $3,250
   C. at least $3,250 but less than $3,350
   D. $3,350 or over

19. Mr. Wall is a candidate for the Bachelor of Arts degree and has completed 126 credits. He registers for the following courses in the spring semester, his final semester at college; French 4, 3 hours a week, 3 credits; Physics (G) 15, 6 hours a week, 3 credits, laboratory fee $80; History (G) 33, 4 hours a week, 3 credits. The TOTAL amount in fees that this candidate must pay is 19.____
   A. less than $2,100
   B. at least $2,100 but less than $2,300
   C. at least $2,300 but less than $2,500
   D. $2,500

20. Mr. Tindall, a candidate for the B.A. degree, has completed 122 credits of undergraduate courses. He registers for the following courses in his final semester: English 31, 3 hours a week, 3 credits; Philosophy 12, 4 hours a week, 4 credits; Anthropology 15, 3 hours a week, 3 credits; Economics (G) 68, 3 hours a week, 3 credits. 20.____
The TOTAL amount in fees that Mr. Tindall must pay in his final semester is
   A. less than $1,200
   B. at least $1,200 but less than $1,400
   C. at least $1,400 but less than $1,600
   D. $1,600

21. Mr. Cantrell, who was graduated from the college a year ago, registers for graduate courses in the fall semester. Each course for which he register carries the same number of credits as the number of hours a week it meets. If he pays a total of $1,530, including a $100 laboratory fee, the number of credits for which he is registered is 21.____
   A. 4 B. 5 C. 6 D. 7

22. Miss Jayson, who is not a candidate for a degree, has registered for several courses including a lecture course in History. She withdraws from the course in History for which she had paid the required course fee of $690. 22.____
The number of hours that this course is scheduled to meet is
   A. 4 B. 5 C. 2 D. 3

23. Mr. Van Arsdale, a graduate of a college in Iowa, registers for the following courses in one semester: Chemistry 35, 5 hours a week, 3 credits; Biology 14, 4 hours a week, 3 credits, laboratory fee $150; Mathematics (G) 179, 3 hours a week, 3 credits. 23.____
The TOTAL amount in fees that Mr. Van Arsdale must pay is
   A. less than $2,400
   B. at least $2,400 but less than $2,500
   C. at least $2,500 but less than $2,600
   D. at least $2,600 or over

Questions 24-25.

DIRECTIONS: Questions 24 and 25 are to be answered SOLELY on the basis of the following passage.

A duplex envelope is an envelope composed of two sections securely fastened together so that they become one mailing piece. This type of envelope makes it possible for a first class letter to be delivered simultaneously with third or fourth class matter and yet not require payment of the much higher first class postage rate on the entire mailing. First class postage is paid only on the letter which goes in the small compartment, third or fourth class postage being paid on the contents of the larger compartment. The larger compartment generally has an ungummed flap or clasp for sealing. The first class or smaller compartment has a gummed flap for sealing. Postal regulations require that the exact amount of postage applicable to each compartment be separately attached to it.

24. On the basis of the above passage, it is MOST accurate to state that 24.____
    A. the smaller compartment is placed inside the larger compartment before mailing
    B. the two compartments may be detached and mailed separately
    C. two classes of mailing matter may be mailed as a unit at two different postage rates
    D. the more expensive postage rate is paid on the matter in the larger compartment

25. When a duplex envelope is used, the 25.____
    A. first class compartment may be sealed with a clasp
    B. correct amount of postage must be placed on each compartment
    C. compartment containing third or fourth class mail requires a gummed flap for sealing
    D. full amount of postage for both compartments may be placed on the larger compartment

KEY (CORRECT ANSWERS)

1.	A	11.	C
2.	D	12.	D
3.	B	13.	A
4.	B	14.	C
5.	C	15.	B
6.	A	16.	D
7.	C	17.	B
8.	B	18.	A
9.	C	19.	B
10.	D	20.	B

21.	C
22.	A
23.	C
24.	C
25.	B

PREPARING WRITTEN MATERIAL

PARAGRAPH REARRANGEMENT COMMENTARY

The sentences that follow are in scrambled order. You are to rearrange them in proper order and indicate the letter choice containing the correct answer at the space at the right.

Each group of sentences in this section is actually a paragraph presented in scrambled order. Each sentence in the group has a place in that paragraph; no sentence is to be left out. You are to read each group of sentences and decide upon the best order in which to put the sentences so as to form a well-organized paragraph.

The questions in this section measure the ability to solve a problem when all the facts relevant to its solution are not given.

More specifically, certain positions of responsibility and authority require the employee to discover connection between events sometimes, apparently, unrelated. In order to do this, the employee will find it necessary to correctly infer that unspecified events have probably occurred or are likely to occur. This ability becomes especially important when action must be taken on incomplete information.

Accordingly, these questions require competitors to choose among several suggested alternatives, each of which presents a different sequential arrangement of the events. Competitors must choose the MOST logical of the suggested sequences.

In order to do so, they may be required to draw on general knowledge to infer missing concepts or events that are essential to sequencing the given events. Competitors should be careful to infer only what is essential to the sequence. The plausibility of the wrong alternatives will always require the inclusion of unlikely events or of additional chains of events which are NOT essential to sequencing the given events.

It's very important to remember that you are looking for the best of the four possible choices, and that the best choice of all may not even be one of the answers you're given to choose from.

There is no one right way to solve these problems. Many people have found it helpful to first write out the order of the sentences, as they would have arranged them, on their scrap paper before looking at the possible answers. If their optimum answer is there, this can save them some time. If it isn't, this method can still give insight into solving the problem. Others find it most helpful to just go through each of the possible choices, contrasting each as they go along. You should use whatever method feels comfortable and works for you.

While most of these types of questions are not that difficult, we've added a higher percentage of the difficult type, just to give you more practice. Usually there are only one or two questions on this section that contain such subtle distinctions that you're unable to answer confidently. And you then may find yourself stuck deciding between two possible choices, neither of which you're sure about.

EXAMINATION SECTION

TEST 1

DIRECTIONS: The following groups of sentences need to be arranged in an order that makes sense. Select the letter preceding the sequence that represents the BEST sentence order. *PRINT THE LETTER OF THE CORRECT ANSWER IN THE SPACE AT THE RIGHT.*

1. I. The keyboard was purposely designed to be a little awkward to slow typists down. 1.____
   II. The arrangement of letters on the keyboard of a typewriter was not designed for the convenience of the typist.
   III. Fortunately, no one is suggesting that a new keyboard be designed right away.
   IV. If one were, we would have to learn to type all over again.
   V. The reason was that the early machines were slower than the typists and would jam easily.
   The CORRECT answer is:
   A. I, III, IV, II, V
   B. II, V, I, IV, III
   C. V, I, II, III, IV
   D. II, I, V, III, IV

2. I. The majority of the new service jobs are part-time or low-paying. 2.____
   II. According to the U.S. Bureau of Labor Statistics, jobs in the service sector constitute 72% of all jobs in this country.
   III. If more and more workers receive less and less money, who will buy the goods and services needed to keep the economy going?
   IV. The service sector is by far the fastest growing part of the United States economy.
   V. Some economists look upon this trend with great concern.
   The CORRECT answer is:
   A. II, IV, I, V, III
   B. II, III, IV, I, V
   C. V, IV, II, III, I
   D. III, I, II, IV, V

3. I. They can also affect one's endurance. 3.____
   II. This can stabilize blood sugar levels, and ensure that the brain is receiving a steady, constant, supply of glucose, so that one is *hitting on all cylinders* while taking the test.
   III. By food, we mean real food, not junk food or unhealthy snacks.
   IV. For this reason, it is important not to skip a meal, and to bring food with you to the exam.
   V. One's blood sugar levels can affect how clearly one is able to think and concentrate during an exam.
   The CORRECT answer is:
   A. V, IV, II, III, I
   B. V, II, I, IV, III
   C. V, I, IV, III, II
   D. V, IV, I, III, II

4. I. Those who are the embodiment of desire are absorbed in material quests, and those who are the embodiment of feeling are warriors who value power more than possession. 4.____
II. These qualities are in everyone, but in different degrees.
III. But those who value understanding yearn not for goods or victory, but for knowledge.
IV. According to Plato, human behavior flows from three main sources: desire, emotion, and knowledge.
V. In the perfect state, the industrial forces would produce but not rule, the military would protect but not rule, and the forces of knowledge, the philosopher kings, would reign.
The CORRECT answer is:
A. IV, V, I, II, III
B. V, I, II, III, IV
C. IV, III, II, I, V
D. IV, II, I, III, V

5. I. Of the more than 26,000 tons of garbage produced daily in New York City, 12,000 tons arrive daily at Fresh Kills. 5.____
II. In a month, enough garbage accumulates there to fill the Empire State Building.
III. In 1937, the Supreme Court halted the practice of dumping the trash of New York City into the sea.
IV. Although the garbage is compacted, in a few years the mounds of garbage at Fresh Kills will be the highest points south of Maine's Mount Desert Island on the Eastern Seaboard.
V. Instead, tugboats now pull barges of much of the trash to Staten Island and the largest landfill in the world, Fresh Kills.
The CORRECT answer is:
A. III, V, IV, I, II
B. III, V, II, IV, I
C. III, V, I, II, IV
D. III, II, V, IV, I

6. I. Communists rank equality very high, but freedom very low. 6.____
II. Unlike communists, conservatives place a high value on freedom and a very low value on equality.
III. A recent study demonstrated that one way to classify people's political beliefs is to look at the importance placed on two words: freedom and equality.
IV. Thus, by demonstrating how members of these groups feel about the two words, the study has proved to be useful for political analysts in several European countries.
V. According to the study, socialists and liberals rank both freedom and equality very high, while fascists rate both very low.
The CORRECT answer is:
A. III, V, I, II, IV
B. V, IV, III, I, II
C. III, V, IV, II, I
D. III, I, II, IV, V

7. I. "Can there be anything more amazing than this?" 7.____
II. If the riddle is successfully answered, his dead brothers will be brought back to life.
III. "Even though man sees those around him dying every day," says Dharmaraj, "he still believes and acts as if he were immortal."
IV. "What is the cause of ceaseless wonder?" asks the Lord of the Lake.
V. In the ancient epic, The Mahabharata, a riddle is asked of one of the Pandava brothers.
The CORRECT answer is:
A. V, II, I, IV, III
B. V, IV, III, I, II
C. V, II, IV, III, I
D. V, II, IV, I, III

8. I. On the contrary, the two main theories—the cooperative (neoclassical) theory and the radical (labor theory)—clearly rest on very different assumptions, which have very different ethical overtones. 8.____
II. The distribution of income is the primary factor in determining the relative levels of material well-being that different groups or individuals attain.
III. Of all issues in economics, the distribution of income is one of the most controversial.
IV. The neoclassical theory tends to support the existing income distribution (or minor changes), while the labor theory ends to support substantial changes in the way income is distributed.
V. The intensity of the controversy reflects the fact that different economic theories are not purely neutral, *detached* theories with no ethical or moral implications.
The CORRECT answer is:
A. II, I, V, IV, III
B. III, II, V, I, IV
C. III, V, II, I, IV
D. III, V, IV, I, II

9. I. The pool acts as a broker and ensures that the cheapest power gets used first. 9.____
II. Every six seconds, the pool's computer monitors all of the generating stations in the state and decides which to ask for more power and which to cut back.
III. The buying and selling of electrical power is handled by the New York Power Pool in Guilderland, New York.
IV. This is to the advantage of both the buying and selling utilities.
V. The pool began operation in 1970, and consists of the state's eight electric utilities.
The CORRECT answer is:
A. V, I, II, III, IV
B. IV, II, I, III, V
C. III, V, I, IV, II
D. V, III, IV, II, I

10. I. Modern English is much simpler grammatically than Old English. 10.____
II. Finnish grammar is very complicated; there are some fifteen cases, for example.
III. Chinese, a very old language, may seem to be the exception, but it is the great number of characters/words that must be mastered that makes it so difficult to learn, not its grammar.
IV. The newest literary language—that is, written as well as spoken—is Finish, whose literary roots go back only to about the middle of the nineteenth century.
V. Contrary to popular belief, the longer a language is been in use the simpler its grammar—not the reverse.

The CORRECT answer is:
A. IV, I, II, III, V
B. V, I, IV, II, III
C. I, II, IV, III, V
D. IV, II, III, I, V

KEY (CORRECT ANSWERS)

1.	D	6.	A
2.	A	7.	C
3.	C	8.	B
4.	D	9.	C
5.	C	10.	B

TEST 2

DIRECTIONS: This type of question tests your ability to recognize accurate paraphrasing, well-constructed paragraphs, and appropriate style and tone. It is important that the answer you select contains only the facts or concepts given in the original sentences. It is also important that you be aware of incomplete sentences, inappropriate transitions, unsupported opinions, incorrect usage, and illogical sentence order. Paragraphs that do not include all the necessary facts and concepts, that distort them, or that add new ones are not considered correct.

The format for this section may vary. Sometimes, long paragraphs are given, and emphasis is placed on style and organization. Our first five questions are of this type. Other times, the paragraphs are shorter, and there is less emphasis on style and more emphasis on accurate representation of information. Our second group of five questions are of this nature.

For each of Questions 1 through 10, select the paragraph that BEST expresses the ideas contained in the sentences above it. *PRINT THE LETTER OF THE CORRECT ANSWER IN THE SPACE AT THE RIGHT.*

1. I. Listening skills are very important for managers. 1.____
   II. Listening skills are not usually emphasized.
   III. Whenever managers are depicted in books, manuals or the media, they are always talking, never listening.
   IV. We'd like you to read the enclosed handout on listening skills and to try to consciously apply them this week.
   V. We guarantee they will improve the quality of your interactions.

   A. Unfortunately, listening skills are not usually emphasized for managers. Managers are always depicted as talking, never listening. We'd like you to read the enclosed handout on listening skills. Please try to apply these principles this week. If you do, we guarantee they will improve the quality of your interactions.
   B. The enclosed handout on listening skills will be important improving the quality of your interactions. We guarantee it. All you have to do is take sometime this week to read and to consciously try to apply the principles. Listening skills are very important for manages, but they are not usually emphasized. Whenever managers are depicted in books, manuals or the media, they are always talking, never listening.
   C. Listening well is one of the most important skills a manager can have, yet it's not usually given much attention. Think about any representation of managers in books, manuals, or in the media that you may have seen. They're always talking, never listening. We'd like you to read the enclosed handout on listening skills and consciously try to apply them the rest of the week. We guarantee you will see a difference in the quality of your interactions.

D. Effective listening, one very important tool in the effective manager's arsenal, is usually not emphasized enough. The usual depiction of managers in books, manuals or the media is one in which they are always talking, never listening. We'd like you to read the enclosed handout and consciously try to apply the information contained therein throughout the rest of the week. We feel sure that you will see a marked difference in the quality of your interactions.

2. I. Chekhov wrote three dramatic masterpieces which share certain themes and formats: Uncle Vanya, The Cherry Orchard, and The Three Sisters. 2.____
II. They are primarily concerned with the passage of time and how this erodes human aspirations.
III. The plays are haunted by the ghosts of the wasted life.
IV. The characters are concerned with life's lesser problems; however, such as the inability to make decisions, loyalty to the wrong cause, and the inability to be clear.
V. This results in sweet, almost aching, type of a sadness referred to as Chekhovian.

A. Chekhov wrote three dramatic masterpieces: Uncle Vanya, The Cherry Orchard, and The Three Sisters. These masterpieces share certain themes and formats: the passage of time, how time erodes human aspirations, and the ghosts of wasted life. Each masterpiece is characterized by a sweet, almost aching, type of sadness that has become known as Chekhovian. The sweetness of this sadness hinges on the fact that it is not the great tragedies of life which are destroying these characters, but their minor flaws: indecisiveness, misplaced loyalty, unclarity.
B. The Cherry Orchard, Uncle Vanya, and The Three Sisters are three dramatic masterpieces written by Chekhov that use similar formats to explore a common theme. Each is primarily concerned with the way that passing time wears down human aspirations, and each is haunted by the ghosts of the wasted life. The characters are shown struggling futilely with the lesser problems of life: indecisiveness, loyalty to the wrong cause, and the inability to be clear. These struggles create a mood of sweet, almost aching, sadness that has become known as Chekhovian.
C. Chekhov's dramatic masterpieces are, along with The Cherry Orchard, Uncle Vanya, and The Three Sisters. These plays share certain thematic and formal similarities. They are concerned most of all with the passage of time and the way in which time erodes human aspirations. Each play is haunted by the specter of the wasted life. Chekhov's characters are caught, however, by life's lesser snares: indecisiveness, loyalty to the wrong cause, and unclarity. The characteristic mood is a sweet, almost aching type of sadness that has come to be known as Chekhovian.
D. A Chekhovian mood is characterized by sweet, almost aching, sadness. The term comes from three dramatic tragedies by Chekhov which revolve around the sadness of a wasted life. The three masterpieces (Uncle Vanya, The Three Sisters, and The Cherry Orchard) share the same

theme and format. The plays are concerned with how the passage of time erodes human aspirations. They are peopled with characters who are struggling with life's lesser problems. These are people who are indecisive, loyal to the wrong causes, or are unable to make themselves clear.

3. I. Movie previews have often helped producers decide which parts of movies they should take out or leave in. 3.____
II. The first 1933 preview of King Kong was very helpful to the producers because many people ran screaming from the theater and would not return when four men first attacked by Kong were eaten by giant spiders.
III. The 1950 premiere of Sunset Boulevard resulted in the filming of an entirely new beginning, and a delay of six months in the film's release.
IV. In the original opening scene, William Holden was in a morgue talking with thirty-six other "corpses" about the ways some of them had died.
V. When he began to tell them of his life with Gloria Swanson, the audience found this hilarious, instead of taking the scene seriously.

A. Movie previews have often helped producers decide what parts of movies they should leave in or take out. For example, the first preview of King Kong in 1933 was very helpful. In one scene, four men were first attacked by Kong and then eaten by giant spiders. Many members of the audience ran screaming from the theater and would not return. The premiere of the 1950 film Sunset Boulevard was also very helpful. In the original opening scene, William Holden was in a morgue with thirty-six other "corpses," discussing the ways some of them had died. When he began to tell them of his life with Gloria Swanson, the audience found this hilarious. They were supposed to take the scene seriously. The result was a delay of six months in the release of the film while a new beginning was added.
B. Movie previews have often helped producers decide whether they should change various parts of a movie. After the 1933 preview of King Kong, a scene in which four men who had been attacked by Kong were eaten by giant spiders was taken out as many people ran screaming from the theater and would not return. The 1950 premiere of Sunset Boulevard also led to some changes. In the original opening scene, William Holden was in a morgue talking with thirty-six other "corpses" about the ways some of them had died. When he began to tell them of his life with Gloria Swanson, the audience found this hilarious, instead of taking the scene seriously.
C. What do Sunset Boulevard and King Kong have in common? Both show the value of using movie previews to test audience reaction. The first 1933 preview of King Kong showed that a scene showing four men being eaten by giant spiders after having been attacked by Kong was too frightening for many people. They ran screaming from the theater and couldn't be coaxed back. The 1950 premiere of Sunset Boulevard was also a scream, but not the kind the producers intended. The movie opens

with William Holden lying in a morgue discussing the ways they had died with thirty-six other "corpses." When he began to tell them of his life with Gloria Swanson, the audience couldn't take him seriously. Their laughter caused a six-month delay while the beginning was rewritten.

D. Producers very often use movie previews to decide if changes are needed. The premiere of Sunset Boulevard in 1950 led to a new beginning and a six-month delay in film release. At the beginning, William Holden and thirty-six other "corpses" discuss the ways some of them died. Rather than taking this seriously, the audience thought it was hilarious when he began to tell them of his life with Gloria Swanson. The first 1933 preview of King Kong was very helpful for its producers because one scene so terrified the audience that many of them ran screaming from the theater and would not return. In this particular scene, four men who had first been attacked by Kong were eaten by giant spiders.

4. I. It is common for supervisors to view employees as "things" to be manipulated. 4.____

II. This approach does not motivate employees, nor does the carrot-and-stick approach because employees often recognize these behaviors and resent them.

III. Supervisors can change these behaviors by using self-inquiry and persistence.

IV. The best managers genuinely respect those they work with, are supportive and helpful, and are interested in working as a team with those they supervise.

V. They disagree with the Golden Rule that says "he or she who has the gold makes the rules."

A. Some managers act as if they think the Golden Rule means "he or she who has the gold makes the rules." They show disrespect to employees by seeing them as "things" to be manipulated. Obviously, this approach does not motivate employees any more than the carrot-and-stick approach motivates them. The employees are smart enough to spot these behaviors and resent them. On the other hand, the managers genuinely respect those they work with, are supportive and helpful, and are interested in working as a team. Self-inquiry and persistence can change even the former type of supervisor into the latter.

B. Many supervisors all into the trap of viewing employees as "things" to be manipulated, or try to motivate them by using a carrot-and-stick approach. These methods do not motivate employees, who often recognize the behaviors and resent them. Supervisors can change these behaviors, however, by using self-inquiry and persistence. The best managers are supportive and helpful, and have genuine respect for those with whom they work. They are interested in working as a team with those they supervise. To them, the Golden Rule is not "he or she who has the gold makes the rules."

C. Some supervisors see employees as "things" to be used or manipulated using a carrot-and-stick technique. These methods don't work. Employees often see through them and resent them. A supervisor who wants to change may do so. The techniques of self-inquiry and persistence can be used to turn him or her into the type of supervisor who doesn't think the Golden Rule is "he or she who has the gold makes the rules." They may become like the best managers who treat those with whom they work with respect and give them help and support. These are the manager who know how to build a team.

D. Unfortunately, many supervisors act as if their employees are objects whose movements they can position at will. This mistaken belief has the same result as another popular motivational technique—the carrot-and-stick approach. Both attitudes can lead to the same result—resentment from those employees who recognize the behaviors for what they are. Supervisors who recognize these behaviors can change through the use of persistence and the use of self-inquiry. It's important to remember that the best managers respect their employees. They readily give necessary help and support and are interested in working as a team with those they supervise. To these managers, the Golden Rule is not "he or she who has the gold makes the rules."

5. I. The first half of the nineteenth century produced a group of pessimistic poets—Byron, De Musset, Heine, Pushkin, and Leopardi. 5.____

II. It also produced a group of pessimistic composers—Schubert, Chopin, Schumann, and even the later Beethoven.

III. Above all, in philosophy, there was the profoundly pessimistic philosopher, Schopenhauer.

IV. The Revolution was dead, the Bourbons were restored, the feudal barons were reclaiming their land, and progress everywhere was being suppressed, as the great age was over.

V. "I thank God," said Goethe, "that I am not young in so thoroughly finished a world."

A. "I thank God," said Goethe, "that I am not young in so thoroughly finished a world." The Revolution was dead, the Bourbons were restored, the feudal barons were reclaiming their land, and progress everywhere was being suppressed. The first half of the nineteenth century produced a group of pessimistic poets: Byron, De Musset, Heine, Pushkin, and Leopardi. It also produced pessimistic composers: Schubert, Chopin, Schumann. Although Beethoven came later, he fits into this group, too. Finally and above all, it also produced a profoundly pessimistic philosopher, Schopenhauer. The great age was over.

B. The first half of the nineteenth century produced a group of pessimistic poets: Byron, De Musset, Heine, Pushkin, and Leopardi. It produced a group of pessimistic composers: Schubert, Chopin, Schumann, and even the later Beethoven. Above all, it produced a profoundly pessimistic philosopher, Schopenhauer. For each of these men, the great age was over. The Revolution was dead, and the Bourbons were restored. The feudal barons were reclaiming their land, and progress everywhere was being suppressed.

C. The great age was over. The Revolution was dead—the Bourbons were restored, and the feudal barons were reclaiming their land. Progress everywhere was being suppressed. Out of this climate came a profound pessimism. Poets, like Byron, De Musset, Heine, Pushkin, and Leopardi; composers, like Schubert, Chopin, Schumann, and even the later Beethoven; and above all, a profoundly pessimistic philosopher, Schopenauer. This pessimism which arose in the first half of the nineteenth century is illustrated by these words of Goethe, "I thank God that I am not young in so thoroughly finished a world."

D. The first half of the nineteenth century produced a group of pessimistic poets, Byron, De Musset, Heine, Pushkin, and Leopardi—and a group of pessimistic composers, Schubert, Chopin, Schumann, and the later Beethoven. Above it all, it produced a profoundly pessimistic philosopher, Schopenhauer. The great age was over. The Revolution was dead, the Bourbons were restored, the feudal barons were reclaiming their land, and progress everywhere was being suppressed. "I thank God," said Goethe, "that I am not young in so thoroughly finished a world."

6. I. A new manager sometimes may feel insecure about his or her competence in the new position. 6.____

II. The new manager may then exhibit defensive or arrogant behavior towards those one supervises, or the new manager may direct overly flattering behavior toward one's new supervisor.

A. Sometimes, a new manager may feel insecure about his or her ability to perform well in this new position. The insecurity may lead him or her to treat others differently. He or she may display arrogant or defensive behavior towards those he or she supervises, or be overly flattering to his or her new supervisor.

B. A new manager may sometimes feel insecure about his or her ability to perform well in the new position. He or she may then become arrogant, defensive, or overly flattering towards those he or she works with.

C. There are times when a new manager may be insecure about how well he or she can perform in the new job. The new manager may also behave defensive or act in an arrogant way towards those he or she supervises, or overly flatter his or her boss.

D. Sometimes a new manager may feel insecure about his or her ability to perform well in the new position. He or she may then display arrogant or defensive behavior towards those they supervise, or become overly flattering towards their supervisors.

7. I. It is possible to eliminate unwanted behavior by bringing it under stimulus control—tying the behavior to a cue, and then never, or rarely, giving the cue. 7.____

II. One trainer successfully used this method to keep an energetic young porpoise from coming out of her tank whenever she felt like it, which was potentially dangerous.

III. Her trainer taught her to do it for a reward, in response to a hand signal, and then rarely gave the signal.

A. Unwanted behavior can be eliminated by tying the behavior to a cue, and then never, or rarely, giving the cue. This is called stimulus control. One trainer was able to use this method to keep an energetic young porpoise from coming out of her tank by teaching her to come out for a reward in response to a hand signal, and then rarely giving the signal.
B. Stimulus control can be used to eliminate unwanted behavior. In this method, behavior is tied to a cue, and then the cue is rarely, if ever, given. One trainer was able to successfully use stimulus control to keep an energetic young porpoise from coming out of her tank whenever she felt like it—a potentially dangerous practice. She taught the porpoise to come out for a reward when she gave a hand signal, and then rarely gave the signal.
C. It is possible to eliminate behavior that is undesirable by bringing it under stimulus control by tying behavior to a signal, and then rarely giving the signal. One trainer successfully used this method to keep an energetic porpoise from coming out of her tank, a potentially dangerous situation. Her trainer taught the porpoise to do it for a reward, in response to a hand signal, and then would rarely give the signal.
D. By using stimulus control, it is possible to eliminate unwanted behavior by tying the behavior to a cue, and then rarely or never give the cue. One trainer was able to use this method to successfully stop a young porpoise from coming out of her tank whenever she felt like it. To curb this potentially dangerous practice, the porpoise was taught by the trainer to come out of the tank for a reward, in response to a hand signal, and then rarely given the signal.

8. I. There is a great deal of concern over the safety of commercial trucks, caused by their greatly increased role in serious accidents since federal deregulation in 1981. 8.____
II. Recently, 60 percent of trucks in New York and Connecticut and 70 percent of trucks in Maryland randomly stopped by state troopers failed safety inspections.
III. Sixteen states in the United States require no training at all for truck drivers.

A. Since federal deregulation in 1981, there has been a great deal of concern over the safety of commercial trucks, and their greatly increased role in serious accidents. Recently, 60 percent of trucks in New York and Connecticut, and 70 percent of trucks in Maryland failed safety inspections. Sixteen states in the United States require no training at all for truck drivers.
B. There is a great deal of concern over the safety of commercial trucks since federal deregulation in 1981. Their role in serious accidents has greatly increased. Recently, 60 percent of trucks randomly stopped in Connecticut and New York and 70 percent in Maryland failed safety inspections conducted by state troopers. Sixteen states in the United States provide no training at all for truck drivers.
C. Commercial trucks have a greatly increased role in serious accidents since federal deregulation in 1981. This has led to a great deal of concern.

Recently, 70 percent of trucks in Maryland and 60 percent of trucks in New York and Connecticut failed inspection of those that were randomly stopped by state troopers. Sixteen states in the United States require no training for all truck drivers.

D. Since federal deregulation in 1981, the role that commercial trucks have played in serious accidents has greatly increased, and this has led to a great deal of concern. Recently, 60 percent of trucks in New York and Connecticut, and 70 percent of trucks in Maryland randomly stopped by state troopers failed safety inspections. Sixteen states in the U.S. don't require any training for truck drivers.

9. I. No matter how much some people have, they still feel unsatisfied and want more, or want to keep what they have forever. 9.____

II. One recent television documentary showed several people flying from New York to Paris for a one-day shopping spree to buy platinum earrings, because they were bored.

III. In Brazil, some people were ordering coffins that cost a minimum of $45,000 and are equipping them with deluxe stereos, televisions, and other graveyard necessities.

A. Some people, despite having a great deal, still feel unsatisfied and want more, or think they can keep what they have forever. One recent documentary on television showed several people enroute from Paris to New York for a one day shopping spree to buy platinum earrings, because they were bored. Some people in Brazil are even ordering coffins equipped with such graveyard necessities as deluxe stereos and televisions. The price of the coffins start at $45,000.

B. No matter how much some people have, they may feel unsatisfied. This leads them to want more, or to want to keep what they have forever. Recently, a television documentary depicting several people flying from New York to Paris for a one day shopping spree to buy platinum earrings. They were bored. Some people in Brazil are ordering coffins that cost at least $45,000 and come equipped with deluxe televisions, stereos and other necessary graveyard items.

C. Some people will be dissatisfied no matter how much they have. They may want more, or they may want to keep what they have forever. One recent television documentary showed several people, motivated by boredom, jetting from New York to Paris for a one-day shopping spree to buy platinum earrings. In Brazil, some people are ordering coffins equipped with deluxe stereos, televisions and other graveyard necessities. The minimum price for these coffins—$45,000.

D. Some people are never satisfied. No matter how much they have they still want more, or think they can keep what they have forever. One television documentary recently showed several people flying from New York to Paris for the day to buy platinum earrings because they were bored. In Brazil, some people are ordering coffins that cost $45,000 and are equipped with deluxe stereos, televisions and other graveyard necessities.

10. I. A television signal or video signal has three parts. 10.____
II. Its parts are the black-and-white portion, the color portion, and the synchronizing (sync) pulses, which keep the picture stable.
III. Each video source, whether it's a camera or a video-cassette recorder contains its own generator of these synchronizing pulses to accompany the picture that it's sending in order to keep it steady and straight.
IV. In order to produce a clean recording, a video-cassette recorder must "lock-up" to the sync pulses that are part of the video it is trying to record, and this effort may be very noticeable if the device does not have gunlock.

A. There are three parts to a television or video signal: the black-and-white part, the color part, and the synchronizing (sync) pulses, which keep the picture stable. Whether it's a video-cassette recorder or a camera, each video source contains its own pulse that synchronizes and generates the picture it's sending in order to keep it straight and steady. A video-cassette recorder must "lock up" to the sync pulses that are part of the video it's trying to record. If the device doesn't have gunlock, this effort must be very noticeable.
B. A video signal or television is comprised of three parts: the black-and-white portion, the color portion, and the sync (synchronizing) pulses, which keep the picture stable. Whether it's a camera or a video-cassette recorder, each video source contains its own generator of these synchronizing pulses. These accompany the picture that it's sending in order to keep it straight and steady. A video-cassette recorder must "lock up" to the sync pulses that are part of the video it is trying to record in order to produce a clean recording. This effort may be very noticeable if the device does not have gunlock.
C. There are three parts to a television or video signal: the color portion, the black-and-white portion, and the sync (synchronizing pulses). These keep the picture stable. Each video source, whether it's a video-cassette recorder or a camera, generates these synchronizing pulses accompanying the picture it's sending in order to keep it straight and steady. If a clean recording is to be produced, a video-cassette recorder must store the sync pulses that are part of the video it is trying to record. This effort may not be noticeable if the device does not have gunlock.
D. A television signal or video signal has three parts: the black-and-white portion, the color portion, and the synchronizing (sync) pulses. It's the sync pulses which keep the picture stable, which accompany it and keep it steady and straight. Whether it's a camera or a video-cassette recorder, each video source contains its own generator of these synchronizing pulses. To produce a clean recording, a video-cassette recorder must "lock up" to the sync pulses that are part of the video it is trying to record. If the device does not have gunlock, this effort may be very noticeable.

KEY (CORRECT ANSWERS)

1.	C	6.	A
2.	B	7.	B
3.	A	8.	D
4.	B	9.	C
5.	D	10.	D

PREPARING WRITTEN MATERIAL

EXAMINATION SECTION

TEST 1

DIRECTIONS: Each of the sentences in this test may be classified under one of the following four categories:

A. Faulty because of incorrect grammar or word usage
B. Faulty because of incorrect punctuation
C. Faulty because of incorrect capitalization or incorrect spelling
D. Correct

Examine each sentence carefully to determine under which of the above four options it is best classified. Then, in the space to the right, print the capital letter preceding the option which is the BEST of the four suggested above. (Note that each faulty sentence contains but one type of error. Consider a sentence to be correct if it contains none of the types of errors mentioned, even though there may be other correct ways of expressing the same thought.)

1. He sent the notice to the clerk who you hired yesterday. 1.____

2. It must be admitted, however that you were not informed of this change. 2.____

3. Only the employee who have served in this grade for at least two years are eligible for promotion. 3.____

4. The work was divided equally between she and Mary. 4.____

5. He thought that you were not available at that time. 5.____

6. When the messenger returns; please give him this package. 6.____

7. The new secretary prepared, typed, addressed, and delivered, the notices. 7.____

8. Walking into the room, his desk can be seen at the rear. 8.____

9. Although John has worked here longer than She, he produces a smaller amount of work. 9.____

10. She said she could of typed this report yesterday. 10.____

11. Neither one of these procedures are adequate for the efficient performance of this task. 11.____

12. The typewriter is the tool of the typist; the cash register, the tool of the cashier. 12.____

13. "The assignment must be completed as soon as possible" said the supervisor. 13.____

14. As you know, office handbooks are issued to all new Employees. 14.____

15. Writing a speech is sometimes easier than to deliver it before an audience. 15.____

16. Mr. Brown our accountant, will audit the accounts next week. 16.____

17. Give the assignment to whomever is able to do it most efficiently. 17.____

18. The supervisor expected either your or I to file these reports. 18.____

KEY (CORRECT ANSWERS)

1.	A	11.	A
2.	B	12.	C
3.	D	13.	B
4.	A	14.	C
5.	D	15.	A
6.	B	16.	B
7.	B	17.	A
8.	A	18.	A
9.	C		
10.	A		

TEST 2

DIRECTIONS: Each of the sentences in this test may be classified under one of the following four categories:

A. Faulty because of incorrect grammar or word usage
B. Faulty because of incorrect punctuation
C. Faulty because of incorrect capitalization or incorrect spelling
D. Correct

Examine each sentence carefully to determine under which of the above four options it is best classified. Then, in the space to the right, print the capital letter preceding the option which is the BEST of the four suggested above. (Note that each faulty sentence contains but one type of error. Consider a sentence to be correct if it contains none of the types of errors mentioned, even though there may be other correct ways of expressing the same thought.)

1. The fire apparently started in the storeroom, which is usually locked. 1.____

2. On approaching the victim, two bruises were noticed by this officer. 2.____

3. The officer, who was there examined the report with great care. 3.____

4. Each employee in the office had a seperate desk. 4.____

5. All employees including members of the clerical staff, were invited to the lecture. 5.____

6. The suggested Procedure is similar to the one now in use. 6.____

7. No one was more pleased with the new procedure than the chauffeur. 7.____

8. He tried to persaude her to change the procedure. 8.____

9. The total of the expenses charged to petty cash were high. 9.____

10. An understanding between him and I was finally reached. 10.____

KEY (CORRECT ANSWERS)

1.	D	6.	C
2.	A	7.	D
3.	B	8.	C
4.	C	9.	A
5.	B	10.	A

TEST 3

DIRECTIONS: Each of the sentences in this test may be classified under one of the following four categories:

A. Faulty because of incorrect grammar or word usage
B. Faulty because of incorrect punctuation
C. Faulty because of incorrect capitalization or incorrect spelling
D. Correct

Examine each sentence carefully to determine under which of the above four options it is best classified. Then, in the space to the right, print the capital letter preceding the option which is the BEST of the four suggested above. (Note that each faulty sentence contains but one type of error. Consider a sentence to be correct if it contains none of the types of errors mentioned, even though there may be other correct ways of expressing the same thought.)

1. They told both he and I that the prisoner had escaped. 1.____

2. Any superior officer, who, disregards the just complaint of his subordinates, is remiss in the performance of his duty. 2.____

3. Only those members of the national organization who resided in the Middle West attended the conference in Chicago. 3.____

4. We told him to give the national organization assignment to whoever was available. 4.____

5. Please do not disappoint and embarass us by not appearing in court. 5.___

6. Although the office's speech proved to be entertaining, the topic was not relevent to the main theme of the conference. 6.____

7. In February all new officers attended a training course in which they were learned in their principal duties and the fundamental operating procedure of the department. 7.____

8. I personally seen inmate Jones threaten inmates Smith and Green with bodily harm if they refused to participate in the plot. 8.____

9. To the layman, who on a chance visit to the prison observes everything functioning smoothly, the maintenance of prison discipline may seem to be a relatively easily realizable objective. 9.____

10. The prisoners in cell block fourty were forbidden to sit on the cell cots during the recreation hour. 10.____

KEY (CORRECT ANSWERS)

1.	A	6.	C
2.	B	7.	A
3.	C	8.	A
4.	D	9.	D
5.	C	10.	C

TEST 4

DIRECTIONS: Each of the sentences in this test may be classified under one of the following four categories:

A. Faulty because of incorrect grammar or word usage
B. Faulty because of incorrect punctuation
C. Faulty because of incorrect capitalization or incorrect spelling
D. Correct

Examine each sentence carefully to determine under which of the above four options it is best classified. Then, in the space to the right, print the capital letter preceding the option which is the BEST of the four suggested above. (Note that each faulty sentence contains but one type of error. Consider a sentence to be correct if it contains none of the types of errors mentioned, even though there may be other correct ways of expressing the same thought.)

1. I cannot encourage you any. 1.____

2. You always look well in those sort of clothes. 2.____

3. Shall we go to the park? 3.____

4. The man whome he introduced was Mr. Carey. 4.____

5. She saw the letter laying here this morning. 5.____

6. It should rain before the Afternoon is over. 6.____

7. They have already went home. 7.____

8. That Jackson will be elected is evident. 8.____

9. He does not hardly approve of us. 9.____

10. It was he, who won the prize. 10.____

KEY (CORRECT ANSWERS)

1.	A	6.	C
2.	A	7.	A
3.	D	8.	D
4.	C	9.	A
5.	A	10.	B

TEST 5

DIRECTIONS: Each of the sentences in this test may be classified under one of the following four categories:

A. Faulty because of incorrect grammar or word usage
B. Faulty because of incorrect punctuation
C. Faulty because of incorrect capitalization or incorrect spelling
D. Correct

Examine each sentence carefully to determine under which of the above four options it is best classified. Then, in the space to the right, print the capital letter preceding the option which is the BEST of the four suggested above. (Note that each faulty sentence contains but one type of error. Consider a sentence to be correct if it contains none of the types of errors mentioned, even though there may be other correct ways of expressing the same thought.)

1. Shall we go to the park. 1.____

2. They are, alike, in this particular way. 2.____

3. They gave the poor man sume food when he knocked on the door. 3.____

4. I regret the loss caused by the error. 4.____

5. The students' will have a new teacher. 5.____

6. They sweared to bring out all the facts. 6.____

7. He decided to open a branch store on 33rd street. 7.____

8. His speed is equal and more than that of a racehorse. 8.____

9. He felt very warm on that Summer day. 9.____

10. He was assisted by his friend, who lives in the next house. 10.____

KEY (CORRECT ANSWERS)

1.	B	6.	A
2.	B	7.	C
3.	C	8.	A
4.	D	9.	C
5.	B	10.	D

TEST 6

DIRECTIONS: Each of the sentences in this test may be classified under one of the following four categories:

A. Faulty because of incorrect grammar or word usage
B. Faulty because of incorrect punctuation
C. Faulty because of incorrect capitalization or incorrect spelling
D. Correct

Examine each sentence carefully to determine under which of the above four options it is best classified. Then, in the space to the right, print the capital letter preceding the option which is the BEST of the four suggested above. (Note that each faulty sentence contains but one type of error. Consider a sentence to be correct if it contains none of the types of errors mentioned, even though there may be other correct ways of expressing the same thought.)

1. The climate of New York is colder than California. 1.____

2. I shall wait for you on the corner. 2.____

3. Did we see the boy who, we think, is the leader. 3.____

4. Being a modest person, John seldom talks about his invention. 4.____

5. The gang is called the smith street bos. 5.____

6. He seen the man break into the store. 6.____

7. We expected to lay still there for quite a while. 7.____

8. He is considered to be the Leader of his organization. 8.____

9. Although I recieved an invitation, I won't go. 9.____

10. The letter must be here some place. 10.____

KEY (CORRECT ANSWERS)

1.	A	6.	A
2.	D	7.	A
3.	B	8.	C
4.	D	9.	C
5.	C	10.	A

TEST 7

DIRECTIONS: Each of the sentences in this test may be classified under one of the following four categories:

A. Faulty because of incorrect grammar or word usage
B. Faulty because of incorrect punctuation
C. Faulty because of incorrect capitalization or incorrect spelling
D. Correct

Examine each sentence carefully to determine under which of the above four options it is best classified. Then, in the space to the right, print the capital letter preceding the option which is the BEST of the four suggested above. (Note that each faulty sentence contains but one type of error. Consider a sentence to be correct if it contains none of the types of errors mentioned, even though there may be other correct ways of expressing the same thought.)

1. I though it to be he. 1.____

2. We expect to remain here for a long time. 2.____

3. The committee was agreed. 3.____

4. Two-thirds of the building are finished. 4.____

5. The water was froze. 5.____

6. Everyone of the salesmen must supply their own car. 6.____

7. Who is the author of Gone With the Wind? 7.____

8. He marched on and declaring that he would never surrender. 8.____

9. Who shall I say called? 9.____

10. Everyone has left but they. 10.____

KEY (CORRECT ANSWERS)

1.	A	6.	A
2.	D	7.	B
3.	D	8.	A
4.	A	9.	D
5.	A	10.	D

TEST 8

DIRECTIONS: Each of the sentences in this test may be classified under one of the following four categories:

A. Faulty because of incorrect grammar or word usage
B. Faulty because of incorrect punctuation
C. Faulty because of incorrect capitalization or incorrect spelling
D. Correct

Examine each sentence carefully to determine under which of the above four options it is best classified. Then, in the space to the right, print the capital letter preceding the option which is the BEST of the four suggested above. (Note that each faulty sentence contains but one type of error. Consider a sentence to be correct if it contains none of the types of errors mentioned, even though there may be other correct ways of expressing the same thought.)

1. Who did we give the order to? 1.____

2. Send your order in immediately. 2.____

3. I believe I paid the Bill. 3.____

4. I have not met but one person. 4.____

5. Why aren't Tom, and Fred, going to the dance? 5.____

6. What reason is there for him not going? 6.____

7. The seige of Malta was a tremendous event. 7.____

8. I was there yesterday I assure you 8.____

9. Your ukulele is better than mine. 9.____

10. No one was there only Mary. 10.____

KEY (CORRECT ANSWERS)

1.	A	6.	A
2.	D	7.	C
3.	C	8.	B
4.	A	9.	C
5.	B	10.	A

TEST 9

DIRECTIONS: In each of the following groups of sentences, one of the four sentences is faulty in grammar, punctuation, or capitalization. Select the INCORRECT sentence in each case.

1. A. If you had stood at home and done your homework, you would not have failed in arithmetic. 1.____
   B. Her affected manner annoyed every member of the audience.
   C. How will the new law affect our income taxes?
   D. The plants were not affected by the long, cold winter, but they succumbed to the drought of summer.

2. A. He is one of the most able men who have been in the Senate. 2.____
   B. It is he who is to blame for the lamentable mistake.
   C. Haven't you a helpful suggestion to make at this time?
   D. The money was robbed from the blind man's cup.

3. A. The amount of children in this school is steadily increasing. 3.____
   B. After taking an apple from the table, she went out to play.
   C. He borrowed a dollar from me.
   D. I had hoped my brother would arrive before me.

4. A. Whom do you think I hear from every week? 4.____
   B. Who do you think is the right man for the job?
   C. Who do you think I found in the room?
   D. He is the man whom we considered a good candidate for the presidency.

5. A. Quietly the puppy laid down before the fireplace. 5.____
   B. You have made your bed; now lie in it.
   C. I was badly sunburned because I had lain too long in the sun.
   D. I laid the doll on the bed and left the room.

KEY (CORRECT ANSWERS)

1. A
2. D
3. A
4. C
5. A

RECORD KEEPING
EXAMINATION SECTION
TEST 1

DIRECTIONS: Each question or incomplete statement is followed by several suggested answers or completions. Select the one that BEST answers the question or completes the statement. *PRINT THE LETTER OF THE CORRECT ANSWER IN THE SPACE AT THE RIGHT.*

Questions 1-7.

DIRECTIONS: In answering Questions 1 through 7, use the following master list. For each question, determine where the name would fit on the master list. Each answer choice indicates right before or after the name in the answer choice.

Aaron, Jane
Armstead, Brendan
Bailey, Charles
Dent, Ricardo
Grant, Mark
Mars, Justin
Methieu, Justine
Parker, Cathy
Sampson, Suzy
Thomas, Heather

1. Schmidt, William 1.____
   A. Right before Cathy Parker
   B. Right after Heather Thomas
   C. Right after Suzy Sampson
   D. Right before Ricardo Dent

2. Asanti, Kendall 2.____
   A. Right before Jane Aaron
   B. Right after Charles Bailey
   C. Right before Justine Methieu
   D. Right after Brendan Armstead

3. O'Brien, Daniel 3.____
   A. Right after Justine Methieu
   B. Right before Jane Aaron
   C. Right after Mark Grant
   D. Right before Suzy Sampson

4. Marrow, Alison 4.____
   A. Right before Cathy Parker
   B. Right before Justin Mars
   C. Right before Mark Grant
   D. Right after Heather Thomas

5. Grantt, Marissa 5.____
   A. Right before Mark Grant
   B. Right after Mark Grant
   C. Right after Justin Mars
   D. Right before Suzy Sampson

6. Thompson, Heath 6.____
   A. Right after Justin Mars
   B. Right before Suzy Sampson
   C. Right after Heather Thomas
   D. Right before Cathy Parker

DIRECTIONS: Before answering Question 7, add in all of the names from Questions 1 through 6. Then fit the name in alphabetical order based on the new list.

7. Francisco, Mildred 7.____
   A. Right before Mark Grant
   B. Right after Marissa Grantt
   C. Right before Alison Marrow
   D. Right after Kendall Asanti

Questions 8-10.

DIRECTIONS: In answering Questions 8 through 10, compare each pair of names and addresses. Indicate whether they are the same or different in any way.

8. William H. Pratt, J.D. / Attourney at Law — William H. Pratt, J.D. / Attorney at Law 8.____
   A. No differences
   B. 1 difference
   C. 2 differences
   D. 3 differences

9. 1303 Theater Drive,; Apt. 3-B — 1330 Theatre Drive,; Apt. 3-B 9.____
   A. No differences
   B. 1 difference
   C. 2 differences
   D. 3 differences

10. Petersdorff, Briana and Mary — Petersdorff, Briana and Mary 10.____
   A. No differences
   B. 1 difference
   C. 2 differences
   D. 3 differences

11. Which of the following words, if any, are misspelled? 11.____
   A. Affordable
   B. Circumstansial
   C. Legalese
   D. None of the above

Questions 12-13.

DIRECTIONS: Questions 12 and 13 are to be answered on the basis of the following table.

Standardized Test Results for High School Students in District #1230

	English	Math	Science	Reading
High School 1	21	22	15	18
High School 2	12	16	13	15
High School 3	16	18	21	17
High School 4	19	14	15	16

The scores for each high school in the district were averaged out and listed for each subject tested. Scores of 0-10 are significantly below College Readiness Standards. 11-15 are below College Readiness, 16-20 meet College Readiness, and 21-25 are above College Readiness.

12. If the high schools need to meet or exceed in at least half the categories in order to NOT be considered "at risk," which schools are considered "at risk"? 12.____
    A. High School 2
    B. High School 3
    C. High School 4
    D. Both A and C

13. What percentage of subjects did the district as a whole meet or exceed College Readiness standards? 13.____
    A. 25%
    B. 50%
    C. 75%
    D. 100%

Questions 14-15.

DIRECTIONS: Questions 14 and 15 are to be answered on the basis of the following information.

You have seven employees working as a part of your team: Austin, Emily, Jeremy, Christina, Martin, Harriet, and Steve. You have just sent an e-mail informing them that there will be a mandatory training session next week. To ensure that work still gets done, you are offering the training twice during the week: once on Tuesday and also on Thursday. This way half the employees will still be working while the other half attend the training. The only other issue is that Jeremy doesn't work on Tuesdays and Harriet doesn't work on Thursdays due to compressed work schedules.

14. Which of the following is a possible attendance roster for the first training session? 14.____
    A. Emily, Jeremy, Steve
    B. Steve, Christina, Harriet
    C. Harriet, Jeremy, Austin
    D. Steve, Martin, Jeremy

15. If Harriet, Christina, and Steve attend the training session on Tuesday, which of the following is a possible roster for Thursday's training session? 15.____
    A. Jeremy, Emily, and Austin
    B. Emily, Martin, and Harriet
    C. Austin, Christina, and Emily
    D. Jeremy, Emily, and Steve

Questions 16-20.

DIRECTIONS: In answering Questions 16 through 20, you will be given a word and will need to choose the answer choice that is MOST similar or different to the word.

16. Which word means the SAME as *annual*? 16.____
    A. Monthly
    B. Usually
    C. Yearly
    D. Constantly

17. Which word means the SAME as *effort*? 17.____
    A. Energy
    B. Equate
    C. Cherish
    D. Commence

18. Which word means the OPPOSITE of *forlorn*? 18.____
    A. Neglected
    B. Lethargy
    C. Optimistic
    D. Astonished

19. Which word means the SAME as *risk*? 19.____
    A. Admire
    B. Hazard
    C. Limit
    D. Hesitant

20. Which word means the OPPOSITE of *translucent*? 20.____
    A. Opaque B. Transparent C. Luminous D. Introverted

21. Last year, Jamie's annual salary was $50,000. Her boss called her today to inform her that she would receive a 20% raise for the upcoming year. How much more money will Jamie receive next year? 21.____
    A. $60,000 B. $10,000 C. $1,000 D. $51,000

22. You and a co-worker work for a temp hiring agency as part of their office staff. You both are given 6 days off per month. How many days off are you and your co-worker given in a year? 22.____
    A. 24 B. 72 C. 144 D. 48

23. If Margot makes $34,000 per year and she works 40 hours per week for all 52 weeks, what is her hourly rate? 23.____
    A. $16.34/hour B. $17.00/hour C. $15.54/hour D. $13.23/hour

24. How many dimes are there in $175.00? 24.____
    A. 175 B. 1,750 C. 3,500 D. 17,500

25. If Janey is three times as old as Emily, and Emily is 3, how old is Janey? 25.____
    A. 6 B. 9 C. 12 D. 15

KEY (CORRECT ANSWERS)

1.	C	11.	B
2.	D	12.	A
3.	A	13.	D
4.	B	14.	B
5.	B	15.	A
6.	C	16.	C
7.	A	17.	A
8.	B	18.	C
9.	C	19.	B
10.	A	20.	A

21.	B
22.	C
23.	A
24.	B
25.	B

TEST 2

DIRECTIONS: Each question or incomplete statement is followed by several suggested answers or completions. Select the one that BEST answers the question or completes the statement. *PRINT THE LETTER OF THE CORRECT ANSWER IN THE SPACE AT THE RIGHT.*

Questions 1-6.

DIRECTIONS: Questions 1 through 6 are to be answered on the basis of the following information.

item	name of item to be ordered
quantity	minimum number that can be ordered
beginning amount	amount in stock at start of month
amount received	amount receiving during month
ending amount	amount in stock at end of month
amount used	amount used during month
amount to order	will need at least as much of each item as used in the previous month
unit price	cost of each unit of an item
total price	total price for the order

Item	Quantity	Beginning	Received	Ending	Amount Used	Amount to Order	Unit Price	Total Price
Pens	10	22	10	8	24	20	$0.11	$2.20
Spiral notebooks	8	30	13	12			$0.25	
Binder clips	2 boxes	3 boxes	1 box	1 box			$1.79	
Sticky notes	3 packs	12 packs	4 packs	2 packs			$1.29	
Dry erase markers	1 pack (dozen)	34 markers	8 markers	40 markers			$16.49	
Ink cartridges (printer)	1 cartridge	3 cartridges	1 cartridge	2 cartridges			$79.99	
Folders	10 folders	25 folders	15 folders	10 folders			$1.08	

1. How many packs of sticky notes were used during the month? 1.____
   A. 16 B. 10 C. 12 D. 14

2. How many folders need to be ordered for next month? 2.____
   A. 15 B. 20 C. 30 D. 40

3. What is the total price of notebooks that you will need to order? 3.____
   A. $6.00 B. $0.25 C. $4.50 D. $2.75

4. Which of the following will you spend the second most money on? 4.____
   A. Ink cartridges B. Dry erase markers
   C. Sticky notes D. Binder clips

5. How many packs of dry erase markers should you order? 5.____
   A. 1 B. 8 C. 12 D. 0

6. What will be the total price of the file folders you order? 6.____
A. $20.16 B. $21.60 C. $10.80 D. $4.32

Questions 7-11.

DIRECTIONS: Questions 7 through 11 are to be answered on the basis of the following table.

Number of Car Accidents, By Location and Cause, for 2014						
	Location 1		Location 2		Location 3	
Cause	Number	Percent	Number	Percent	Number	Percent
Severe Weather	10		25		30	
Excessive Speeding	20	40	5		10	
Impaired Driving	15		15	25	8	
Miscellaneous	5		15		2	4
TOTALS	50	100	60	100	50	100

7. Which of the following is the third highest cause of accidents for all three locations? 7.____
A. Severe Weather
B. Impaired Driving
C. Miscellaneous
D. Excessive Speeding

8. The average number of Severe Weather accidents per week at Location 3 for the year (52 weeks) was MOST NEARLY 8.____
A. 0.57 B. 30 C. 1 D. 1.25

9. Which location had the LARGEST percentage of accidents caused by Impaired Driving? 9.____
A. 1 B. 2 C. 3 D. Both A and B

10. If one-third of the accidents at all three locations resulted in at least one fatality, what is the LEAST amount of deaths caused by accidents last year? 10.____
A. 60 B. 106 C. 66 D. 53

11. What is the percentage of accidents caused by miscellaneous means from all three locations in 2014? 11.____
A. 5% B. 10% C. 13% D. 25%

12. How many pairs of the following groups of letters are exactly alike? 12.____

ACDOBJ	ACDBOJ
HEWBWR	HEWRWB
DEERVS	DEERVS
BRFQSX	BRFQSX
WEYRVB	WEYRVB
SPQRZA	SQRPZA

A. 2 B. 3 C. 4 D. 5

Questions 13-19.

DIRECTIONS: Questions 13 through 19 are to be answered on the basis of the following information.

In 2012, the most current information on the American population was finished. The information was compiled by 200 volunteers in each of the 50 states. The territory of Puerto Rico, a sovereign of the United States, had 25 people assigned to compile data. In February of 2010, volunteers in each state and sovereign began collecting information. In Puerto Rico, data collection finished by January 31st, 2011, while work in the United States was completed on June 30, 2012. Each volunteer gathered data on the population of their state or sovereign. When the information was compiled, volunteers sent reports to the nation's capital, Washington, D.C. Each volunteer worked 20 hours per month and put together 10 reports per month. After the data was compiled in total, 50 people reviewed the data and worked from January 2012 to December 2012.

13. How many reports were generated from February 2010 to April 2010 in Illinois and Ohio? 13.____
    A. 3,000 B. 6,000 C. 12,000 D. 15,000

14. How many volunteers in total collected population data in January 2012? 14.____
    A. 10,000 B. 2,000 C. 225 D. 200

15. How many reports were put together in May 2012? 15.____
    A. 2,000 B. 50,000 C. 100,000 D. 100,250

16. How many hours did the Puerto Rican volunteers work in the fall (September-November)? 16.____
    A. 60 B. 500 C. 1,500 D. 0

17. How many workers were compiling or reviewing data in July 2012? 17.____
    A. 25 B. 50 C. 200 D. 250

18. What was the total amount of hours worked by Nevada volunteers in July 2010? 18.____
    A. 500 B. 4,000 C. 4,500 D. 5,000

19. How many reviewers worked in January 2013? 19.____
    A. 75 B. 50 C. 0 D. 25

20. John has to file 10 documents per shelf. How many documents would it take for John to fill 40 shelves? 20.____
    A. 40 B. 400 C. 4,500 D. 5,000

21. Jill wants to travel from New York City to Los Angeles by bike, which is approximately 2,772 miles. How many miles per day would Jill need to average if she wanted to complete the trip in 4 weeks? 21.____
    A. 100 B. 89 C. 99 D. 94

22. If there are 24 CPU's and only 7 monitors, how many more monitors do you need to have the same amount of monitors as CPU's? 22.____
    A. Not enough information
    B. 17
    C. 31
    D. 0

23. If Gerry works 5 days a week and 8 hours each day, and John works 3 days a week and 10 hours each day, how many more hours per year will Gerry work than John? 23.____
    A. They work the same amount of hours.
    B. 450
    C. 520
    D. 832

24. Jimmy gets transferred to a new office. The new office has 25 employees, but only 16 are there due to a blizzard. How many coworkers was Jimmy able to meet on his first day? 24.____
    A. 16
    B. 25
    C. 9
    D. 7

25. If you do a fundraiser for charities in your area and raise $500 total, how much would you give to each charity if you were donating equal amounts to 3 of them? 25.____
    A. $250.00
    B. $167.77
    C. $50.00
    D. $111.11

KEY (CORRECT ANSWERS)

1.	D	11.	C
2.	B	12.	B
3.	A	13.	C
4.	C	14.	A
5.	D	15.	C
6.	B	16.	C
7.	D	17.	B
8.	A	18	B
9.	A	19.	C
10.	D	20.	B

21.	C
22.	B
23.	C
24.	A
25.	B

TEST 3

DIRECTIONS: Each question or incomplete statement is followed by several suggested answers or completions. Select the one that BEST answers the question or completes the statement. *PRINT THE LETTER OF THE CORRECT ANSWER IN THE SPACE AT THE RIGHT.*

Questions 1-3.

DIRECTIONS: In answering Questions 1 through 3, choose the correctly spelled word.

1. A. allusion B. alusion C. allusien D. allution 1.____

2. A. altitude B. alltitude C. atlitude D. altlitude 2.____

3. A. althogh B. allthough C. althrough D. although 3.____

Questions 4-9.

DIRECTIONS: In answering Questions 4 through 9, choose the answer that BEST completes the analogy.

4. Odometer is to mileage as compass is to 4.____
   A. speed B. needle C. hiking D. direction

5. Marathon is to race as hibernation is to 5.____
   A. winter B. dream C. sleep D. bear

6. Cup is to coffee as bowl is to 6.____
   A. dish B. spoon C. food D. soup

7. Flow is to river as stagnant is to 7.____
   A. pool B. rain C. stream D. canal

8. Paw is to cat as hoof is to 8.____
   A. lamb B. horse C. lion D. elephant

9. Architect is to building as sculptor is to 9.____
   A. museum B. chisel C. stone D. statue

Questions 10-14.

DIRECTIONS: Questions 10 through 14 are to be answered on the basis of the following graph.

Population of Carroll City Broken Down by Age and Gender (in Thousands)			
Age	Female	Male	Total
Under 15	60	60	120
15-23		22	
24-33		20	44
34-43	13	18	31
44-53	20		67
64 and Over	65	65	130
TOTAL	230	232	462

10. How many people in the city are between the ages of 15-23? 10.____
    A. 70 B. 46,000 C. 70,000 D. 225,000

11. Approximately what percentage of the total population of the city was female aged 24-33? 11.____
    A. 10% B. 5% C. 15% D. 25%

12. If 33% of the males have a job and 55% of females don't have a job, which of the following statements is TRUE? 12.____
    A. Males have approximately 2,600 more jobs than females.
    B. Females have approximately 49,000 more jobs than males.
    C. Females have approximately 26,000 more jobs than males.
    D. None of the above statements are true.

13. How many females between the ages of 15-23 live in Carroll City? 13.____
    A. 67,000 B. 24,000 C. 48,000 D. 91,000

14. Assume all males 44-53 living in Carroll City are employed. If two-thirds of males age 44-53 work jobs outside of Carroll City, how many work within city limits? 14.____
    A. 31,333
    B. 15,667
    C. 47,000
    D. Cannot answer the question with the information provided

Questions 15-16.

DIRECTIONS: Questions 15 and 16 are labeled as shown. Alphabetize them for filing. Choose the answer that correctly shows the order.

15. (1) AED 15.____
(2) OOS
(3) FOA
(4) DOM
(5) COB

A. 2-5-4-3-2 B. 1-4-5-2-3 C. 1-5-4-2-3 D. 1-5-4-3-2

16. Alphabetize the names of the people. Last names are given last. 16.____
(1) Lindsey Jamestown
(2) Jane Alberta
(3) Ally Jamestown
(4) Allison Johnston
(5) Lyle Moreno

A. 2-1-3-4-5 B. 3-4-2-1-5 C. 2-3-1-4-5 D. 4-3-2-1-5

17. Which of the following words is misspelled? 17.____
A. disgust
B. whisper
C. locale
D. none of the above

Questions 18-21.

DIRECTIONS: Questions 18 through 21 are to be answered on the basis of the following list of employees.

Robertson, Aaron
Bacon, Gina
Jerimiah, Trace
Gillette, Stanley
Jacks, Sharon

18. Which employee name would come in third in alphabetized list? 18.____
A. Robertson, Aaron
B. Jerimiah, Trace
C. Gillette, Stanley
D. Jacks, Sharon

19. Which employee's first name starts with the letter in the alphabet that is five letters after the first letter of their last name? 19.____
A. Jerimiah, Trace
B. Bacon, Gina
C. Jacks, Sharon
D. Gillette, Stanley

20. How many employees have last names that are exactly five letters long? 20.____
A. 1 B. 2 C. 3 D. 4

21. How many of the employees have either a first or last name that starts with the letter "G"? 21.____
A. 1 B. 2 C. 4 D. 5

Questions 22-25.

DIRECTIONS: Questions 22 through 25 are to be answered on the basis of the following chart.

Bicycle Sales (Model #34JA32)							
Country	May	June	July	August	September	October	Total
Germany	34	47	45	54	56	60	296
Britain	40	44	36	47	47	46	260
Ireland	37	32	32	32	34	33	200
Portugal	14	14	14	16	17	14	89
Italy	29	29	28	31	29	31	177
Belgium	22	24	24	26	25	23	144
Total	176	198	179	206	208	207	1166

22. What percentage of the overall total was sold to the German importer? 22.____
A. 25.3% B. 22% C. 24.1% D. 23%

23. What percentage of the overall total was sold in September? 23.____
A. 24.1% B. 25.6% C. 17.9% D. 24.6%

24. What is the average number of units per month imported into Belgium over the first four months shown? 24.____
A. 26 B. 20 C. 24 D. 31

25. If you look at the three smallest importers, what is their total import percentage? 25.____
A. 35.1% B. 37.1% C. 40% D. 28%

KEY (CORRECT ANSWERS)

1. A
2. A
3. D
4. D
5. C
6. D
7. A
8. B
9. D
10. C
11. B
12. C
13. C
14. B
15. D
16. C
17. D
18. D
19. B
20. B
21. B
22. A
23. C
24. C
25. A

TEST 4

DIRECTIONS: Each question or incomplete statement is followed by several suggested answers or completions. Select the one that BEST answers the question or completes the statement. *PRINT THE LETTER OF THE CORRECT ANSWER IN THE SPACE AT THE RIGHT.*

Questions 1-6.

DIRECTIONS: In answering Questions 1 through 6, choose the sentence that represents the BEST example of English grammar.

1. A. Joey and me want to go on a vacation next week. 1.____
   B. Gary told Jim he would need to take some time off.
   C. If turning six years old, Jim's uncle would teach Spanish to him.
   D. Fax a copy of your resume to Ms. Perez and me.

2. A. Jerry stood in line for almost two hours. 2.____
   B. The reaction to my engagement was less exciting than I thought it would be.
   C. Carlos and me have done great work on this project.
   D. Two parts of the speech needs to be revised before tomorrow.

3. A. Arriving home, the alarm was tripped. 3.____
   B. Jonny is regarded as a stand up guy, a responsible parent, and he doesn't give up until a task is finished.
   C. Each employee must submit a drug test each month.
   D. One of the documents was incinerated in the explosion.

4. A. As soon as my parents get home, I told them I finished all of my chores. 4.____
   B. I asked my teacher to send me my missing work, check my absences, and how did I do on my test.
   C. Matt attempted to keep it concealed from Jenny and me.
   D. If Mary or him cannot get work done on time, I will have to split them up.

5. A. Driving to work, the traffic report warned him of an accident on Highway 47. 5.____
   B. Jimmy has performed well this season.
   C. Since finishing her degree, several job offers have been given to Cam.
   D. Our boss is creating unstable conditions for we employees.

6. A. The thief was described as a tall man with a wiry mustache weighing approximately 150 pounds. 6.____
   B. She gave Patrick and I some more time to finish our work.
   C. One of the books that he ordered was damaged in shipping.
   D. While talking on the rotary phone, the car Jim was driving skidded off the road.

Questions 7-9.

DIRECTIONS: Questions 7 through 9 are to be answered on the basis of the following graph.

Ice Lake Frozen Flight (2002-2013)		
Year	Number of Participants	Temperature (Fahrenheit)
2002	22	4°
2003	50	33°
2004	69	18°
2005	104	22°
2006	108	24°
2007	288	33°
2008	173	9°
2009	598	39°
2010	698	26°
2011	696	30°
2012	777	28°
2013	578	32°

7. Which two year span had the LARGEST difference between temperatures? 7.____
   A. 2002 and 2003
   B. 2011 and 2012
   C. 2008 and 2009
   D. 2003 and 2004

8. How many total people participated in the years after the temperature reached at least 29°? 8.____
   A. 2,295
   B. 1,717
   C. 2,210
   D. 4,543

9. In 2007, the event saw 288 participants, while in 2008 that number dropped to 173. Which of the following reasons BEST explains the drop in participants? 9.____
   A. The event had not been going on that long and people didn't know about it.
   B. The lake water wasn't cold enough to have people jump in.
   C. The temperature was too cold for many people who would have normally participated.
   D. None of the above reasons explain the drop in participants.

10. In the following list of numbers, how many times does 4 come just after 2 when 2 comes just after an odd number? 10.____
    2365247653898632488572486392424
    A. 2
    B. 3
    C. 4
    D. 5

11. Which choice below lists the letter that is as far after B as S is after N in the alphabet? 11.____
    A. G
    B. H
    C. I
    D. J

Questions 12-15.

DIRECTIONS: Questions 12 through 15 are to be answered on the basis of the following directory and list of changes.

Directory		
Name	Emp. Type	Position
Julie Taylor	Warehouse	Packer
James King	Office	Administrative Assistant
John Williams	Office	Salesperson
Ray Moore	Warehouse	Maintenance
Kathleen Byrne	Warehouse	Supervisor
Amy Jones	Office	Salesperson
Paul Jonas	Office	Salesperson
Lisa Wong	Warehouse	Loader
Eugene Lee	Office	Accountant
Bruce Lavine	Office	Manager
Adam Gates	Warehouse	Packer
Will Suter	Warehouse	Packer
Gary Lorper	Office	Accountant
Jon Adams	Office	Salesperson
Susannah Harper	Office	Salesperson

Directory Updates:

- Employee e-mail addresses will adhere to the following guidelines: lastnamefirstname@apexindustries.com (ex. Susannah Harper is harpersusannah@apexindustries.com). Currently, employees in the warehouse share one e-mail, distribution@apexindustries.com.
- The "Loader" position will now be referred to as "Specialist I"
- Adam Gates has accepted a Supervisor position within the Warehouse and is no longer a Packer. All warehouse employees report to the two Supervisors and all office employees report to the Manager.

12. Amy Jones tried to send an e-mail to Adam Gates, but it wouldn't send. Which of the following offers the BEST explanation? 12.____
    A. Amy put Adam's first name first and then his last name.
    B. Adam doesn't check his e-mail, so he wouldn't know if he received the e-mail or not.
    C. Adam does not have his own e-mail.
    D. Office employees are not allowed to send e-mails to each other.

13. How many Packers currently work for Apex Industries? 13.____
    A. 2 B. 3 C. 4 D. 5

14. What position does Lisa Wong currently hold? 14.____
    A. Specialist I
    B. Secretary
    C. Administrative Assistant
    D. Loader

15. If an employee wanted to contact the office manager, which of the following e-mails should the e-mail be sent to? 15.____
    A. officemanager@apexindustries.com
    B. brucelavine@apexindustries.com
    C. lavinebruce@apexindustries.com
    D. distribution@apexindustries.com

Questions 16-19.

DIRECTIONS: In answering Questions 16 through 19, compare the three names, numbers or addresses.

16. Smiley Yarnell   Smiley Yarnel   Smily Yarnell 16.____
    A. All three are exactly alike.
    B. The first and second are exactly alike.
    C. The second and third are exactly alike.
    D. All three are different.

17. 1583 Theater Drive   1583 Theater Drive   1583 Theatre Drive 17.____
    A. All three are exactly alike.
    B. The first and second are exactly alike.
    C. The second and third are exactly alike.
    D. All three are different.

18. 3341893212   3341893212   3341893212 18.____
    A. All three are exactly alike.
    B. The first and second are exactly alike.
    C. The second and third are exactly alike.
    D. All three are different.

19. Douglass Watkins   Douglas Watkins   Douglass Watkins 19.____
    A. All three are exactly alike.
    B. The first and third are exactly alike.
    C. The second and third are exactly alike.
    D. All three are different.

Questions 20-24.

DIRECTIONS: In answering Questions 20 through 24, you will be presented with a word. Choose the synonym that BEST represents the word in question.

20. Flexible 20.____
    A. delicate   B. inflammable   C. strong   D. pliable

21. Alternative 21.____
    A. choice   B. moderate   C. lazy   D. value

22. Corroborate — 22.____
    A. examine   B. explain   C. verify   D. explain

23. Respiration — 23.____
    A. recovery   B. breathing   C. sweating   D. selfish

24. Negligent — 24.____
    A. lazy   B. moderate   C. hopeless   D. lax

25. Plumber is to Wrench as Painter is to — 25.____
    A. pipe   B. shop   C. hammer   D. brush

KEY (CORRECT ANSWERS)

1.	D	11.	A
2.	A	12.	C
3.	D	13.	A
4.	C	14.	A
5.	B	15.	C
6.	C	16.	D
7.	C	17.	B
8.	B	18.	A
9.	C	19.	B
10.	C	20.	D

21.	A
22.	C
23.	B
24.	D
25.	D

PHILOSOPHY, PRINCIPLES, PRACTICES, AND TECHNICS OF SUPERVISION, ADMINISTRATION, MANAGEMENT, AND ORGANIZATION

TABLE OF CONTENTS

PHILOSOPHY, PRINCIPLES, PRACTICES, AND TECHNICS
OF
SUPERVISION, ADMINISTRATION, MANAGEMENT, AND ORGANIZATION

MEANING OF SUPERVISION

The extension of the democratic philosophy has been accompanied by an extension in the scope of supervision. Modern leaders and supervisors no longer think of supervision in the narrow sense of being confined chiefly to visiting employees, supplying materials, or rating the staff. They regard supervision as being intimately related to all the concerned agencies of society, they speak of the supervisor's function in terms of "growth," rather than the "improvement" of employees.

This modern concept of supervision may be defined as follows: Supervision is leadership and the development of leadership within groups which are cooperatively engaged in inspection, research, training, guidance, and evaluation.

THE OLD AND THE NEW SUPERVISION

TRADITIONAL
1. Inspection
2. Focused on the employee
3. Visitation
4. Random and haphazard
5. Imposed and authoritarian
6. One person usually

MODERN
1. Study and analysis
2. Focused on aims, materials, methods, supervisors, employees, environment
3. Demonstrations, intervisitation, workshops, directed reading, bulletins, etc.
4. Definitely organized and planned (scientific)
5. Cooperative and democratic
6. Many persons involved (creative)

THE EIGHT (8) BASIC PRINCIPLES OF THE NEW SUPERVISION

I. Principle of Responsibility
Authority to act and responsibility for acting must be joined.
   A. If you give responsibility, give authority.
   B. Define employee duties clearly.
   C. Protect employees from criticism by others.
   D. Recognize the rights as well as obligations of employees.
   E. Achieve the aims of a democratic society insofar as it is possible within the area of your work.
   F. Establish a situation favorable to training and learning.
   G. Accept ultimate responsibility for everything done in your section, unit, office, division, department.
   H. Good administration and good supervision are inseparable.

II. Principle of Authority
The success of the supervisor is measured by the extent to which the power of authority is not used.
A. Exercise simplicity and informality in supervision
B. Use the simplest machinery of supervision
C. If it is good for the organization as a whole, it is probably justified.
D. Seldom be arbitrary or authoritative.
E. Do not base your work on the power of position or of personality.
F. Permit and encourage the free expression of opinions.

III. Principle of Self-Growth
The success of the supervisor is measured by the extent to which, and the speed with which, he is no longer needed.
A. Base criticism on principles, not on specifics.
B. Point out higher activities to employees.
C. Train for self-thinking by employees to meet new situations.
D. Stimulate initiative, self-reliance, and individual responsibility
E. Concentrate on stimulating the growth of employees rather than on removing defects.

IV. Principle of Individual Worth
Respect for the individual is a paramount consideration in supervision.
A. Be human and sympathetic in dealing with employees.
B. Don't nag about things to be done.
C. Recognize the individual differences among employees and seek opportunities to permit best expression of each personality.

V. Principle of Creative Leadership
The best supervision is that which is not apparent to the employee.
A. Stimulate, don't drive employees to creative action.
B. Emphasize doing good things.
C. Encourage employees to do what they do best.
D. Do not be too greatly concerned with details of subject or method.
E. Do not be concerned exclusively with immediate problems and activities.
F. Reveal higher activities and make them both desired and maximally possible.
G. Determine procedures in the light of each situation but see that these are derived from a sound basic philosophy.
H. Aid, inspire, and lead so as to liberate the creative spirit latent in all good employees.

VI. Principle of Success and Failure
There are no unsuccessful employees, only unsuccessful supervisors who have failed to give proper leadership.
A. Adapt suggestions to the capacities, attitudes, and prejudices of employees.
B. Be gradual, be progressive, be persistent.
C. Help the employee find the general principle; have the employee apply his own problem to the general principle.
D. Give adequate appreciation for good work and honest effort.
E. Anticipate employee difficulties and help to prevent them.
F. Encourage employees to do the desirable things they will do anyway.
G. Judge your supervision by the results it secures.

VII. Principle of Science
Successful supervision is scientific, objective, and experimental. It is based on facts, not on prejudices.
A. Be cumulative in results.
B. Never divorce your suggestions from the goals of training.
C. Don't be impatient of results.
D. Keep all matters on a professional, not a personal, level.
E. Do not be concerned exclusively with immediate problems and activities.
F. Use objective means of determining achievement and rating where possible.

VIII. Principle of Cooperation
Supervision is a cooperative enterprise between supervisor and employee.
A. Begin with conditions as they are.
B. Ask opinions of all involved when formulating policies.
C. Organization is as good as its weakest link.
D. Let employees help to determine policies and department programs.
E. Be approachable and accessible—physically and mentally.
F. Develop pleasant social relationships.

WHAT IS ADMINISTRATION

Administration is concerned with providing the environment, the material facilities, and the operational procedures that will promote the maximum growth and development of supervisors and employees. (Organization is an aspect and a concomitant of administration.)

There is no sharp line of demarcation between supervision and administration; these functions are intimately interrelated and, often, overlapping. They are complementary activities.

I. Practices Commonly Classed as "Supervisory"
A. Conducting employees' conferences
B. Visiting sections, units, offices, divisions, departments
C. Arranging for demonstrations
D. Examining plans
E. Suggesting professional reading
F. Interpreting bulletins
G. Recommending in-service training courses
H. Encouraging experimentation
I. Appraising employee morale
J. Providing for intervisitation

II. Practices Commonly Classified as "Administrative"
A. Management of the office
B. Arrangement of schedules for extra duties
C. Assignment of rooms or areas
D. Distribution of supplies
E. Keeping records and reports
F. Care of audio-visual materials
G. Keeping inventory records
H. Checking record cards and books

I. Programming special activities
J. Checking on the attendance and punctuality of employees

III. Practices Commonly Classified as Both "Supervisory" and "Administrative"
A. Program construction
B. Testing or evaluating outcomes
C. Personnel accounting
D. Ordering instructional materials

RESPONSIBILITIES OF THE SUPERVISOR

A person employed in a supervisory capacity must constantly be able to improve his own efficiency and ability. He represent the employer to the employees and only continuous self-examination can make him a capable supervisor.

Leadership and training are the supervisor's responsibility. An efficient working unit is one in which the employees work with the supervisor. It is his job to bring out the best in his employees. He must always be relaxed, courteous, and calm in his association with his employees. Their feelings are important, and a harsh attitude does not develop the most efficient employees.

COMPETENCES OF THE SUPERVISOR

I. Complete knowledge of the duties and responsibilities of his position.
II. To be able to organize a job, plan ahead, and carry through.
III. To have self-confidence and initiative.
IV. To be able to handle the unexpected situation and make quick decisions.
V. To be able to properly train subordinates in the positions they are best suited for.
VI. To be able to keep good human relations among his subordinates.
VII. To be able to keep good human relations between his subordinates and himself and to earn their respect and trust.

THE PROFESSIONAL SUPERVISOR-EMPLOYEE RELATIONSHIP

There are two kinds of efficiency: one kind is only apparent and is produced in organizations through the exercise of mere discipline; this is but a simulation of the second, or true, efficiency which springs from spontaneous cooperation. If you are a manager, no matter how great or small your responsibility, it is your job, in the final analysis, to create and develop this involuntary cooperation among the people whom you supervise. For, no matter how powerful a combination of money, machines, and materials a company may have, this is a dead and sterile thing without a team of willing, thinking, and articulate people to guide it.

The following 21 points are presented as indicative of the exemplary basic relationship that should exist between supervisor and employee:

1. Each person wants to be liked and respected by his fellow employee and wants to be treated with consideration and respect by his superior.
2. The most competent employee will make an error. However, in a unit where good relations exist between the supervisor and his employees, tenseness and fear do not exist. Thus, errors are not hidden or covered up, and the efficiency of a unit is not impaired.

3. Subordinates resent rules, regulations, or orders that are unreasonable or unexplained.
4. Subordinates are quick to resent unfairness, harshness, injustices, and favoritism.
5. An employee will accept responsibility if he knows that he will be complimented for a job well done, and not too harshly chastised for failure; that his supervisor will check the cause of the failure, and, if it was the supervisor's fault, he will assume the blame therefore. If it was the employee's fault, his supervisor will explain the correct method or means of handling the responsibility.
6. An employee wants to receive credit for a suggestion he has made, that is used. If a suggestion cannot be used, the employee is entitled to an explanation. The supervisor should not say "no" and close the subject.
7. Fear and worry slow up a worker's ability. Poor working environment can impair his physical and mental health. A good supervisor avoids forceful methods, threats, and arguments to get a job done.
8. A forceful supervisor is able to train his employees individually and as a team, and is able to motivate them in the proper channels.
9. A mature supervisor is able to properly evaluate his subordinates and to keep them happy and satisfied.
10. A sensitive supervisor will never patronize his subordinates.
11. A worthy supervisor will respect his employees' confidences.
12. Definite and clear-cut responsibilities should be assigned to each executive.
13. Responsibility should always be coupled with corresponding authority.
14. No change should be made in the scope or responsibilities of a position without a definite understanding to that effect on the part of all persons concerned.
15. No executive or employee, occupying a single position in the organization, should be subject to definite orders from more than one source.
16. Orders should never be given to subordinates over the head of a responsible executive. Rather than do this, the officer in question should be supplanted.
17. Criticisms of subordinates should, whoever possible, be made privately, and in no case should a subordinate be criticized in the presence of executives or employees of equal or lower rank.
18. No dispute or difference between executives or employees as to authority or responsibilities should be considered too trivial for prompt and careful adjudication.
19. Promotions, wage changes, and disciplinary action should always be approved by the executive immediately superior to the one directly responsible.
20. No executive or employee should ever be required, or expected, to be at the same time an assistant to, and critic of, another.
21. Any executive whose work is subject to regular inspection should, wherever practicable, be given the assistance and facilities necessary to enable him to maintain an independent check of the quality of his work.

MINI-TEXT IN SUPERVISION, ADMINISTRATION, MANAGEMENT, AND ORGANIZATION

I. Brief Highlights

Listed concisely and sequentially are major headings and important data in the field for quick recall and review.

A. Levels of Management

Any organization of some size has several levels of management. In terms of a ladder, the levels are:

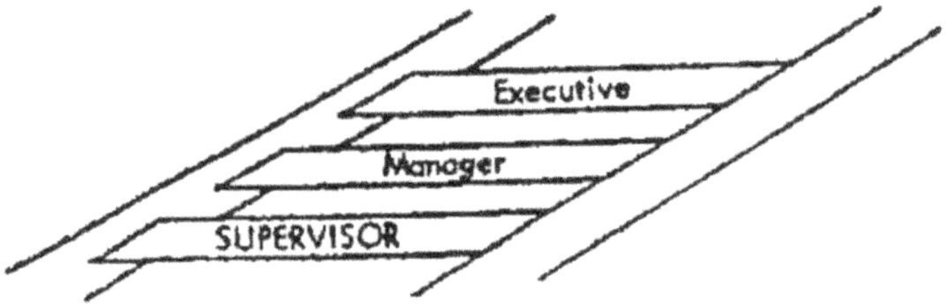

The first level is very important because it is the beginning point of management leadership.

B. What the Supervisor Must Learn

A supervisor must learn to:

1. Deal with people and their differences
2. Get the job done through people
3. Recognize the problems when they exist
4. Overcome obstacles to good performance
5. Evaluate the performance of people
6. Check his own performance in terms of accomplishment

C. A Definition of Supervisor

The term supervisor means any individual having authority, in the interests of the employer, to hire, transfer, suspend, lay-off, recall, promote, discharge, assign, reward, or discipline other employees or responsibility to direct them, or to adjust their grievances, or effectively to recommend such action, if, in connection with the foregoing, exercise of such authority is not of a merely routine or clerical nature but requires the use of independent judgment.

D. Elements of the Team Concept

What is involved in teamwork? The component parts are:

1. Members
2. A leader
3. Goals
4. Plans
5. Cooperation
6. Spirit

E. Principles of Organization

1. A team member must know what his job is.
2. Be sure that the nature and scope of a job are understood.
3. Authority and responsibility should be carefully spelled out.
4. A supervisor should be permitted to make the maximum number of decisions affecting his employees.
5. Employees should report to only one supervisor.
6. A supervisor should direct only as many employees as he can handle effectively.
7. An organization plan should be flexible.

8. Inspection and performance of work should be separate.
9. Organizational problems should receive immediate attention.
10. Assign work in line with ability and experience.

F. The Four Important Parts of Every Job
1. Inherent in every job is the *accountability* for results.
2. A second set of factors in every job is *responsibilities*.
3. Along with duties and responsibilities one must have the *authority* to act within certain limits without obtaining permission to proceed.
4. No job exists in a vacuum. The supervisor is surrounded by key *relationships*.

G. Principles of Delegation
Where work is delegated for the first time, the supervisor should think in terms of these questions:
1. Who is best qualified to do this?
2. Can an employee improve his abilities by doing this?
3. How long should an employee spend on this?
4. Are there any special problems for which he will need guidance?
5. How broad a delegation can I make?

H. Principles of Effective Communications
1. Determine the media.
2. To whom directed?
3. Identification and source authority.
4. Is communication understood?

I. Principles of Work Improvement
1. Most people usually do only the work which is assigned to them.
2. Workers are likely to fit assigned work into the time available to perform it.
3. A good workload usually stimulates output.
4. People usually do their best work when they know that results will be reviewed or inspected.
5. Employees usually feel that someone else is responsible for conditions of work, workplace layout, job methods, type of tools/equipment, and other such factors.
6. Employees are usually defensive about their job security.
7. Employees have natural resistance to change.
8. Employees can support or destroy a supervisor.
9. A supervisor usually earns the respect of his people through his personal example of diligence and efficiency.

J. Areas of Job Improvement
The areas of job improvement are quite numerous, but the most common ones which a supervisor can identify and utilize are:
1. Departmental layout
2. Flow of work
3. Workplace layout
4. Utilization of manpower
5. Work methods
6. Materials handling

7. Utilization
8. Motion economy

K. Seven Key Points in Making Improvements
1. Select the job to be improved
2. Study how it is being done now
3. Question the present method
4. Determine actions to be taken
5. Chart proposed method
6. Get approval and apply
7. Solicit worker participation

I. Corrective Techniques of Job Improvement

Specific Problems
1. Size of workload
2. Inability to meet schedules
3. Strain and fatigue
4. Improper use of men and skills
5. Waste, poor quality, unsafe conditions
6. Bottleneck conditions that hinder output
7. Poor utilization of equipment and machine
8. Efficiency and productivity of labor

General Improvement
1. Departmental layout
2. Flow of work
3. Work plan layout
4. Utilization of manpower
5. Work methods
6. Materials handling
7. Utilization of equipment
8. Motion economy

Corrective Techniques
1. Study with scale model
2. Flow chart study
3. Motion analysis
4. Comparison of units produced to standard allowance
5. Methods analysis
6. Flow chart and equipment study
7. Down time vs. running time
8. Motion analysis

M. A Planning Checklist
1. Objectives
2. Controls
3. Delegations
4. Communications
5. Resources
6. Manpower

7. Equipment
8. Supplies and materials
9. Utilization of time
10. Safety
11. Money
12. Work
13. Timing of improvements

N. Five Characteristics of Good Directions

In order to get results, directions must be:

1. Possible of accomplishment
2. Agreeable with worker interests
3. Related to mission
4. Planned and complete
5. Unmistakably clear

O. Types of Directions

1. Demands or direct orders
2. Requests
3. Suggestion or implication
4. volunteering

P. Controls

A typical listing of the overall areas in which the supervisor should establish controls might be:

1. Manpower
2. Materials
3. Quality of work
4. Quantity of work
5. Time
6. Space
7. Money
8. Methods

Q. Orienting the New Employee

1. Prepare for him
2. Welcome the new employee
3. Orientation for the job
4. Follow-up

R. Checklist for Orienting New Employees

	Yes	No
1. Do you appreciate the feelings of new employees when they first report for work?	___	___
2. Are you aware of the fact that the new employee must make a big adjustment to his job?	___	___
3. Have you given him good reasons for liking the job and the organization?	___	___
4. Have you prepared for his first day on the job?	___	___
5. Did you welcome him cordially and make him feel needed?	___	___

	Yes	No
6. Did you establish rapport with him so that he feels free to talk and discuss matters with you?	___	___
7. Did you explain his job to him and his relationship to you?	___	___
8. Does he know that his work will be evaluated periodically on a basis that is fair and objective?	___	___
9. Did you introduce him to his fellow workers in such a way that they are likely to accept him?	___	___
10. Does he know what employee benefits he will receive?	___	___
11. Does he understand the importance of being on the job and what to do if he must leave his duty station?	___	___
12. Has he been impressed with the importance of accident prevention and safe practice?	___	___
13. Does he generally know his way around the department?	___	___
14. Is he under the guidance of a sponsor who will teach the right way of doing things?	___	___
15. Do you plan to follow-up so that he will continue to adjust successfully to his job?	___	___

S. Principles of Learning
1. Motivation
2. Demonstration or explanation
3. Practice

T. Causes of Poor Performance
1. Improper training for job
2. Wrong tools
3. Inadequate directions
4. Lack of supervisory follow-up
5. Poor communications
6. Lack of standards of performance
7. Wrong work habits
8. Low morale
9. Other

U. Four Major Steps in On-The-Job Instruction
1. Prepare the worker
2. Present the operation
3. Tryout performance
4. Follow-up

V. Employees Want Five Things
1. Security
2. Opportunity
3. Recognition
4. Inclusion
5. Expression

W. Some Don'ts in Regard to Praise
1. Don't praise a person for something he hasn't done.
2. Don't praise a person unless you can be sincere.
3. Don't be sparing in praise just because your superior withholds it from you.
4. Don't let too much time elapse between good performance and recognition of it

X. How to Gain Your Workers' Confidence
Methods of developing confidence include such things as:
1. Knowing the interests, habits, hobbies of employees
2. Admitting your own inadequacies
3. Sharing and telling of confidence in others
4. Supporting people when they are in trouble
5. Delegating matters that can be well handled
6. Being frank and straightforward about problems and working conditions
7. Encouraging others to bring their problems to you
8. Taking action on problems which impede worker progress

Y. Sources of Employee Problems
On-the-job causes might be such things as:
1. A feeling that favoritism is exercised in assignments
2. Assignment of overtime
3. An undue amount of supervision
4. Changing methods or systems
5. Stealing of ideas or trade secrets
6. Lack of interest in job
7. Threat of reduction in force
8. Ignorance or lack of communications
9. Poor equipment
10. Lack of knowing how supervisor feels toward employee
11. Shift assignments

Off-the-job problems might have to do with:
1. Health
2. Finances
3. Housing
4. Family

Z. The Supervisor's Key to Discipline
There are several key points about discipline which the supervisor should keep in mind:
1. Job discipline is one of the disciplines of life and is directed by the supervisor.
2. It is more important to correct an employee fault than to fix blame for it.
3. Employee performance is affected by problems both on the job and off.
4. Sudden or abrupt changes in behavior can be indications of important employee problems.
5. Problems should be dealt with as soon as possible after they are identified.
6. The attitude of the supervisor may have more to do with solving problems than the techniques of problem solving.
7. Correction of employee behavior should be resorted to only after the supervisor is sure that training or counseling will not be helpful.

8. Be sure to document your disciplinary actions.
9. Make sure that you are disciplining on the basis of facts rather than personal feelings.
10. Take each disciplinary step in order, being careful not to make snap judgments, or decisions based on impatience.

AA. Five Important Processes of Management

1. Planning
2. Organizing
3. Scheduling
4. Controlling
5. Motivating

BB. When the Supervisor Fails to Plan

1. Supervisor creates impression of not knowing his job
2. May lead to excessive overtime
3. Job runs itself—supervisor lacks control
4. Deadlines and appointments missed
5. Parts of the work go undone
6. Work interrupted by emergencies
7. Sets a bad example
8. Uneven workload creates peaks and valleys
9. Too much time on minor details at expense of more important tasks

CC. Fourteen General Principles of Management

1. Division of work
2. Authority and responsibility
3. Discipline
4. Unity of command
5. Unity of direction
6. Subordination of individual interest to general interest
7. Remuneration of personnel
8. Centralization
9. Scalar chain
10. Order
11. Equity
12. Stability of tenure of personnel
13. Initiative
14. Esprit de corps

DD. Change

Bringing about change is perhaps attempted more often, and yet less well understood, than anything else the supervisor does. How do people generally react to change? (People tend to resist change that is imposed upon them by other individuals or circumstances.

Change is characteristic of every situation. It is a part of every real endeavor where the efforts of people are concerned.

1. Why do people resist change?
   People may resist change because of:
   a. Fear of the unknown
   b. Implied criticism
   c. Unpleasant experiences in the past
   d. Fear of loss of status
   e. Threat to the ego
   f. Fear of loss of economic stability

2. How can we best overcome the resistance to change?
   In initiating change, take these steps:
   a. Get ready to sell
   b. Identify sources of help
   c. Anticipate objections
   d. Sell benefits
   e. Listen in depth
   f. Follow up

II. Brief Topical Summaries

A. Who/What is the Supervisor?
   1. The supervisor is often called the "highest level employee and the lowest level manager."
   2. A supervisor is a member of both management and the work group. He acts as a bridge between the two.
   3. Most problems in supervision are in the area of human relations, or people problems.
   4. Employees expect: Respect, opportunity to learn and to advance, and a sense of belonging, and so forth.
   5. Supervisors are responsible for directing people and organizing work. Planning is of paramount importance.
   6. A position description is a set of duties and responsibilities inherent to a given position.
   7. It is important to keep the position description up-to-date and to provide each employee with his own copy.

B. The Sociology of Work
   1. People are alike in many ways; however, each individual is unique.
   2. The supervisor is challenged in getting to know employee differences. Acquiring skills in evaluating individuals is an asset.
   3. Maintaining meaningful working relationships in the organization is of great importance.
   4. The supervisor has an obligation to help individuals to develop to their fullest potential.
   5. Job rotation on a planned basis helps to build versatility and to maintain interest and enthusiasm in work groups.
   6. Cross training (job rotation) provides backup skills.

7. The supervisor can help reduce tension by maintaining a sense of humor, providing guidance to employees, and by making reasonable and timely decisions. Employees respond favorably to working under reasonably predictable circumstances.
8. Change is characteristic of all managerial behavior. The supervisor must adjust to changes in procedures, new methods, technological changes, and to a number of new and sometimes challenging situations.
9. To overcome the natural tendency for people to resist change, the supervisor should become more skillful in initiating change.

C. Principles and Practices of Supervision

1. Employees should be required to answer to only one superior.
2. A supervisor can effectively direct only a limited number of employees, depending upon the complexity, variety, and proximity of the jobs involved.
3. The organizational chart presents the organization in graphic form. It reflects lines of authority and responsibility as well as interrelationships of units within the organization.
4. Distribution of work can be improved through an analysis using the "Work Distribution Chart."
5. The "Work Distribution Chart" reflects the division of work within a unit in understandable form.
6. When related tasks are given to an employee, he has a better chance of increasing his skills through training.
7. The individual who is given the responsibility for tasks must also be given the appropriate authority to insure adequate results.
8. The supervisor should delegate repetitive, routine work. Preparation of recurring reports, maintaining leave and attendance records are some examples.
9. Good discipline is essential to good task performance. Discipline is reflected in the actions of employees on the job in the absence of supervision.
10. Disciplinary action may have to be taken when the positive aspects of discipline have failed. Reprimand, warning, and suspension are examples of disciplinary action.
11. If a situation calls for a reprimand, be sure it is deserved and remember it is to be done in private.

D. Dynamic Leadership

1. A style is a personal method or manner of exerting influence.
2. Authoritarian leaders often see themselves as the source of power and authority.
3. The democratic leader often perceives the group as the source of authority and power.
4. Supervisors tend to do better when using the pattern of leadership that is most natural for them.
5. Social scientists suggest that the effective supervisor use the leadership style that best fits the problem or circumstances involved.
6. All four styles—telling, selling, consulting, joining—have their place. Using one does not preclude using the other at another time.

7. The theory X point of view assumes that the average person dislikes work, will avoid it whenever possible, and must be coerced to achieve organizational objectives.
8. The theory Y point of view assumes that the average person considers work to be a natural as play, and, when the individual is committed, he requires little supervision or direction to accomplish desired objectives.
9. The leader's basic assumptions concerning human behavior and human nature affect his actions, decisions, and other managerial practices.
10. Dissatisfaction among employees is often present, but difficult to isolate. The supervisor should seek to weaken dissatisfaction by keeping promises, being sincere and considerate, keeping employees informed, and so forth.
11. Constructive suggestions should be encouraged during the natural progress of the work.

E. Processes for Solving Problems

1. People find their daily tasks more meaningful and satisfying when they can improve them.
2. The causes of problems, or the key factors, are often hidden in the background. Ability to solve problems often involves the ability to isolate them from their backgrounds. There is some substance to the cliché that some persons "can't see the forest for the trees."
3. New procedures are often developed from old ones. Problems should be broken down into manageable parts. New ideas can be adapted from old one.
4. People think differently in problem-solving situations. Using a logical, patterned approach is often useful. One approach found to be useful includes these steps:
   a. Define the problem
   b. Establish objectives
   c. Get the facts
   d. Weigh and decide
   e. Take action
   f. Evaluate action

F. Training for Results

1. Participants respond best when they feel training is important to them.
2. The supervisor has responsibility for the training and development of those who report to him.
3. When training is delegated to others, great care must be exercised to insure the trainer has knowledge, aptitude, and interest for his work as a trainer.
4. Training (learning) of some type goes on continually. The most successful supervisor makes certain the learning contributes in a productive manner to operational goals.
5. New employees are particularly susceptible to training. Older employees facing new job situations require specific training, as well as having need for development and growth opportunities.
6. Training needs require continuous monitoring.
7. The training officer of an agency is a professional with a responsibility to assist supervisors in solving training problems.

8. Many of the self-development steps important to the supervisor's own growth are equally important to the development of peers and subordinates. Knowledge of these is important when the supervisor consults with others on development and growth opportunities.

G. Health, Safety, and Accident Prevention
1. Management-minded supervisors take appropriate measures to assist employees in maintaining health and in assuring safe practices in the work environment.
2. Effective safety training and practices help to avoid injury and accidents.
3. Safety should be a management goal. All infractions of safety which are observed should be corrected without exception.
4. Employees' safety attitude, training and instruction, provision of safe tools and equipment, supervision, and leadership are considered highly important factors which contribute to safety and which can be influenced directly by supervisors.
5. When accidents do occur, they should be investigated promptly for very important reasons, including the fact that information which is gained can be used to prevent accidents in the future.

H. Equal Employment Opportunity
1. The supervisor should endeavor to treat all employees fairly, without regard to religion, race, sex, or national origin.
2. Groups tend to reflect the attitude of the leader. Prejudice can be detected even in very subtle form. Supervisors must strive to create a feeling of mutual respect and confidence in every employee.
3. Complete utilization of all human resources is a national goal. Equitable consideration should be accorded women in the work force, minority-group members, the physically and mentally handicapped, and the older employee. The important question is: "Who can do the job?"
4. Training opportunities, recognition for performance, overtime assignments, promotional opportunities, and all other personnel actions are to be handled on an equitable basis.

I. Improving Communications
1. Communications is achieving understanding between the sender and the receiver of a message. It also means sharing information—the creation of understanding.
2. Communication is basic to all human activity. Words are means of conveying meanings; however, real meanings are in people.
3. There are very practical differences in the effectiveness of one-way, impersonal, and two-way communications. Words spoken face-to-face are better understood. Telephone conversations are effective, but lack the rapport of person-to-person exchanges. The whole person communicates.
4. Cooperation and communication in an organization go hand in hand. When there is a mutual respect between people, spelling out rules and procedures for communicating is unnecessary.
5. There are several barriers to effective communications. These include failure to listen with respect and understanding, lack of skill in feedback, and misinterpreting the meanings of words used by the speaker. It is also common

practice to listen to what we want to hear, and tune out things we do not want to hear.

6. Communication is management's chief problem. The supervisor should accept the challenge to communicate more effectively and to improve interagency and intra-agency communications.
7. The supervisor may often plan for and conduct meetings. The planning phase is critical and may determine the success or the failure of a meeting.
8. Speaking before groups usually requires extra effort. Stage fright may never disappear completely, but it can be controlled.

J. Self-Development

1. Every employee is responsible for his own self-development.
2. Toastmaster and toastmistress clubs offer opportunities to improve skills in oral communications.
3. Planning for one's own self-development is of vital importance. Supervisors know their own strengths and limitations better than anyone else.
4. Many opportunities are open to aid the supervisor in his developmental efforts, including job assignments; training opportunities, both governmental and non-governmental—to include universities and professional conferences and seminars.
5. Programmed instruction offers a means of studying at one's own rate.
6. Where difficulties may arise from a supervisor's being away from his work for training, he may participate in televised home study or correspondence courses to meet his self-development needs.

K. Teaching and Training

1. The Teaching Process

   Teaching is encouraging and guiding the learning activities of students toward established goals. In most cases this process consists of five steps: preparation, presentation, summarization, evaluation, and application.

   a. Preparation

      Preparation is two-fold in nature; that of the supervisor and the employee. Preparation by the supervisor is absolutely essential to success. He must know what, when, where, how, and whom he will teach. Some of the factors that should be considered are:

      1) The objectives
      2) The materials needed
      3) The methods to be used
      4) Employee participation
      5) Employee interest
      6) Training aids
      7) Evaluation
      8) Summarization

      Employee preparation consists in preparing the employee to receive the material. Probably the most important single factor in the preparation of the employee is arousing and maintaining his interest. He must know the objectives of the training, why he is there, how the material can be used, and its importance to him.

b. Presentation
In presentation, have a carefully designed plan and follow it. The plan should be accurate and complete, yet flexible enough to meet situations as they arise. The method of presentation will be determined by the particular situation and objectives.

c. Summary
A summary should be made at the end of every training unit and program. In addition, there may be internal summaries depending on the nature of the material being taught. The important thing is that the trainee must always be able to understand how each part of the new material relates to the whole.

d. Application
The supervisor must arrange work so the employee will be given a chance to apply new knowledge or skills while the material is still clear in his mind and interest is high. The trainee does not really know whether he has learned the material until he has been given a chance to apply it. If the material is not applied, it loses most of its value.

e. Evaluation
The purpose of all training is to promote learning. To determine whether the training has been a success or failure, the supervisor must evaluate this learning.
In the broadest sense, evaluation includes all the devices, methods, skills, and techniques used by the supervisor to keep himself and the employees informed as to their progress toward the objectives they are pursuing. The extent to which the employee has mastered the knowledge, skills, and abilities, or changed his attitudes, as determined by the program objectives, is the extent to which instruction has succeeded or failed.
Evaluation should not be confined to the end of the lesson, day, or program but should be used continuously. We shall note later the way this relates to the rest of the teaching process.

2. Teaching Methods
A teaching method is a pattern of identifiable student and instructor activity used in presenting training material.
All supervisors are faced with the problem of deciding which method should be used at a given time.

a. Lecture
The lecture is direct oral presentation of material by the supervisor. The present trend is to place less emphasis on the trainer's activity and more on that of the trainee.

b. Discussion
Teaching by discussion or conference involves using questions and other techniques to arouse interest and focus attention upon certain areas, and by doing so creating a learning situation. This can be one of the most

valuable methods because it gives the employees an opportunity to express their ideas and pool their knowledge.

c. Demonstration
The demonstration is used to teach how something works or how to do something. It can be used to show a principle or what the results of a series of actions will be. A well-staged demonstration is particularly effective because it shows proper methods of performance in a realistic manner.

d. Performance
Performance is one of the most fundamental of all learning techniques or teaching methods. The trainee may be able to tell how a specific operation should be performed but he cannot be sure he knows how to perform the operation until he has done so.
As with all methods, there are certain advantages and disadvantages to each method.

e. Which Method to Use
Moreover, there are other methods and techniques of teaching. It is difficult to use any method without other methods entering into it. In any learning situation, a combination of methods is usually more effective than any one method alone.

Finally, evaluation must be integrated into the other aspects of the teaching-learning process.

It must be used in the motivation of the trainees; it must be used to assist in developing understanding during the training; and it must be related to employee application of the results of training.

This is distinctly the role of the supervisor.

GLOSSARY OF PERSONNEL TERMS

CONTENTS

GLOSSARY OF PERSONNEL TERMS

A

Abandonment of Position—When an employee quits work without resigning. (715)

Absence Without Leave (AWOL) Absence — without prior approval, therefore without pay, that may be subject to disciplinary action. See also, *Leave Without Pay,* which is an approved absence. (630)

Administrative Workweek— A period of seven consecutive calendar days designated in advance by the head of the agency. Usually an administrative workweek coincides with a calendar week. (610)

Admonishment— Informal reproval of an employee by a supervisor; usually oral, but some agencies require written notice. (751)

Adverse Action— A removal, suspension, furlough without pay for 30 days or less, or reduction-in-grade or pay. An adverse action may be taken against an employee for disciplinary or non-disciplinary reasons. However, if the employee is covered by FPM part 752, the action must be in accordance with those procedures. Removals or reductions-in-grade based solely on unacceptable performance are covered by Part 432. Actions taken for reductions-in-force reasons are covered by Part 351. (752)

Affirmative Action — A policy followed closely by the Federal civil service that requires agencies to take positive steps to insure equal opportunity in employment, development, advancement, and treatment of all employees and applicants for employment regardless of race, color, sex, religion, national origin, or physical or mental handicap. Affirmative action also requires that specific actions be directed at the special problems and unique concerns in assuring equal employment opportunity for minorities, women and other disadvantaged groups.

Agreement—See *Collective Bargaining.*

Annuitant—A retired Federal civil service employee or a survivor (spouse or children) being paid an annuity from the Retirement Fund. (831)

Annuity—Payments to a former employee who retired, or to the surviving spouse or children. It is computed as an annual rate but paid monthly. (831)

Appeal—A request by an employee for review of an agency action by an outside agency: The right to such review-is provided by law or regulation and may include an adversary-type hearing and a written decision in which a finding of facts is made and applicable law, Executive order and regulations are applied.

Appointing Officer—A person having power by law or lawfully delegated authority to make appointments. (210, 311)

Appointment, Noncompetitive— Employment without competing with others, in the sense that it is done without regard to civil service registers, etc. Includes reinstatements, transfers, reassignments, demotions, and promotion. (335)

Appointment, Superior Qualifications—Appointment of a candidate to a position in grade 11 or above of the General Schedule at a rate above the minimum because of the candidate's superior qualifications. A rate above the minimum for the grade must be justified by the applicant's unusually high or unique qualifications, a special need of the Government for the candidate's services, or because the candidate's current pay is higher than the minimum for the grade which he or she is offered. (338, 531)

Appointment, TAPER—Abbreviation for "temporary appointment pending establishment of a register." Employment made under an OPM authority granted to an agency when there are insufficient eligibles on a register appropriate to fill the position involved. (316)

Appointment, Temporary Limited—Nonpermanent appointment of an employee hired for a specified time of one year or less, or for seasonal or intermittent positions. (316)

Appointment, Term—Nonpermanent appointment of an employee hired to work on a project expected to last over one year, but less than four years. (316)

Appropriate Unit —A group of employees which a labor organization seeks to represent for the purpose of negotiating agreements; an aggregation of employees which has a clear and identifiable community of interest and which promotes effective dealings and efficiency of operations. It may be established on a plant or installation, craft, functional or other basis. (Also known as bargaining unit, appropriate bargaining unit.) (711)

Arbitration—Final step of the negotiated grievance procedure which may be invoked by the agency or the union (not the employee) if the grievance has not been resolved. Involves use of an impartial arbitrator selected by the agency and union to render a binding award to resolve the grievance. (711)

Arbitrator—An impartial third party to whom disputing parties submit their differences for decision (award). An *ad hoc* arbitrator is one selected to act in a specific case or a limited group of cases. A permanent arbitrator is one selected to serve for the life of the agreement or a stipulated term, hearing all disputes that arise during this period. (711)

Area Office (OPM)—Forcal point for administering and implementing all OPM programs, except investigations, in the geographic area assigned. Provides personnel management advice and assistance to agencies, and personnel evaluation, recruiting and examining and special program leadership. Principal source of employment information for agencies and the public.

Audit, Work—Visit to an employee or his supervisor to verify or gather information about a position. Sometimes called "desk audit."

B

Bargaining Rights—Legally recognized right of the labor organization to represent employees in negotiations with employers. (711)

Bargaining Unit—An appropriate grouping of employees represented on an exclusive basis by a labor organization. "Appropriate" for this purpose means that it is a grouping of employees who share a community of interest and which promotes effective union and agency dealings and efficient agency operations. (711)

Basic Workweek—For a full-time employee, the 40-hour non overtime work schedule within an administrative workweek. The usual workweek consists of five 8-hour days, Monday through Friday. (610)

Break in Service—The time between separation and reemployment that may cause a loss of rights or privileges. For transfer purposes, it means not being on an agency payroll for one working day or more. For the three-year career conditional period or for reinstatement purposes, it means not being on an agency payroll for over 30 calendar days. (315)

Bumping—During reduction-in-force, the displacement of one employee by another employee in a higher group or subgroup. (351)

C

Career—Tenure of a permanent employee in the competitive service who has completed three years of substantially continuous creditable Federal service. (315)

Career-Conditional—Tenure of a permanent employee in the competitive service who *has not* completed three years of substantially continuous creditable Federal service. (315)

Career Counseling—Service available to employees to assist them in: (1) assessing their skills, abilities, interests, and aptitudes; (2) determining qualifications required for occupations within the career system and how the requirements relate to their individual capabilities; (3) defining their career goals and developing plans for reaching the goals; (4) identifying and assessing education and training opportunities and enrollment procedures; (5) identifying factors which may impair career development; and (6) learning about resources, inside or outside the agency, where additional help is available. (250)

Career Development—Systematic development designed to increase an employee's potential for advancement and career change. It may include classroom training, reading, work experience, etc. (410)

Career Ladder—A career ladder is a series of developmental positions of increasing difficulty in the same line of work, through which an employee may progress to a journeyman level on his or her personal development and performance in that series.

Career Reserved Position—A position within SES that has a specific requirement for impartiality. May be filled" only by career appointment. (920)

Ceiling, Personnel—The maximum number of employees authorized at a given time. (312)

Certification—The process by which eligibles are ranked, according to regulations, for appointment or promotion consideration. (332, 335)

Certification, Selective—Certifying only the names of eligibles who have special qualifications required to fill particular vacant positions. (332)

Certification, Top of the Register—Certifying in regular order, beginning with the eligibles at the top of the register. (332)

Change in Duty Station—A personnel action that changes an employee from one geographical location to another in the same agency. (296)

Change to Lower Grade—Downgrading a position or reducing an employee's grade. See *Demotion.* (296)

Class of Positions—All positions sufficiently similar in: (1) kind or subject matter of work; (2) level of difficulty and responsibility; and (3) qualification requirements, so as to warrant similar treatment in personnel and pay administration. For example, all Grade GS-3 Clerk-Typist positions. (511)

Classified Service—See *Competitive Service* (212)

Collective Bargaining—Performance of the mutual obligation of the employer and the exclusive (employee) representative to meet at reasonable times, to confer and negotiate in good faith, and to execute a written agreement with respect to conditions of employment, except that by any such obligation neither party shall be compelled to agree to proposals, or be required to make concessions. (Also known as collective negotiations, negotiations, and negotiation of agreement.) (711)

Collective Bargaining Agreement—A written agreement between management and a labor-organization which is usually for a definite term, and usually defines conditions of employment, and includes grievance and arbitration procedures. The terms "collective bargaining agreement" and "contract" are synonymous. (711)

Collective Bargaining Unit—A group of employees recognized as appropriate for representation by a labor organization for collective bargaining. (See *Appropriate Unit)* (711)

Compensatory Time Off—Time off (hour-for-hour) granted an employee in lieu of overtime pay. (550)

Competitive Area—For reduction-in-force, that part of an agency within which employees are in competition for retention. Generally, it is that part of an agency covered by a single appointing office. (351)

Competitive Service—Federal positions normally filled through open competitive examination (hence the term "competitive service") under civil service rules and regulations. About 86 percent of all Federal positions are in the competitive service. (212)

Competitive Status—Basic eligibility of a person to be selected to fill a position in the competitive service without open competitive examination. Competitive status may be acquired by career-conditional or career appointment through open competitive examination, or may be granted by statute, executive order, or civil service rules without competitive examination. A person with competitive status may be promoted, transferred, reassigned, reinstated, or demoted subject to the conditions prescribed by civil service rules and regulations. (212)

Consultant—An advisor to an officer or instrumentality of the Government, as distinguished from an officer or employee who carries out the agency's duties and responsibilities. (304)

Consultation—The obligation of an agency to consult the labor organization on particular personnel issues. The process of consultation lies between notification to the labor organization, which may amount simply to providing information, and negotiation, which implies agreement on the part of the labor organization. (711)

Conversion—The process of changing a person's tenure from one type of appointment to another (e.g., conversion from temporary to career-conditional). (315)

D

Demotion—A change of an employee, while serving continuously with the same agency:
(a) To a lower grade when both the old and the new positions are in the General Schedule or under the same type graded wage schedule; or
(b) To a position with a lower rate of pay when both the old and the new positions are under the same type ungraded wage schedule, or are in different pay method categories. (335, 752)

Detail—A temporary assignment of an employee to different duties or to a different position for a specified time, with the employee returning to his/her regular duties at the end of the detail. (300)

Differentials—Recruiting incentives in the form of compensation adjustments justified by: (1) extraordinarily difficult living conditions; (2) excessive physical hardship; or (3) notably unhealthful conditions. (591)

Disciplinary Action—Action taken to correct the conduct of an employee; may range from an admonishment through reprimand, suspension, reduction in grade or pay, to removal from the service. (751, 752)

Displaced Employee Program—(DEP)— A system to help find jobs for career and career-conditional employees displaced either through reduction-in-force or by an inability to accept assignment to another commuting area. (330)

Downgrading—Change of a position to a lower grade. (511, 532)

Dual Compensation—When an employee receives compensation for more than one Federal position if he/she worked more than 40 hours during the week. The term is also used in connection with compensation from a full-time Federal position as well as a retirement annuity for prior military service. (550)

Duty Station—The specific geographical area in which an employee is permanently assigned. (296)

E

Eligible—Any applicant for appointment or promotion who meets the minimum qualification requirements. (337)

Employee Development—A term which may include *career development* and *upward mobility.* It may be oriented toward development for better performance on an employee's current job, for learning a new policy or procedure, or for enhancing an employee's potential for advancement. (410, 412)

Employee, Exempt—An employee exempt from the overtime provisions of the Fair Labor Standards Act. (551)

Employee, Nonexempt—An employee subject to the overtime provision of the Fair Labor Standards Act. (551)

Employee Organization— See *Labor Organization.*

Employee Relations—The personnel function which centers upon the relationship between the supervisor and individual employees. (711)

Entrance Level Position—A position in an occupation at the beginning level grade. (511)

Environmental Differential—Additional pay authorized for a duty involving unusually severe hazards or working conditions. (532, 550)

Equal Employment Opportunity—Federal policy to provide equal employment opportunity for all; to prohibit discrimination on the grounds of age, race, color, religion, sex, national origin, or physical or mental handicap; and to promote the full realization of employees' potential through a continuing affirmative action program in each executive department and agency. (713)

Equal Employment Opportunity Commission—Regulates and enforces the Federal program for insuring equal employment opportunity, and oversees the development and implementation of Federal agencies' affirmative action programs.

Equal Pay for Substantially Equal Work—An underlying principle that provides the same pay level for work at the same level of difficulty and responsibility. (271)
Examination, Assembled—An examination which includes as one of its parts a written or performance test for which applicants are required to assemble at appointed times and places. (337)

Examination— A means of measuring, in a practical and suitable manner, qualifications of applicants for employment in specific positions. (337)

Examination, Fitness-For-Duty—An agency directed examination given by a Federal medical officer or an employee-designated, agency-approved physician to determine the employee's physical, mental, or emotional ability to perform assigned duties safely and efficiently. (339, 831)

Examination, Unassembled—An examination in which applicants are rated on their education, experience, and other qualifications as shown in the formal application and any supportive evidence that may be required, without assembling for a written or performance test. (337)

Excepted Service—Positions in the Federal civil service not subject to the appointment requirements of the competitive service. Exceptions to the normal, competitive requirements are authorized by law, executive order, or regulation. (213, 302)

Exclusive Recognition—The status conferred on a labor organization which receives a majority of votes cast in a representation election, entitling it to act for and negotiate agreements covering all employees included in an appropriate bargaining unit. The labor organization enjoying this status is known as the exclusive representative, exclusive bargaining representative, bargaining agent, or exclusive bargaining agent. (711)

Executive Inventory—An OPM computerized file which contains background information on all members of the Senior Executive Service and persons in positions at GS-16 through GS-18 or the equivalent, and individuals at lower grades who have been certified as meeting the managerial criteria for SES. It is used as an aid to agencies in executive recruiting and as a planning and management tool. (920)

Executive Resources Board—Panel of top agency executives responsible under the law for conducting the merit staffing process for career appointment to Senior Executive Service (SES) positions in the agency. Most Boards are also responsible for setting policy on and overseeing such areas as SES position planning and executive development. (920)

F

Federal Labor Relations Authority (FLRA)—Administers the Federal service labor-management relations program. It resolves questions of union representation of employees; prosecutes and adjudicates allegations of unfair labor practices; decides questions of what is or is not negotiable; and on appeal, reviews decisions of arbitrators. (5 USC 7104)

Federal Personnel Manual (FPM)—The official publication containing Federal personnel regulations and guidance. Also contains the code of Federal civil service law, selected Executive orders pertaining to Federal employment, and civil service rules. (171)

Federal Service Impasses Panel (FSIP)—Administrative body created to resolve bargaining impasses in the Federal service. The Panel may recommend procedures, including arbitration, for settling impasses, or may settle the impasse itself. Considered the legal alternative to strike in the Federal sector. (711)

Federal Wage System (FWS)—A body of laws and regulations governing the administrative processes related to trades and laboring occupations in the Federal service. (532)

Full Field Investigation—Personal investigation of an applicant's background to determine whether he/she meets fitness standards for a critical-sensitive Federal position. (736)

Function—All, or a clearly identifiable segment, of an agency's mission, including all the parts of the mission (e.g. procurement), regardless of how performed. (351)

G

General Position—A position within the Senior Executive Service that may be filled by a career, noncareer, or limited appointment. (920)

General Schedule—(GS)The graded pay system as presented by Chapter 51 of Title 5, United States Code, for classifying positions. **(511)**

Grade—All classes of positions which, although different with respect to kind or subject matter of work, are sufficiently equivalent as to (1) level of difficulty and responsibility, and (2) level of qualification requirements of the work to warrant the inclusion of such classes of positions within one range of rates of basic compensation. (511, 532)

Grade Retention—The right of a General Schedule or prevailing rate employee, when demoted for certain reasons, to retain the higher grade for most purposes for two years. (536)

Grievance, (Negotiated Procedure)—Any complaint or expressed dissatisfaction by an employee against an action by management in connection with his job, pay or other aspects of employment. Whether such complaint or expressed dissatisfaction is formally recognized and handled as a "grievance" under a negotiated procedure depends on the scope of that procedure. (711)

Grievance (Under Agency Administrative Procedure)—A request by an employee or by a group of employees acting as individuals, for personal relief in a matter of concern or dissatisfaction to the employee, subject to the control of agency management.

Grievance Procedure—A procedure, either administrative or negotiated, by which employees may seek redress of any matter subject to the control of agency management. (711, 771)

H

Handbook X-118— The official qualification standard a manual for General Schedule Positions. (338)

Handbook X-118C—The official qualification standards manual for Wage System positions. (338)

Hearing—The opportunity for contending parties under a grievance, complaint, or other remedial process, to introduce testimony and evidence and to confront and examine or cross examine witnesses. (713, 771, 772)

I

Impasse Procedures—Procedures for resolving deadlocks between agencies and union in collective bargaining. (711)

Incentive Awards—An all-inclusive term covoring awards granted under Part 451 or OPM regulations. Includes an award for a suggestion submitted by an employee and adopted by management; a special achievement award for performance exceeding job requirements, or an honorary award in the form of a certificate, emblem, pin or other item. (451)

Indefinite—Tenure of a nonpermanent employee hired for an unlimited time. (316)

Injury, Work Related—For compensation under the Federal Employees' Compensation Act, a personal injury sustained while in the performance of duty. The term "injury" includes diseases proximately caused by the employment. (810)

Injury, Traumatic—Under the Federal Employees' Compensation Act, for continuation of pay purposes, a wound or other condition of the body caused by external force, including stress or strain. The injury must be identifiable by time and place of occurrence and member or function of the body affected, and be caused by a specific event or incident or series of events or incidents within a single day or work shift. (810)

Intergovernmental Personnel Assignment—Assignments of personnel to and from the Executive Branch of the Federal Government, state and local government agencies, and institutions of higher education up to two years, although a two-year extension may be permitted. The purpose is to provide technical assistance or expertise where needed for short periods of time. (334)

Intermittent—Less than full-time employment requiring irregular work hours which cannot be prescheduled. (610)

J

Job Analysis—Technical review and evaluation of a position's duties, responsibilities, and level of work and of the skills, abilities, and knowledge needed to do the work. (511, 532)

Job Enrichment—Carefully planned work assignments and/or training to use and upgrade employee skills, abilities, and interests; and to provide opportunity for growth, and encourage self-improvement. (312)

Job Freeze—A restriction on hiring and/or promotion by administrative or legislative action. (330)

Job Title— The formal name of a position as determined by official classification standards. (511, 532)

Journeyman Level—(Full Performance Level)The lowest level of a career ladder position at which an employee has learned the full range of duties in a specific occupation. All jobs below full performance level are developmental levels, through which each employee in the occupation may progress to full performance. (511)

L

Labor-Management Relations—Relationships and dealings between employee unions and management. (711)

Labor Organization—An organization composed in whole or in part of employees, in which employees participate and pay dues, and which has as a purpose dealing with an agency concerning grievances and working conditions of employment. (711)

Lead Agency—Under the Federal Wage-System, the Federal agency with the largest number of Federal wage workers in a geographical area; consequently, it has the primary role for determining wage rates for all Federal employees who work in that area and are covered by the System. (532)

Leave, Annual—Time allowed to employees for vacation and other absences for personal reasons. (630)

Leave, Court—Time allowed to employees for jury and certain types of witness service. (630)

Leave, Military—Time allowed to employees for certain types of military service. (630)

Leave, Sick—Time allowed to employees for physical incapacity, to prevent the spread of contagious diseases, or to obtain medical, dental or eye examination or treatment. (630)

Leave Without Pay (LWOP)—A temporary nonpay status and absence from duty, requested by an employee. The permissive nature of "leave without pay" distinguishes it from "absence without leave." (630)

Level of Difficulty—A classification term used to indicate the relative ranking of duties and responsibilities. (511, 532)

M

Maintenance Review—A formal, periodic review (usually annual) of all positions in an organization, or portion of an organization, to insure that classifications are correct and position descriptions are current. (511)

Major Duty—Any duty or responsibility, or group of closely related tasks, of a position which (1) determines qualification requirements for the position, (2) occupies a significant amount of the employee's time, and (3) is a regular or recurring duty. (511)

Management Official—An individual employed by an agency in a position whose duties and responsibilities require or authorize the individual to formulate, determine or influence the policies of the agency. (711)

Management Rights—The right of management to make day-today personnel decisions and to direct the work force without mandatory negotiation with the exclusive representative. (See "Reserved Rights Doctrine.") Usually a specific list of management authorities not subject to the obligation to bargain. (117)

Mediation—Procedure using a third-party to facilitate the reaching of an agreement voluntarily. (711)

Merit Promotion Program—The system under which agencies consider an employee for internal personnel actions on the basis of personal merit. (335)

Merit Systems Protection Board (MSPB)—An independent agency which monitors the administration of the Federal civil service system, prosecutes and adjudicates allegations of merit principle abuses, and hears and decides other civil service appeals. (5 USC 1205)

N

National Agency Check and Inquiry (NACI)—The Investigation of applicants for nonsensitive Federal positions by means of a name check through national investigative files and voucher inquiries. (731)

National Consultation Rights—A relationship established between the headquarters of a Federal agency and the national office of a union under criteria of the Federal Labor Relations Authority. When a union holds national consultation rights, the agency must give the union notice of proposed new substantive personnel policies, and of proposed changes in personnel policies, and an opportunity to comment on such proposals. The union has a right to: (1) suggest changes in personnel policies and have those suggestions carefully considered; (2) consult at reasonable times with appropriate officials about personnel policy matters; and (3) submit its views in writing on personnel policy matters at any time. The agency must provide the union with a written statement (which need not be detailed) of reasons for taking its final action on a policy. (711)

Negotiability—A determination as to whether a matter is within the obligation to bargain. (711)

Negotiated Grievance Procedure—A procedure applicable to members of a bargaining unit for considering grievances. Coverage and scope are negotiated by the parties to the agreement, except that the procedures may not cover certain matters designated in Title VII of the CSRA as excluded from the scope of negotiated grievance procedures. (711)

Negotiations—The bargaining process used to reach a settlement between labor and management over conditions of employment. (711)

Nominating Officer—A subordinate officer of an agency to whom authority has been delegated by the head of the agency to nominate for appointment but not actually appoint employees. (311)

O

Objection—A written statement by an agency of the reasons why it believes an eligible whose name is on a certificate is not qualified for the position to which referred. If the Examining Office sustains the objection, the agency may eliminate the person from consideration. (332)

Occupational Group—Positions of differing kinds but within the same field of work. For example, the GS-500 Accounting and Budget Occupational Group includes: General Accounting Clerical and Administrative Series; Financial Management; Internal Revenue Agent Accounting Technician; Payroll; etc. (511, 532)

Office of Personnel Management (OPM)—Regulates, administers, and evaluates the civil service program according to merit principles. (5 USC 1103)

Office of Workers Compensation Programs (OWCP)—In the Department of Labor, administers statutes that allow compensation to employees and their survivors for work-related injuries and illnesses. Decides and pays claims. (810)

Official Personnel Folder (OPF)—The official repository of employment records and documents affecting personnel actions during an employee's Federal civilian service. (293)

Overtime Work—Under Title 5, U.S. Code, officially ordered or approved work performed in excess of eight hours in a day or 40 hours in a week. Under the Fair Labor Standards Act, work in excess of 40 hours in a week by a nonexempt employee. (550, 551)

P

Pass Over—Elimination from appointment consideration of a veteran preference eligible on a certificate (candidate list), to appoint a lower ranking nonveteran, when the agency submits reasons which OPM finds sufficient. (332)

Pay Retention—The right of a General Schedule or prevailing rate employee (following a grade retention period or at other specified times when the rate of basic pay would otherwise be reduced) to continue to receive the higher rate. Pay is retained indefinitely. (536)

Pay, Severance—Money paid to employees separated by reduction-in-force and not eligible for retirement. The following formula is used, but the amount cannot be more than one year's pay:

Basic Severance Pay— One week's pay for each year of civilian service up to 10 years, and two weeks' pay for each year served over 10 years, plus

Age Adjustment Allowance —10 percent of the basic severance pay for each year over age 40. (550)

Performance Appraisal—The comparison, under a performance appraisal system, of an employee's actual performance against the performance standards previously established for the position. (430)

Personal Action— The process necessary to appoint, separate, reinstate, or make other changes affecting an employee (e.g., change in position assignment, tenure, etc.). (296)

Personnel Management—Management of human resources to accomplish a mission and provide individual job satisfaction. It is the line responsibility of the operating supervisor and the staff responsibility of the personnel office. (250)

Position—A specific job consisting of all the current major duties and responsibilities assigned or delegated by management. (312)

Position Change—A promotion, demotion, or reassignment. (335)

Position Classification—Analyzing and categorizing jobs by occupational group, series, class, and grade according to like duties, responsibilities, and qualification requirements. (511, 532)

Position Classifier—A specialist in job analysis who determines the titles, occupational groups, series, and grades of positions. (312)

Position Description—An official written statement of the major duties, responsibilities and supervisory relationships of a position. (312)

Position Management—The process of designing positions to combine logical and consistent duties and responsibilities into an orderly, efficient, and productive organization to accomplish agency mission. (312)

Position Survey—Agency review of positions to determine whether the positions are still needed and, if so, whether the classification and position description are correct. (312)

Position, "PL 313 Type"—Positions established under Public Law 80-313 of August 1, 1947, or similar authorities. A small group of high level professional and scientific positions generally in the competitive service, but not filled through competitive examinations. Salaries are set between GS-12 and GS-18. (534)

Preference, Compensable Disability ("CP")—Ten-point preference awarded to a veteran separated under honorable conditions from active duty, who receives compensation of 10 percent or more for a service-connected disability. Eligible "CP" veterans are placed at the top of civil service lists of eligibles for positions at GS-9 or higher. (211)

Preference, 30 Percent or More, Disabled ("CPS")—A disabled veteran whose disability is rated at 30 percent or more, entitled to special preference in appointment and during reduction in force.

Preference, Disability ("XP")—Ten-point preference in hiring for a veteran separated under honorable conditions from active duty and who has a service-connected disability or receives compensation, pension, or disability retirement from the VA or a uniformed service. (211)

Preference, Mother ("XP")—Ten-point preference to which the mother of a deceased or disabled military veteran may be entitled. (211)

Preference, Spouse ("XP")—Ten-point preference to which a disabled military veteran's spouse may be entitled. (211)

Preference, Tentative ("TP")— Five-point veteran preference tentatively awarded an eligible who served on active duty during specified periods and was separated from military service under honorable conditions. It must be verified by the appointing officer. (211)

Preference, Veteran—The statutory right to special advantage in appointments or separations; based on a person's discharge under honorable conditions from the armed forces, for a service-connected disability. *Not* applicable to the Senior Executive Service. (211)

Preference, Widow or Widower ("XP")—Ten-point preference to which a military veteran's widow or widower may be entitled. (211)

Premium Pay—Additional pay for overtime, night, Sunday and holiday work. (550)

Prevailing Rate System—A subsystem of the Federal Wage System used to determine the employee's pay in a particular wage area. The determination requires, comparing. the_. rate of pay with the private sector for similar duties and responsibilities. (532)

Probationary Period—A trial period which is a condition of the initial competitive appointment. Provides the final indispensable test of ability, that of actual performance on the job. (315)

Promotion—A change of an employee to a higher grade when both the old and new positions are under the same job classification system and pay schedule, or to a position with higher pay in a different job classification system and pay schedule. (335)

Promotion, Career—Promotion of an employee without current competition when: (1) he/ she had earlier been competitively selected from a register or under competitive promotion procedures for an assignment intended as a matter of record to be preparation for the position being filled; or (2) the position is reconstituted at a higher grade because of additional duties and responsibilities. (335)

Promotion, Competitive—Selection of a current or former Federal civil service employee for a higher grade position, using procedures that compare the candidates on merit. (335)

Promotion Certificate—A list of best qualified candidates to be considered to fill a position under competitive promotion procedures. (335)

Q

Qualifications Review Board—A panel attached to OPM that determines whether a candidate for career appointment in the Senior Executive Service meets the managerial criteria established by law.

Qualification Requirements—Education, experience, and other prerequisites to employment or placement in a position. (338)

Quality Graduate—College graduate who was a superior student and can be hired at a higher grade than the one to which he/she would otherwise be entitled '(338)

Quality Increase—An additional within-grade increase granted to General Schedule employees for high quality performance above that ordinarily found in the type of position concerned (531).

R

Reassignment—The change of an employee, while serving continuously within the same agency, from one position to another, without promotion or demotion. (210)

Recognition—Employer acceptance of a labor organization as authorized to negotiate, usually for all members of a bargaining unit. (711) Also, used to refer to incentive awards granted under provisions of Parts 451 and 541 of OPM Regulations, and Quality Increases granted under Part 531.

Recruitment—Process of attracting a supply of qualified eligibles for employment consideration. (332)

Reduction-in-Force (RIF)—A personnel action that may be required due to lack of work or funds, changes resulting from reorganization, downward reclassification of a position, or the need to make room for an employee with reemployment or restoration rights. Involves separating an employee from his/her present position, but does not necessarily result in separation or downgrading. (351) (See also *Tenure Groups.)*

Reemployment Priority List—Career and career-conditional employees, separated by reduction-in-force, who are identified, in priority order, for reemployment to competitive positions in the agency in the commuting area where the separations occurred. (330)

Reemployment Rights—Right of an employee to return to an agency after detail, transfer, or appointment to: (1) another Executive agency during an emergency; (2) an international organization; or (3) other statutorily covered employment, e.g., the Peace Corps. (352)

Register—A list of eligible applicants compiled in the order of their relative standing for referral to Federal jobs, after competitive civil service examination. (332,210)

Reinstatement— Noncompetitive reemployment in the competitive service based on previous service under a career or career-conditional appointment. (315)

Removal—Separation of an employee for cause or because of continual unacceptable performance. (432, 752)

Representation—Actions and rights of the labor organization to consult and negotiate with management on behalf of the bargaining unit and represent employees in the unit. (711)

Representation Election—Election conducted to determine whether the employees in an appropriate unit (See *Bargaining Unit)* desire a labor organization to act as their exclusive representative. (711)

Reprimand—An official rebuke of an employee. Normally in writing and placed in the temporary side of an employee's OPF-(751)

"Reserved Rights Doctrine"—Specific functions delegated to management by Title VII of CSRA that protect management's ability to perform its necessary functions and duties. (See Management Rights.) Delegates to management specific functions not subject to negotiation except as to procedures and impact. (711)

Resignation—A separation, prior to retirement, in response to an employee's request for the action. It is a voluntary expression of the employee's desire to leave the organization and must not be demanded as an alternative to some other action to be taken or withheld. (715)

Restoration Rights—Employees who enter military service or sustain a compensable job-related injury or disability are entitled to be restored to the same or higher employment status held prior to their absence. (353)

Retention Preference—The relative standing of employees competing in a reduction-inforce. Their standing is determined by veteran's preference, tenure group, length of service, and performance appraisal. (351)

Retention Register—A list of all employees, arranged by competitive level, describing their retention preference during reductions-in-force. (351)

Retirement—Payment of an annuity after separation from a position under the Civil Service Retirement System and based on meeting age and length of service requirements. The types of retirement are:

Deferred - An employee with five years civilian service who separates or transfers to a position not under the Retirement Act, may receive an annuity, does not withdraw from the Retirement Fund. (.83:1)

Disability - An immediate annuity paid to an employee under the retirement system who has completed five years of civilian service and has suffered a mental, emotional, or physical disability not the result of the employee's vicious habits, intemperance, or willful misconduct, (831)

Discontinued Service - An immediate annuity paid to an employee who is involuntarily separated, through no personal fault of the employee, after age 50 and 20 years of service, or at any age with 25 years of service. This annuity is reduced by 1/6 of one percent for each full month under age 55 (two percent per year). (831)

Optional - The minimum combinations of age and service for this kind of immediate annuity are: age 62 with five years of service; age 60 with 20 years of service; age 55 with 30 years of service. (831)

Review, Classification—An official written request for reclassification of a position. Previously called a classification appeal.

S

Schedules A, B, and C—Categories of positions excepted from the competitive service by regulation. (213)

Schedule A—Positions other than confidential or policy determining, for which it is not practical to examine.

Schedule B— Positions other than confidential or policy determining for which it is not practical to hold a competitive examination.

Schedule C—Positions of a confidential or policy determining character.

Senior Executive Service—A separate personnel system for persons who set policy and administer programs at the top levels of the Government (equivalent to GS-16 through Executive Level IV). (920)

Service Computation Date-Leave—The date, either actual or adjusted, from which service credit is accumulated for determining the rate of leave accrual; it may be different from the service computation date, which determines relative standing in a subgroup for reduction-in-force, or service computation date for retirement. (296)

Service Record Card (Standard Form 7)—A brief of the employee's service history. It is kept on file in accordance with agency disposition instructions. (295)

Special Salary Rates—Salary rates higher than regular statutory schedule; established for occupations in which private enterprise pays substantially more than the regular Federal Schedule. (530)

Spoils System—The personnel system characterized by the political appointment and removal of employees without regard to merit. (212)

Staffing—Use of available and projected personnel through recruitment, appointment, reassignment, promotion, reduction-in-force, etc., to provide the work force required to fulfill the agency's mission. (250)

Standard Form—171 ("Personal Qualification Statement") Used in applying for a Federal position through a competitive examination. (295)

Standards of Conduct For Labor Organization—In the Federal sector, a code governing internal democratic practices and fiscal responsibility, and procedures to which a labor organization must adhere to be eligible to receive any recognition. (711)

Steward (Union Steward)—A local union's representative in a plant or department, appointed by the union to carry out union duties, adjust grievances, collect dues and solicit new members. Stewards are employees trained by the union to carry out their duties.

Strike—Temporary stoppage of work by a group of employees to express a grievance, enforce a demand for changes in conditions of employment, obtain recognition, or resolve a dispute with management. *Wildcat strike-* a strike not sanctioned by union and which may violate a collective agreement. *Quickie strike-* a spontaneous or unannounced strike of short duration. *Slowdown-a* deliberate reduction of output without an actual strike in order to force concessions from *an* employer. *Walkout* -same as strike. Strikes are illegal for Federal employees. (711)

Suitability—An applicant's or employee's fitness for Federal employment as indicated by character and conduct. (731)

Supervisor—An individual employed by an agency having authority, in the interest of the agency, to hire, direct, assign, promote, reward, transfer, furlough, lay off, recall, suspend, discipline-or remove employees, to adjust their grievances, or to effectively recommend such action-if the exercise of the authority is not merely routine or clerical in nature but requires the consistent exercise of independent judgment. With respect to any unit which includes firefighters or nurses, the term "supervisor" includes only those individuals who devote a preponderance of their employment time to exercising such authority. (711).

Survey, Classification—An intensive study of all positions in an organization or organizational segment to insure their correct classification.

Suspension—Placing an employee, for disciplinary reasons, in a temporary status without duties and pay. (751, 752)

T

Tenure—The time an employee may reasonably expect to serve under a current appointment. It is governed by the type of appointment, without regard to whether the employee has competitive status. (210)

Tenure Groups—Categories of employees ranked in priority order for retention during reduction in force . Within each group, veterans are ranked above nonveterans. For the competitive service, the tenure groups are, in descending order:

Group I—Employees under career appointments and not serving probation.

Group II—Employees serving probation, career-conditional employees, and career employees in obligated positions.

Group III—Employees with indefinite appointments, status quo employees under any other nonstatus, nontemporary appointment. (351)

For the *excepted service,* they are in descending order:

Group I—Permanent employees, not serving a trial period, whose appointments carry no restriction or condition, such as "indefinite" or "time-limited".

Group II—Employees serving trial periods, those whose tenure is indefinite because they occupy obligated positions, and those whose tenure is equivalent to career-conditional in the competitive service.

Group III—Employees whose tenure is indefinite, but not potentially permanent, and temporary employees who have completed one year of current continuous employment. (351)

Tenure Subgroups—The ranking of veterans above nonveterans in each tenure group, as follows:

Subgroup AD—Veterans with service-connected disability of 30% or more.
Subgroup A— All other veterans
Subgroup B—Nonveterans

Time-in-Grade Restriction—A requirement intended to prevent excessively rapid promotions in the General Schedule. Generally, an employee may not be promoted more than two grades within one year to positions up to GS-5. At GS-5 and above, an employee must serve a minimum of one year in grade, and cannot be promoted more than one grade, or two grades if that is the normal progression. (300)

Tour of Duty—The hours of a day (a daily tour of duty) and the day of an administrative workweek (weekly tour of duty) scheduled in advance and during which an employee is required to work regularly. (610)

Training—Formal instruction or controlled and planned exposure to learning. (410)

Transfer—A change of an employee, without a break in service of one full workday, from a position in one agency to a position in another agency. (315)

Transfer of Function—For reduction-in-force, the transfer of a continuing function from one agency or competitive area to another, or when the competitive area in which work is performed is moved to another commuting area. (315)

U

Unemployment Compensation—Income maintenance payments to former Federal employees who: (1) are unemployed; (2) file a claim at a local employment office for unemployment compensation; and (3) register for work assignment. The program is administered through state and D.C. employment service offices, which determine eligibility and make the payments. (850)

Unfair Labor Practices—Prohibited actions by agency management and labor organizations. (711)

Union—See *Labor Organization.*

Upward Mobility—Systematic career development requiring competitive selection in positions that provide experience and training leading to future assignments in other, more responsible positions.(410)

V

Veteran—A person entitled to preference under 5 USC 2108, including a spouse, widow, widower, or mother entitled to preference under the law. (211)

Voucher—In staffing terms, a formal inquiry to employers, references, professors, and others who presumably know a job applicant well enough to describe job qualifications and personal character. (337)

19

W

Wage Employees—Those employees-in trades, crafts, or labor occupations covered by the Federal Wage System, whose pay is fixed and adjusted periodically in accordance with prevailing rates. (532)

Within-Grade Increase—A salary increase provided in certain Government pay plans based upon time-in-grade and acceptable or satisfactory work performance. Also known as "periodic increase" or "step increase." (531)

NOTE:

Numbers in parentheses after the definitions refer to the appropriate FEDERAL PERSONNEL MANUAL (FPM) Chapter indicated.

www.ingramcontent.com/pod-product-compliance
Lightning Source LLC
Chambersburg PA
CBHW082037300426
44117CB00015B/2513
9781799328674